RLE

Publishers Comp's.
May 22, 1968

THE SOCIOLOGY
OF RELIGIOUS BELONGING

THE SOCIOLOGY OF RELIGIOUS BELONGING

HERVÉ CARRIER S.J.

HERDER AND HERDER

1965
HERDER AND HERDER NEW YORK
232 Madison Avenue, New York 16, N.Y.

Original edition: *Psycho-sociologie de l'appartenance religieuse*
(Rome: Presses de l'Université Gregorienne).
Translated by Arthur J. Arrieri in cooperation with the author.

Imprimi potest:

        R. P. Paulus Muñoz Vega S.J.
        Rector Universitatis
        die 28 Maii, 1960

Nihil obstat:

        Patrick A. Barry
        Censor Librorum

Imprimatur:

        † Robert F. Joyce
        Bishop of Burlington
        December 28, 1963

Library of Congress Catalog Card Number: 64-13684
© 1965 by Herder and Herder, Incorporated
Printed in the United States of America

Contents

PART ONE

CONCEPTUAL SCHEME

ONE RELIGIOUS BELONGING AS AN ATTITUDE
     RELATED TO BEHAVIOR

PART TWO
FORMATION OF
THE RELIGIOUS ATTITUDE

PART THREE

DIFFERENTIATION OF
THE RELIGIOUS ATTITUDE

LIST OF TABLES

List of Figures

"This book should be translated into English" was the remark made by Gillian Lindt Gollin in reviewing Père Carrier's French text for the *American Journal of Sociology* in 1961. I welcome the opportunity to second the motion, for I know of no book which presents such a clear and systematic statement of the sociological and the psychological factors involved in the process of becoming and remaining affiliated to religious groups, or of withdrawing from them.

Hervé Carrier's work is essentially one of synthesis, and as such fills a gap in the field of religious sociology. We have accumulated, and are accumulating, a great deal of information about religious behavior: who attend church or synagogue and how often, what do they believe, how is attendance or belief related to age and sex, church and sect, education and social class. We have some excellent typologies for the analysis of religious groups: Fichter's parish-based division of types within religious groups—the nuclear, modal, marginal and dormant member; Troeltsch's familiar division between religious groups—church and sect, with the added notion of the relation of denomination to each polar type. But what does it all mean? How can the data and the concepts be brought together to form a construct which will integrate what we already know and—at least as important—point to our most crucial areas of ignorance?

12

Carrier's work does this for the field of religious affiliation.

A principal key to Carrier's systematic statement and to the integration of data within it is a word at which many of us on this side of the Atlantic may boggle: psycho-sociology. By the term he does not mean social psychology, that elastic phrase which is stretched to cover personality studies, attitude and value studies, small group studies, public opinion surveys—and almost anything else that the diehard psychologists disavow and that the hard core sociologists cannot fit under one of the social system rubrics. I personally hope that some day soon the term will snap and curl itself around the study of personality as seen in its relationship to the social and cultural systems within which personality is developed.

Pragmatically enough, Père Carrier informs me that "the prefix 'psycho' was meant to add the personal and the psychological dimension to current research in religious sociology as it stood when I started to work on [religious affiliation] in 1957 in Europe." From the shifting ground of the social science disciplines, however, with the word psychosociology he wants to focus our attention on the "complementary approach:" religious affiliation must be seen from "the member's point of view as well as from the community's." In this he is not far from Alex Inkeles' suggested use of the term psychosociology in his essay in *Sociology Today,* for he is dealing with the structure and the functioning of the religious group as a social system and relating it to the modal personality types and the personal needs of the system's members. The relationship is most welcome.

Aside from the excellence of the synthesis which it presents, this book possesses other strong points. One is the imaginative and yet careful way in which it relates the

13

personal needs and the institutional stances of religious organizations during the process of socialization. Another may stem from the writer's dual status as priest and sociologist: a deft balance between religious insight and methodological rigor. Such qualities make the book something special in sociological literature, and establish its author as a man of sociological vision.

Arthur Arrieri's translation of *Psycho-sociologie de l'appartenance religieuse* puts an important contribution to social science literature before the eyes of English language readers.

ROBERT J. MCNAMARA, S.J., PH.D.

Department of Sociology and Anthropology
Fordham University, New York

PREFACE

Is it possible to retrace the genesis of a book? If someone were to ask us what preoccupations, what curiosities have inspired the present work, it would be difficult for us to give a simple explanation. Would it suffice, for example, to point out that we came to religious sociology by the indirect way of rather general sociological studies, and that, becoming professionally interested in group religious behavior, we quite naturally made it the object of research? This is only part of the explanation. Frankly, it would be necessary to search further.

We confess that our interest in religious sociology dates precisely from the time when, in sociological circles, there was a desire for more studies of "mentality," qualitative analyses of religious sentiment, and intimate probings of socioreligious attitudes. The statistical descriptions of religious mores, the sociography of sects, of denominations, of groups, of parishes, of dioceses, had developed to a large extent during the preceding few years. But if anyone wished to penetrate to the "heart of groups," to socioreligious attitudes and motivations, there was scarce aid from the general data of psychosociology. There was relatively abundant information on the structures of political attitudes, on electoral behavior, on the phenomena of public opinion, of industrial psychology: but with regard to the structures of religious behavior, there was scarcely anything comparable

15

to this. Was applied psychosociology able to tell us nothing about the structure of religious behavior, about the specificity of religious attitudes?

Is it our aim, then, to fill this need? If such were the case, this claim would certainly be a vain boast. It is well known how modern syntheses in the human sciences are formulated; they rely essentially upon a great number of previous monographs. When these latter have gradually elucidated the different aspects of a problem, they permit in the second stage the elaboration of theories or universal explanations on the empirical level. Undoubtedly, the time has not yet come to think of this type of explanation as more or less definitive; and, in the present state of research, to make such a claim would be rash.

Nevertheless, an impressive number of monographs have been published in several countries lately on the precise subject of religious behavior. Thus, there came the idea of bringing together in a systematic presentation the findings produced by numerous although individually limited studies already in existence and relating to the psychosociology of religious behavior. After gathering these scattered findings, we have integrated them into a conceptual schema which we believe can be drawn from the available information. Our working hypothesis consisted in the proposition that religious behavior has characteristics which clearly distinguish it, on the psychosocial level, from other forms of human behavior. In the course of our analysis this hypothesis appeared to be confirmed by the data, as we hope to demonstrate in the following pages and particularly in the concluding chapter. In the course of our analysis, the answer to this question appeared positive, and we here attempt to justify this answer, especially in the concluding chapter. All this will soon be presented to the reader.

At this point, clergymen and scientists will perhaps ask

us some other questions. "Are you speaking to us in theological language?" the first group will inquire. "Do you remain on the level of observation?" the second group will ask. These are fair questions, and require a statement of the exact limits of our work. Our perspective, through the whole course of our analysis, has been exclusively that of psychosociology. In other words, we have limited ourselves to observable facts, without searching for a total explanation of religious behavior.

Religious historians, metaphysicians and theologians would have much more to say on each of our descriptions and our conclusions. Let us note, however, that in accepting the limitations of an empirical perspective it became possible for us to identify certain structures and certain norms of socioreligious behavior; and these data, we believe, will enlighten the theologian and religious leader interested in the various phenomena inherent in the conduct of believers. Religious belonging is both spiritual and psychosocial; individual and group bases for human behavior are found and interrelated according to specific structures. This type of analysis is, moreover, familiar enough to contemporary theologians who are acquainted with studies in pastoral psychology or with the earlier research work of Schmidt or of Pinard de la Boullaye. We wish in this work precisely to reopen one of the chapters of *L'Etude comparée des religions,* whose author was formerly a professor at the Gregorian University.

A scientist will understand that this book, written by a Catholic priest, was inspired from the start by a preoccupation which was both scientific and pastoral. This postulate of apostolic utility, we believe, will not have diverted our attention from valid observation. In any event, it is on their empirical value alone that our results are to be judged. At a time when the interdependence of various disciplines has become unavoidable, it may be hoped that the work of a priest sociologist will, of its very nature, facilitate the dialogue between theology and the human sciences.

It is not without great pleasure that we mention in the first pages of this book the name of Jean Stoetzel, a professor at the Sorbonne, whose advice and encouragement have been so helpful to us throughout the course of this work. We express to him here our deepest thanks.

INTRODUCTION TOWARD A RELIGIOUS PSYCHOSOCIOLOGY

From the beginning of its history, sociology was oriented toward religious phenomena, and this tendency was strengthened as the new discipline steadily made headway and its methods of research improved. French tradition is very clear in this respect. Auguste Comte, who was to give the young science its definitive name, published the first *Treatise on Sociology* in 1854, which eventually bore in its subtitle the word "Religion." His perspective, it is true, was that of a rather arbitrary philosophy of history which consequently was abandoned by sociologists, but the interesting point is that sociology from its very birth showed itself immediately concerned with the role and the function of religion in the dynamism of societies.

Among the scholars who in their turn have brought fame to French sociological studies, it suffices to mention a few names in order to recall the vast amount of research dedicated, in whole or in part, to the observation of religious data. One might think, for example, of Durkheim, of Hubert, of Mauss, of Lévy-Bruhl. Or one might recall that the first issue of *L'Année Sociologique,* which appeared in 1896, inaugurated within its pages a "Chronique de sociologie religieuse" which continues to the present. Undoubtedly some amazing discoveries would be available to the scholar who would go methodically through these reviews.

Another rich source of information would be found in another French collection, that of the *Science Sociale,* a review in which the disciples of Le Play and of H. de Tourville published, from 1886 to 1924, hundreds of monographs, almost all of them containing thought-provoking data concerning religious sociology.

About 1930 a new line of research developed in France with the publication of the first work of Gabriel Le Bras, whose work, as we know, was favorably received by sociologists. These efforts bore fruit after the war, when France witnessed a remarkable development in religious sociology, both in the field of teaching and in that of applied research. The results of these new developments are periodically evaluated by the "Groupe de Sociologie des Religions" in the *Archives de Sociologie des Religions.* Some critical evaluations have begun to appear which help to estimate the present directions of this movement and to place it in the totality of sociological research.[1]

The other European schools of sociology, especially those of England and Germany, allow similar comments. The scholars of these two countries have constantly shown a marked interest in religious sociology. In Germany, since Troeltsch and Weber, and from Sombart to Mensching and Wach, a solid tradition has been established. England too can claim a long series of contributions extending from the research of Tylor, Spencer and Frazer to that of Malinowski, Tawney, Thouless and Grensted.

An identical course can be seen in the history of American sociology. For example, the *American Journal of Sociology* at the end of the last century encouraged research both on secular and research on ethicoreligious problems. A

[1] J. Stoetzel, "Sociology in France: An Empiricist View" in H. Becker and A. Boskoff (ed.), *Modern Sociological Theory* (New York: 1957), 623–657; see also J. Maître, "Les sociologies du catholicisme en France" in *Cahiers Intern. Sociol.,* 1958, 24, 104–124.

remarkable fact in this tradition is that the research of the first sociologists and psychologists were complementary and sometimes parallel. Thus, the work of Leuba and Starbuck led the way for that of William James, and all three contributed to the first formulation of a religious psychosociology. Here we should add the names of Kidd, Ellwood and Ross, the sociologists who gradually refined the functionalistic interpretation which has been constantly improved and modified down to the present time.[2] These trends were already foreshadowing the work of G. W. Allport, Yinger and Fichter.

A methodical history of the advances in religious sociology remains to be written. As a specialized branch of sociology, it has become a separate entity, which today has its own growing number of professional sociologists. Socioreligious research centers are being established and specialized periodicals are being published in several countries. When one becomes aware of the particularly rapid development in this science, especially since the war, one feels the need for an evaluation of results and of new developments. At first glance, the whole picture remains somewhat confused; the direction of the movement is barely discernible. Though Joachim Wach[3] was able to claim for religious sociology an "autonomous existence" independent of the traditional sciences, it is necessary, however, to recognize that the methodology, the fundamental concepts, and the

[2] See W. L. Kolb, "Values, Positivism, and the Functional Theory of Religion: The Growth of a Moral Dilemma" in *Social Forces,* 1953, 31, 305–311; cf. P. Tufari, S.J., "Functional Analysis in the Sociology of Religion" in *Social Compass,* 1960, 1, 9–20; 2, 121–137; and A. W. Eister, "Religious Institutions in Complex Societies: Difficulties in the Theoretic Specification of Functions" in *Amer. Sociol. Rev.,* 1957, 22, 387–391.

[3] See J. Wach, *Sociology of Religion* (Chicago: 1944); also G. Gurvitch and W. E. Moore (ed.), *La sociologie au XXe siècle,* 1 (Paris: 1947).

objectives of religious sociology remain rather vague.[4] Let us note, however, that there is now a deeper awareness of these problems.

In using the term "religious sociology" one runs the risk of causing confusion, for it is indiscriminately attached to many scientific undertakings which are quite different from each other. An over-all view of the works which are ordinarily considered as religious sociology would undoubtedly justify a rather complex classification. We would distinguish three principal types of religious sociology. The first type could be called formal religious sociology. This approach, represented by Wach or Mensching, is based on the history of religions, the comparative method and classical ethnology; it attempts to arrive at a general sociology of religion. These authors, and those who followed them, remain for the most part rather aloof from the methods of positive sociology and, if by chance they rely on the parallel research of the positive sociologist, their interpretation tends to lack any critical sense. Mensching, for example, still had recourse, in 1947 and in 1951, to the psychology of Gustave Le Bon as if it were current theory. It is true that Wach, at Chicago, did become better acquainted with his fellow sociologists; and, of all the authors who are associated with the "formal" trend, he is the most open to the work of professional sociologists.

A second type of research, religious morphology, in contrast to the preceding type, does not propose, as yet, general conclusions. Through descriptive methods, statistics on religious practice, and the historical study of institutions, this

---

[4] See, on this subject, the remarks of T. Parsons, "The Theoretical Development of the Sociology of Religion," in *Journal of the History of Ideas,* 1944, 5, 176–190; and those of J. M. Yinger, "Areas of Research in the Sociology of Religion" in *Sociology and Social Research,* 1958, 42, 466–472; see R. R. Dynes, "Toward the Sociology of Religion" in *Sociology and Social Research,* 1954, 38, 227–232.

approach attempts to understand specific situations and to develop practical programs for influencing religious action. Although it does not refuse to come to grips with the problems which the differences among the religions pose for sociologists, these authors proceed only progressively and by stages "from morphology to typology." Gabriel Le Bras and Boulard are representatives of this trend.[5]

It is difficult to characterize the third approach in a few words, but, as a matter of convenience, it could be called *religious psychosociology*. It is more a general orientation of studies than a branch of research; this orientation becomes more apparent the more one surveys the work published in the principal sociological and social psychological reviews during the past fifteen years or so. Even outside the scope of an explicit religious sociology, studies frequently deal with the religious phenomenon from a sociological point of view. It is still difficult to speak of a unified area of research, although a great number of monographs and research reports have appeared. Social psychology has not as yet formulated any synthesis on religious behavior, and this deficiency is lamented by several scholars.[6] There is a growing need to determine and define a special branch of research devoted to this topic; this branch would be analogous to branches which already exist for such phenomena as public opinion, communications, electoral behavior, etc. The general treatises on social psychology, or the great collective works like those of Lindzey or Murchison, give

---

[5] For the work of Gabriel Le Bras, consult H. Desroche, "Domaines et méthodes de la sociologie religieuse dans l'œuvre de Gabriel Le Bras" in *Revue d'Histoire et de Philosophie religieuses*, 1954, 34, 128–158; and F. A. Isambert, "Développement et dépassement de l'étude de la pratique chez Gabriel Le Bras" in *Cahiers Intern. Socio.*, 1956, 20, 149–169.

[6] See W. E. Gregory, "The Psychology of Religion: Some Suggested Areas of Research of Significance to Psychology" in *Journ. Abn. Soc. Psychol.*, 1952, 47, 256–258.

only occasional references to religious psychosociological works. It would seem, however, that the breadth of detailed research justifies at least a provisory synthesis. Perhaps, in the multiplication of these endeavors, social psychology will eventually be provided with its missing chapter on religious behavior.

Let us acknowledge for the exoneration of the psychosociologists, that the undertaking involves some particular difficulties. It poses delicate problems of methodology, and it requires constant attention to the postulates and presuppositions of research. Two stumbling blocks seem particularly serious. The first, that of wishing to find a total explanation of the religious phenomenon solely on the level of social psychology, involves a metaphysical position and may be tantamount to eradicating the phenomenon that one wishes to study in its specificity. This type of religious sociologism, which has kept the discussions of the past alive for a long time, seems to have yielded today to a more truly objective approach.[7]

A second methodological deviation is a more subtle threat to the objectivity of research. The error consists in assimilating or confusing, a priori, facts which more careful observation would demand be distinguished one from the other; this may involve confusion, for example, in the interpretation of religious conduct or beliefs. In this Le Bras recognized one of the most serious reasons for the "bottlenecks of religious sociology."[8] We would be able to cite numerous research works which made the same initial mistake. For example, in order to evaluate the sense of religious

[7] In this regard, consult the following authors: H. Becker, "Supreme Values and the Sociologist" in *Amer. Sociol. Rev.,* 1941, 6, 155–172; C. C. Bowman, "Must the Social Sciences Foster Moral Skepticism?" in *Amer. Sociol. Rev.,* 1945, 10, 709–715; W. L. Kolb, "Values, Positivism, and the Functional Theory of Religion: The Growth of a Moral

[8] G. Le Bras, *Études de sociologie religieuse* (Paris: 1956), II, 790. Dilemma" in *Social Forces,* 1953, 31, 305–311.

liberty or tolerance or doctrinal orthodoxy in a mixed population, the questions proposed often have meanings which are clearly different according to the religious beliefs of the subjects. The fact of vaguely asking a population composed of Protestants, Catholics and Jews the same doctrinal or moral questions does not in any way lead to valid conclusions on the orthodoxy, conservatism or progress of the groups studied. The negative response of a Jew to a question on the divinity of Christ has scarcely any significance for the evaluation of his Jewish orthodoxy. A Catholic who answers in a questionnaire that he does not claim the right of personally choosing another demonation than his own should not be grouped, on this alone, with the intolerant. If one religious denomination prohibits mixed marriages or divorce, this is no necessary proof of a faithful member's conservatism when he opts for the ordinary opinion of his coreligionists.[9]

These difficulties lead to the question of collaboration between the sciences, for there can scarcely be an adequate solution to these difficult problems without a dialogue between sociologists and theologians well informed on the exigencies of research. Progress in this matter can be seen by comparing, for example, the first extensive religious survey by the Institut Français d'Opinion Publique in 1952 with the survey the same organization ran six years later on the religious attitude of French youth. The first, although it was received with interest, stirred up reservations and criticisms on the part of theologians; but the second was

[9] In the way of some examples, let us cite, respectively, the three following studies from which we extracted the three questions stated above: D. C. Brown, and W. L. Lowe, "Religious Beliefs and Personality Characteristics of College Students" in *Journ. Soc. Psychol.*, 1951, 33, 103–129; H. Woolston, "Religious Consistency" in *Amer. Sociol. Rev.*, 1937, 2, 380–388; L. W. Ferguson, "The Stability of the Primary Social Attitudes: I. Religionism and Humanitarianism" in *Journ. of Psychol.*, 1941, 12, 283–288.

requested by a Catholic magazine and involved a direct collaboration with theologians.

Let us also acknowledge the fact that the instruments of analysis available to social psychology today permit a more precise observation of the different aspects of religious behavior. The now classic distinction between verbal attitude and real attitude, the more exact determination of perceptive, motivational and emotional factors of behavior, as well as the discovery of the relationships between beliefs and attitudes, make it possible for psychosociologists to analyze moral or religious conduct more closely. Until recently, religious sociology had scarcely been able to utilize the methods of research of social psychology, and it had concentrated on the analysis of groups (size, structure, evolution), rather than the phenomena of behavior properly so called. It is still too early to expect broad generalizations on religious behavior from psychosociology. In the present state of research, however, some partial syntheses do not seem impossible.

From the multiple analyses which have been published up to the present time, we would like to attempt a synthesis concerning a phenomenon which seemed fundamental to us, namely, religious belonging. What is the sociological significance of religious belonging? One speaks of the "sense of belonging" to, of "identification" with, a religious group. What phenomenon do these concepts express? There is frequently, in surveys, a question about the "religious membership" of subjects and, most of the time, the sociologist is satisfied with general answers like "Catholic," "Protestant," etc. Do such answers justify the generalizations which are habitually drawn from them? Can we presuppose, in this case, that religious belonging, once labeled, reveals to us a factor which is invariable and always the same?

The answer to these questions is of interest to the practical sociologist as well as to the theoretician. Both are interested in learning more about the psychosociological components and the factors of differentiation of religious belonging. But before we begin our differential analysis of the phenomenon, it is essential to state precisely the conceptual schema of our research and to define the operational meaning of the fundamental concepts that we shall use.

PART ONE
CONCEPTUAL SCHEME

Our first step will consist in stating the precise methodological limits which will guide us throughout this work. We have arranged, in the present chapter which outlines our conceptual scheme, the data which will allow us to analyze religious belonging in its psychosocial dimensions. This analysis, we believe, will justify our treatment of religious belonging as an attitude related to behavior.

First, we will determine in what sense religious belonging can be considered as an empirical phenomenon. Next, we will see how the fact of religious belonging situates the faithful member with regard to various aspects of social reality; categories; and we will examine more particularly the communal bonds which permit a specific definition of religious belonging. Finally, religious belonging will be considered in the precise perspective of psychosocial attitudes. We will distinguish here two complementary aspects: religious membership will appear either as a creator of subsequent attitudes, or as the object of a specific attitude, namely, that of a member of a church.

Religious belonging will thus be analyzed in three stages in this chapter: (1) as an empirical phenomenon; (2) in its relations to the "communal order;" (3) as a psychosociological attitude.

CHAPTER I

RELIGIOUS BELONGING AS AN ATTITUDE
RELATED TO BEHAVIOR

I Religious Belonging:
an Empirical Phenomenon

1 Comprehensiveness of the religious attitude. 2 Religious experience and its expression. 3 Choice of an analytic schema. 4 The "communal," the "civil," the "supranatural."

1 COMPREHENSIVENESS OF THE RELIGIOUS ATTITUDE

One of the first problems which is presented to the religious psychosociologist is that of stating a precise aspect of research or a branch of analysis which is not arbitrarily delimited. This problem, which is common to all sociological analyses, is even more difficult when it concerns religious conduct. A great number of scholars have noted the comprehensive character of religious attitude and feelings. As we shall see in speaking of religious education, the attitude of the believer tends to organize and to unify all aspects of behavior; and Allport has wondered if there can even exist, with the exception of a religious feeling acquired in

31

maturity, one sole feeling comprehensive enough to integrate the totality of interests and leave no residue unassimilated.[1] We will return to these findings later, but these first indications already warn us to be particularly careful when one wishes to delimit a specific sector within an area which, from the outset, strikes one as being so comprehensive. As we shall see, several authors have utilized different conceptual schemes in an effort to analyze this phenomenon in all its comprehensivness.

2 RELIGIOUS EXPERIENCE AND ITS EXPRESSION

In order to avoid any confusion on this subject in the course of our analysis, it seems wise to make use of Wach's well known typology. Wach begins by carefully distinguishing between religious experience and its forms of expression.[2] The religious experience properly so called, or the personal experience of things religious, seems to him irreducible to sociological analysis. Sociology, as he explains, would not be able to attain the religious act in itself: "Those among us who study the sociological implications of religion would be deceived if they imagined that their works are capable of revealing the nature and the essence of religion in itself."[3] The psychosociologist who would break through this frontier would assume the functions of the philosopher or the theologian. Religious sociology, then, imposes on its researchers limitations analogous to those which researchers encounted in the sociology of art or in the sociology of knowledge; even the experience of artistic inspiration or the

[1] G. W. Allport, *The Individual and His Religion: A Psychological Interpretation* (London: 1951), 77.
[2] J. Wach, *op. cit.,* 21.
[3] *Ibid.,* 9.

32

intimate act of knowledge, as well as the religious experience, cannot be interiorly analyzed by psychosociology alone. The phenomenological studies of esthetic experience undertaken by Dufrenne[4] have shown the frontier which delimits the two orders of facts.

Once this reservation has been made, it must be added that the expression, or the phenomenological forms of things religious, are not to be considered as outside the religious sphere. It is sufficient to think of ritual manifestations, of forms of prayer, to be convinced that "religious expression" itself is within the religious order. First, the expressive forms of behavior may indirectly reveal to us the intimate experience of the subject, for example, an act of liturgical participation; but even here our observation of the internal fact is only mediate and reconstituted from the exterior: "The experiences of the subject, it has been observed, can be for the observer only the object of a reconstruction."[5] Moreover, the expression itself gets its value from the point of view of the believer.

Foregoing the direct analysis of religious experience, and methodologically considering it as a positively unverifiable datum, is not to limit, to the same degree, the scope of psychosociological observation; on the contrary, all that is observable externally pertains to it, as Pinard de la Boullaye has shown so well.[6] We have but to refer to this author whoever would wish to delve further into the problems of method posed by religious psychology or sociology. He has made a considerable effort to reconcile positive research with methodological studies on these questions.

[4] See M. Dufrenne, *La phénoménologie de l'expérience esthétique,* 2 vol. (Paris: 1953).

[5] J. Stoetzel, "La psychologie sociale et la théorie des attitudes" in *Annales Sociologiques,* 1941, fasc. 4, 1–24; see 18.

[6] E. Pinard de la Boullaye, S.J., *L'étude comparée des religions* (Paris: 1929), third edition, II, x.

3 CHOICE OF AN ANALYTIC SCHEMA

As we have noted above, numerous schemata have been proposed by researchers to delimit the areas of socioreligious observation. In addition to distinguishing between religious experience and religious expression, Wach has formulated a tripartite division of the phenomena of religious expression:[7] (a) theoretical expression or doctrine; (b) practical expression or cult; (c) sociological expression or the community of believers.

This typology has the advantage of closely adhering to the divisions traditionally accepted by the religious sciences, but it also creates several inconveniences. The border lines are not sufficiently delineated between the sociological and the theological; on the other hand, it seems arbitrary to reserve the sociological criterion solely for the social tie between the believer and his religious community. Several critics have remarked that it is possible to have a sociology not only of community but also of cult, of practice or of doctrine. Le Bras[8] maintains clearly that sociology "can do more"; among the objectives he holds possible is "the examination of the social conditions of the development of beliefs and rites, of collective relations with other societies, religious or secular and also with the societies of the Beyond . . ." Even if one wished to confine the analysis to the formal sociology of Wach, the typology proposed would stir up numerous methodological criticisms, as Desroche has shown.[9]

In the work of Penido, a psychologist of religion, one finds an analytical division revolving about the linear development of the religious life:[10] (a) the beginning: con-

[7] J. Wach, *op. cit.*, chapter 2.

[8] See G. Le Bras, "Présentation—La sociologie du catholicisme en France" in *Lumen Vitae*, 1951, 6, 13–42.

[9] H. Desroche, "Sociologie et théologie dans la typologie religieuse de Joachim Wach" in *Arch. Sociol. des Relig.*, 1956, 1, 41–63.

[10] M. T.-L. Penido, *La conscience religieuse: Essai systématique suivi d'illustrations* (Paris: 1935), v–vi.

version; (b) the advancement: asceticism; (c) the apex: mystical experience.

This framework seems to limit research to strictly religious phenomena, but its immediate perspectives are more suited for the study of individual conduct than for that of socioreligious behavior. Later, we shall emphasize some of the interesting points of Penido's analyses, especially when we discuss conversion. But his general schema seems inadequate for grasping the totality of the phenomena of religious sociology and, therefore, is insufficient for the methodological delimitation of analysis.

In a long chapter on the "Sociological Method," which he added to the latest edition of his work, Pinard de la Boullaye[11] proposed to study religious phenomena starting with the three following points of view: (a) psychology of the collective life; (b) influence of organization in the community; (c) relations of the religious communities with society.

The plan was promising and one would have liked to see how the author would have used it. But, in actuality, he was drawn to combine these three points of view and to treat them together. It is true that thirty years ago sociology and social psychology had not yet at their disposal the methods of analysis which would have permitted a more systematic treatment of the immense documentation which Pinard de la Boullaye wished to interpret. Let us say, however, in all fairness to his "sociological method," that it finds its complement in an earlier chapter on psychological methods.

4 THE COMMUNAL, THE CIVIL, THE SUPRANATURAL

Several other conceptual schemas have been used by recent sociologists, such as Gregory, Dynes, Yinger and

[11] E. Pinard de la Boullaye, *op. cit.,* II, 386 f.

Hoult.[12] The schema we want to consider is Le Bras'. The author has made use of it several times during the course of the last few years. We have at hand four or five versions of his analytical plan, which we believe can be traced back to the broad outline that follows. Le Bras distinguishes three major areas in religious sociology; these he conventionally calls "communal," "civil" and "supranatural."[13]

(a) The *communal* concerns the community of the faithful or the assembly of those belonging to one church; it seeks the composition, the structure and the dynamism of religious societies as such.

(b) The *civil* concerns the relations of religion and secular societies, and the collective relations with surroundings which are not specifically religious; here are studied the interactions of religious groups and secular groups.

(c) The *supranatural* is reserved for outward manifestations of sacred powers, for systems of law, and for prescribed patterns of behavior which are judged appropriate for bringing one into contact with the invisible world.

Without prejudging the refinements that the author may yet make on this schema of analysis, and even wishing that more detailed explanations were available for each of the categories, we believe that it can provide us with an ade-

[12] W. E. Gregory, "The Psychology of Religion: Some Suggested Areas of Research of Significance to Psychology" in *Journ. Abn. Soc. Psychol.*, 1952, 47, 256–258; R. R. Dynes, "Toward the Sociology of Religion" in *Sociology and Social Research*, 1954, 38, 227–232; J. M. Yinger, *Religion, Society and the Individual:* "An Introduction to the Sociology of Religion" (New York: 1958).

[13] For this problem see the works of G. Le Bras, "Note sur la structure de la sociologie religieuse" in *L'Année Sociologique*, 1948–1949, 3e série, 287–294; "Présentation—La sociologie du catholicisme en France" in *Lumen Vitae*, 1951, 6, 13–42; "Sociologie des religions: tendances actuelles de la recherche" in *Current Sociology*, 1956, 5, 5–17; "Sociologie religieuse et science des religions" in *Arch. Sociol. des Relig.*, 1956, 1, 3–17; "La sociologie religieuse parmi les sciences humaines" in *Recherches et Débats*, 1958, 25, 11–25.

quate conceptual framework. The schema has in its favor the distinction of having been conceived a posteriori and it arises, as it were, from multiple studies whose purpose was precisely the incorporation of the plurality of religious phenomena, the omission of none of the forms of belief, and the retention, nevertheless, of the indispensable distinctions between different orders of phenomena.[14]

For the purpose of testing this schema, we have tried an experiment; we have applied the plan of Le Bras to the abundant material on religion with which the sociologists have presented us during these last few years. Thereby we have observed that each of these studies, and even the detailed analyses, could be related, without being too much arbitrariness, to the communal, the civil, or the supranatural. Without judging the theoretical or definitive value of Le Bras' schema, we can use it as a working plan to situate better our particular analyses in their relation to the totality of socioreligious phenomena. The proposed framework should be used in a sufficiently flexible manner; these methodological categories should not be considered hermetic, for there is a continual overlap between one category and another. The only purpose of this first analysis is to establish a perspective which, while being quite clear, avoids being arbitrarily exclusive.

II Religious Belonging: Communal Aspects

1 Religious belonging at the level of the communal. 2 Religious belonging at the level of behavior. 3 The concept of religious behavior. 4 The specificity of the religious.

[14] These requirements are clearly expressed in each of the studies cited above; see the preceding note.

37

1 RELIGIOUS BELONGING AT THE LEVEL OF THE COMMUNAL

To begin the study of religious belonging we situate the phenomenon at the level of what Le Bras calls the communal.[15] Immediately our center of interest becomes clear, and likewise we see the numerous phenomena which will be dropped from consideration emerge. Thus we will concentrate our observations on the religious community as such; our explicit object will be to elucidate the bonds which unite a believer with an organized religion. Belonging will be considered as the identification with the communal or with the religious community. The exact sense of this proposition will appear later.

Our perspective leads us to make an abstraction from a certain number of the phenomena which we would classify as supranatural. It is not that we wish to minimize the interactions of the communal and the supranatural; and if we do not deal explicitly with such phenomena as manifestations of culture, liturgical and sacramental participation, or symbolizations of the sacred, etc., it is not that we consider them as necessarily independent of religious belonging. We believe that belonging to an organized religion can legitimately be considered a relatively stable fact, one endowed with a particular psychosociological consistency, which endures beyond transitory manifestations of worship. This will not, on the other hand, prevent us from underlining the intimate relations between communal and supranatural which shed light on the psychosociology of religious belonging. By assigning the phenomenon of belonging to the order of the communal, we indicate our intention of studying the fact according to its societal and collective specificity rather than from a ritual or symbolical point of view.

[15] The communal order designates community relations which are established within the religious group as such. See the definitions of the communal, the civil and the supranatural, given above.

38

Religious belonging also has relationships with the political, socioeconomic and cultural spheres, as is evidenced by the emphasis given it, for example, by the studies of political sociology or the work of the Weber school. This last order of facts, which we assign to the area of the civil, will be discussed when the occasion warrants it; it does not constitute the immediate object of our study. We will not first consider religious belonging as related to secular structures; we wish to examine the fact of belonging to a religious body in its specificity. We will, in fact, give some consideration to the interaction of the communal and the civil, and we wish to abstract from the secular concomitances of religious belonging only to the degree in which they divert our attention from the central phenomenon to be studied.

2 RELIGIOUS BELONGING AT THE LEVEL OF BEHAVIOR

In our chosen perspective, religious belonging is situated in the immediate and lasting relation of the believer with his church or with his community of faithful members. If our point of view were solely sociographical, we would dwell more on a description of structures as such. Behavior, properly so called, and the psychosocial conduct would be of only secondary interest to us. It should be realized that, up to this time, studies of religious sociology have been almost exclusively written from this sociographical point of view. There have been numerous investigations on the composition of groups, establishing correlations according to age, the level of practice, socio-professional categories, ethnic origin, etc. But behavior, conduct and, in general, the phenomena which are proper to psychosociologists have scarcely been touched upon, except in fragmentary studies.

The relevance of this point of view, however, seems evident, especially at a time when Protestant and Catholic sociologists are inquiring to what degree Christian communities of twenty or forty thousand members, as found in the cities, can continue to be designated real sociological groups. A controversy has even occurred here, the consequences of which we shall examine from the point of view of religious belonging. We only wish to stress that we shall consider religious belonging in the perspective of social participation, identification, or behavior, rather than from the perspective of the composition or structure of groups. The one, moreover, does not exclude the other and we shall take this into account, despite our formal intention of first considering the psychosociological point of view.

This now leads us to a more precise statement of the meaning of a fundamental concept, namely religious behavior. In current terminology there is great confusion about this subject, as Brien[16] has shown, and frequently enough the psychosociologists themselves are content with explanations or interpretations which are too shallow or superficial to be truly objective.[17]

3 THE CONCEPT OF RELIGIOUS BEHAVIOR

The progress of social psychology today invites us to analyze religious behavior within the framework of a widely comprehensive theory of human behavior. A limited perspective, whether it be psychological, or even moral, could not of itself take into account the particularly complex structure of socioreligious behavior. Fortunately, more comprehensive explanations of psychosociological behavior

[16] A. Brien, "Valeur religieuse et équivoques du sens du sacré" in *Recherches et Débats*, 1957, 20, 111–130.

[17] This is well expressed in the article of W. H. Clark, "How Do Social Scientists Define Religion?" in *Journ. Soc. Psychol.*, 1958, 47, 143–147.

permit us to overcome the limitations of a one-dimensional perspective.

It is generally accepted that the French term *"comportement"* (behavior) was borrowed from Pascal and introduced into psychology by Piéron, who defined it as "the objective manifestation of total activity."[18] The generic term, behavior, is used as frequently in animal psychology as in human psychology. When dealing with man's activities, one often uses the word "conduct" (in French *conduite*). This latter expression, used first by Janet, more clearly brings out the intentional and volitional aspect of human activity. But the different nuances of the two terms "conduct" and "behavior" do not prevent their common use as synonyms. Henceforth, unless otherwise stated, we will use these two terms interchangeably. Our intention will be to insist on the total and integral character of the activity considered.

Interdisciplinary research in recent years has illuminated the integrated and synthetic aspect of human conduct. In these studies the primary object is to consider all the dimensions of conduct viewed within a psychological as well as a sociocultural framework. We refer particularly to the discussions since 1951 which periodically have brought together medical research teams composed of psychologists, sociologists, ethnologists, doctors, etc. Grinker published the first synthesis of these works in progress in *Toward a Unified Theory of Human Behavior.*[19] In some ways, these studies verify the original theories of Mauss concerning the interdependence of all orders, beginning from the psychoorganic to the social, and the necessity of studying the totality of behavior at the same time.

[18] One will find a complete definition as well as some historical and technical notations in H. Piéron, *Vocabulaire de la psychologie* (Paris: 1957), under the word "comportement."

[19] See R. R. Grinker (ed.), *Toward a Unified Theory of Human Behavior* (New York: 1957).

The new approach offers us an explanation of human behavior conceived as a dynamic and evolutionary balance of behavioral patterns associated with interdependent systems of the somatic, psychological, cultural and sociological orders. The subject of behavior must be analyzed in the structure of his personal characteristics, in his role within the group, and in the total social structure. "The behavior of the individual is not understandable," writes Grinker, "if detached from the culture of which he is a part, and culture cannot be understood without considering the individuals in it."[20]

Special consideration will be given to the idea of "change, development and evolution," which can introduce into one's observation a dynamic element, itself linked with the spatio-temporal or sociocultural aspects of behavior. For such a perspective, multiple sociopsychological disciplines are joined and they are called upon to collate their complementary analyses to obtain a unified and coherent explanation.

This is not the place to detail the work undertaken by Grinker and his associates. Our purpose is simply that of situating our study of behavior within a perspective which is well known, already official in the field of education, and which seems to us particularly adapted for the numerous aspects of religious behavior. On the other hand, we do not intend to link our analysis to an exclusive theory of behavior. The one point we wish to emphasize here is the need to place religious conduct within a general framework of human behavior. The explanations of Allport, for example, would also furnish us with such a comprehensive framework.

The principal reason for a general framework is that it permits us to avoid the one-sided emphases of a sociological, a psychological, or even a legal approach. If it is admitted

20 *Op. cit.,* 368.

that the religious attitude is one of the most comprehensive that can exist, the advantages of obtaining an explanation of behavior to which moralists as well as psychosociologists can subscribe will be readily evident.

4 THE SPECIFICITY OF THE RELIGIOUS

Once the general notion of behavior has been explained, there remains the task of determining what one understands by specifically religious behavior. The question leads us to a problem which has never ceased to be debated by specialists in the human sciences. How should "religion" be defined? What criteria should a researcher use to discern what he ought to retain or reject when he studies religious phenomena?

It will be recalled that Durkheim believed he could arrive at an answer by proceeding from the observation of the "primitives."[21] He was later led to alter his first definition considerably.[22] More serious doubts were later raised by researchers such as Malinowski,[23] who also took as his starting point the religion of "primitives," but proposed basic objections to the religious sociology of the Durkheim school. No sociologist today would think it justifiable to maintain Durkheim's position exclusively; no one, however, would deny the service that the work of the Durkheim school rendered by drawing attention to the social nature of religious behavior.

Leuba, who was more eclectic, desired to cull further information from the work which had been attempted before him, and he did his utmost to reconcile, in an acceptable

[21] E. Durkheim, "De la définition des phénomènes religieux" in L'Année Sociologique, 1897–1898, 2, 1–28.
[22] In Elementary Forms of the Religious Life (Chicago: 1954).
[23] B. Malinowski, "Social and Individual Sources of Primitive Religions" in J. Needham (ed.), Science, Religion and Reality (New York: 1925), 52–64.

formula, the propositions of his predecessors. Thus he collected forty-eight definitions, with two of his own added; but he was not pleased with the results of his work and consequently abandoned the whole project.[24]

The method of symposia and discussion such as those organized by the *Journal of Religion* in 1927, hardly achieved the minimum of agreement anticipated.[25] The six reports which were published at that time, emphasized the considerable differences between one author and another. Clark[26] has recently reported on a similar investigation. He asked sixty-three specialists in the social sciences the following question: "What is the object of your research when you study religion? In other words, how do you define religion?" The answers were extremely varied. For example, twenty-nine of the group had recourse to a supernatural element; twenty-one made use of the concept of group; fifteen spoke of institutionalized belief, etc. There evidently exist similarities and points of contact among some of the proposed definitions, but no unanimity developed from this. One often met irreconcilable definitions.

Attempts to evaluate present-day efforts of sociologists to discern the criteria of religious phenomena lead ultimately to two principal points of view. The first group of researchers begin with the personal subject, in the manner of William James who stated that "it is in the individual feeling that the very essence of religion lies."[27] Moving further in this direction, one will come to postulate a kind of universal need for religion, which is defined as the funda-

[24] J. H. Leuba, *La psychologie des phénomènes religieux* (Paris: 1914), 397.

[25] "The Definition of Religion: A Symposium" in *Journal of Religion*, 1927, 7, 112–135; 284–314.

[26] W. H. Clark, "How Do Social Scientists Define Religion?" in *Journ. Soc. Psychol.*, 1958, 47, 143–147.

[27] W. James, *The Varieties of Religious Experience* (New York: 1902), 420.

mental orientation of the personality, or as an object of devotion. Fromm, a representative of this tendency, believes that the religious element is always present in all individuals. "The question," he says, "is not religion or not but which kind of religion."[28] Neurosis itself will consequently be considered "a form of private religion" (*ibid.*). Even within the realm of the purely subjective aspect of religious behavior, this conceptualization raises some serious difficulties. Allport in his *The Individual and His Religion* notes that the major weakness of this kind of an explanation is that it leads us to some unverifiable postulates; it has recourse to theories of the unconscious whose proof or refutation, in this matter, is impossible; they omit above all the whole domain of conscious and objective motivations whose role has been emphasized in socioreligious studies like those of Glick and Young or Braden.[29]

A second method consists in symbolically assigning an "ultraphenomenal" pole to religious behavior and in defining this pole as an object of belief, which is transcendental, "numinous," or "supernatural." Religion is then psychologically conceived as a totality of cognitive, volitive and emotional relationships between the subject and the content of his belief. Grafton, for example, defines religion as the interaction of a personality and a supernatural order, in which one believes and which is represented in symbolic forms transmitted socially.[30] As is evident, definitions of this type attempt to respect the element "belief" as a component of religious behavior, but unfortunately there is also introduced into the discussion the notion of "supernatural"

[28] E. Fromm, *Psychoanalysis and Religion* (New Haven: 1950), 26.
[29] P. C. Glick and K. Young, "Justifications for Religious Attitudes and Habits" in *Journ. Soc. Psychol.*, 1943, 17, 45–68; C. S. Braden, "Why People are Religious: A Study in Religious Motivation" in *The Journal of Bible and Religion*, 1947, 15, 38–45.
[30] T. H. Grafton, "Religious Origins and Sociological Theory" in *Amer. Sociol. Rev.*, 1945, 10, 726–738.

which, sooner or later in the course of the analysis, will lead to positions which the social psychologist alone would not be able to account for. How long, apropos the "supernatural," can one avoid metaphysical judgments?

It is not that it is necessary to challenge a priori the collaboration of the psychosociologist and the metaphysician, but we think that this collaboration should be openly admitted, and methodical in nature. We even believe, after a careful study of the various attempts which have been made by sociologists since Durkheim, that a strictly empirical and universal definition of religion is impossible. Despite his efforts William James clearly realized the difficulty and declared that it was useless to look for a definition of religion; he stated that he himself would be content with a definition which was "entirely arbitrary."[31]

A purely arbitrary definition, however, could not be the solution. The illusions and aberrations of religious feeling, studied by Lowe or Rapaport,[32] ought not, even in the strictest terms of psychosociology, be confused a priori with the mature religious feelings which Allport has analyzed so well.[33] The practical solution which we will follow is the one which Pinard de la Boullaye adopted for his own studies. At the outset, therefore, we opt for a definition—metaphysical in origin and therefore incapable of ultimate justification by empirical data—which will nevertheless allow us to concentrate our analysis upon an order of facts which is clearly identified. We will not prejudge the possibility of determining criteria which may be different from ours, and we will concede beforehand that the conclusions

[31] *Op. cit.,* 27.

[32] W. L. Lowe, "Group Beliefs and Socio-cultural Factors in Religious Delusions" in *Journ. Soc. Psychol.,* 1954, 40, 267–274; I. Rapaport, *Introduction à la psychopathologie collective:* "la secte mystique des Skoptzy" (Paris: 1948?).

[33] G. W. Allport, *The Individual and His Religion:* "A Psychological Interpretation" (London: 1951), 58–83.

46

of our research may not be extended beyond the scope delimited by our concept of religion.

Pinard de la Boullaye begins with the following provisional statements. One gives a nominal definition of objective religion, the other applies it to the subject. "Objectively," he writes, "religion is a totality of beliefs and practices [or practical attitudes] concerning an objective reality or at least conceived as such, individual or collective, but supreme to a certain degree and in some manner personal—a reality on which man, in some way or other, recognizes his dependence and with which he wishes to maintain a relationship."[34] Let us note in passing that in his first edition, the author preferred the expression "personal or impersonal." In the subjective sense religion means "the manner of thinking, feeling, acting, in short, the mentality which corresponds to the beliefs and the conduct that we have just indicated."[35] In addition, he suggests the following psychological definition: "The orientation of man toward an ultraphenomenal principle upon which he feels dependence."[36] This last statement is rather similar to one made by Jung for whom "the expression 'religion' signifies the particular attitude of a consciousness which has been modified by the experience of the numinous."[37]

Two methodological questions are worth asking apropos of the definitions we have given. Are these formulations comprehensive enough to comprise all the religious data? Do they sufficiently stress the psychosocial aspect of religious behavior?

The objective definition as stated evidently includes only those religions which offer worship to a personal God; consequently it excludes from the scope of psychoreligious

[34] *Op. cit.*, II, 5.
[35] *Ibid.*, II, 5.
[36] *Ibid.*, II, 321.
[37] C. G. Jung, *Psychology and Religion* (New Haven: 1960).

observation a whole range of phenomena and behavior in which other authors would readily recognize a sacred or mystical character, such as the fervor of humanitarian causes which can command ardent devotion. That there can exist in these adhesions to an impersonal mystique a semblance of religious behavior is not for us either to deny or to postulate. We do not treat these latter phenomena as negligible or without importance, but, methodologically, we are adopting the more restricted point of view of Pinard de la Boullaye. This view provides a certain basic unity of our subject matter; and it is broad enough to comprehend the majority of existing research, which is concentrated in the area of Judeo-Christian religions.

With regard to the second question raised, it seems evident that these definitions can be understood in a sense which extends beyond the individual, even if they do not formally introduce the socioreligious element. In speaking of practices, attitudes, mentality and conduct, we are situated at the meeting point of the individual and the collective. Pinard de la Boullaye leaves no doubt that religion is an object for sociological observation and analysis,[38] and he can well claim that his definition will be useful to discern societies and sects which are specifically religious, that is, collective forms of religious behavior.[39] We do not have to debate at this time the question whether a strictly personal and subjective religion is within the realm of the possible. Durkheim foresaw the difficulty and wondered what the sociologist's position would be concerning "contemporary aspirations toward a religion which would consist entirely of interior and subjective states and which would be freely constructed by each individual." But the problem scarcely made him pause and these undefined tendencies, which he

---

[38] *Op. cit.*, **II, 387 f.**
[39] *Ibid.*, II, 5.

termed "uncertain virtualities,"[40] were brushed aside as being too vague to be included in his concept of religion.

Recent studies, such as those of Fromm, Allport and Grensted, irrespective of how their final conclusions are received, present data indicating that we should not reject without examination the possiblity of religious behavior which is relatively independent of organized worship or institutionalized religion. If this behavior meet the criteria which we have stated above, we cannot exclude it a priori from our concept of religion. Our analysis of religious belonging will orient us rather toward the collective aspect of religious behavior, but the data which we will encounter and the comparisons which we will be led to make between individual attitudes and institutional attitudes, suggest a methodological position which does not deny in advance the possibility of behavior that is inspired by a purely individualized personal form of religion.

III Religious Belonging: a Psychosociological Attitude

1 Religious belonging as viewed by theologians: the "church member." 2 The psychosociologist's point of view: the religious attitude and identification with a religious group. 3 Religious belonging as the source of attitude and as the object of attitude. 4 Specification of belonging and of religious groups.

1 RELIGIOUS BELONGING AS VIEWED BY THEOLOGIANS

What is religious belonging? The very asking of the question immediately evokes rather different answers. A first approach to a solution is afforded us by current expressions

[40] *Op. cit.,* 65.

like "feeling of belonging," "religious preferences," and "religious affiliation." Thus a general phenomenon appears in which one can see the formulation of complementary perspectives: among others, the theologian's viewpoint and the sociologist's. The latter will be particularly interested in the manifestations of collective psychology which accompany the fact of belonging to a religion. The theologian for his part will strive to determine the norms as well as the doctrinal significance of religious belonging.

Before coming to the sociologist's particular point of view, it may be useful, in order to orient our observations, to consider the perspective of the theologian. Social psychologists may well find important clues regarding the nature of religious belonging in the insigts of the theologians. As a starting point they will find that there exist theologico-juridical criteria of religious membership. Who is a member of such and such a church? According to what criteria is adhesion defined? What causes a loss of membership? In the last analysis, the question depends on theology; but the consequences of this theology have visible effects which the social observer cannot ignore without the risk of neglecting the motivational aspect of religious behavior.

At this time we are less concerned with presenting a theology of religious belonging than with recalling methodologically the necessity of considering as a preliminary datum the interpretation that the churches themselves furnish of the reality under study. Let us call to mind what is recounted in the Book of Numbers. The census of the Chosen People was an act properly religious, and it could not be undertaken except in accordance with an order from on high; God gave his people to multiply and he only might know their number. To count them was a divine prerogative and no one had the right to usurp it, not even the king.[41] These

[41] A. George, "Fautes contre Yahweh dans les Livres de Samuel" in *Revue Biblique,* 1946, 53, 161–184.

ancient prescriptions aid us in understanding the jealous care with which religious groups themselves define the conditions of belonging and the criteria which permit a distinction between members and nonmembers. The idea which the religious community possesses of itself is in this case decisive. Two examples will allow us to show this; one applies to Protestant churches, the other to the Catholic Church.

Apropos of the Protestants, we will avoid generalizations and content ourselves with the data furnished by Léonard[42] in his book on the French Protestant in which there can be found interesting insights into Protestant doctrines on religious belonging. The author distinguishes between the "church of those who profess their religion" and the "church of the multitude." The first expression applies especially to pietist communities in which only the adherents and the communicants, that is, those converts or faithful members who have lived the "experience of salvation," are considered members. Membership in these communities tends, therefore, to be unstable; for it depends on the dispositions of the faithful."[43] In the church of the multitude, on the contrary, all the baptized of the denomination, even those "not attached," are considered members; and this last grouping can account for a third of the membership of the French Reformed Church.[44] The notion of church member, as is shown by Léonard, will vary considerably according to the concept of the church proper to each denomination; and it is from this that there spring the sociological effects which he has carefully analyzed.

With regard to Catholics, the official theology of belonging has found its expression in a document coming from Rome: the encyclical *Mystici Corporis*. From its contents,

[42] E. G. Léonard, *Le Protestant français* (Paris: 1955).
[43] *Ibid.*, 150.
[44] *Ibid.*, 82, 149.

the Catholic position can be thus summarized: If in a sense every baptized person becomes a subject of the Church (Canon 87), "only those are to be accounted really members of the Church who have been regenerated in the waters of baptism and profess the Catholic faith, and who have not cut themselves off from the structure of the Body by their own unhappy act or been severed therefrom, for very grave faults, by the legitimate authority."[45] Specifically, a Catholic parish priest will count as a member of his parish every baptized person professing the Catholic faith and residing within the confines of his parish (Canon 94); however, provisions are made for several exceptions, such as the case of the faithful belonging to ethnic minorities who are attached to national parishes, etc.

Although theological comparisons could be indefinitely developed, these brief examples help us to understand that religious belonging cannot be conceived as a univocal attachment to any religious body whatsoever. One does not, in the same way, "belong" to a Catholic community or to a Protestant denomination. Even within a single church, belonging exists with notable variations ranging from regular participation in worship to sporadic identification. The differentiation of religious behavior will obviously absorb the attention of the moralists, but it is also of interest to the sociologist; for it reveals manifestations of collective psychology that the observer believes he can study with the ordinary instruments of analysis.

2 THE PSYCHOSOCIOLOGIST'S POINT OF VIEW

Several approaches are available to the psychosociologist who undertakes an analysis of the data of religious belong-

[45] *Mystici Corporis* (encyclical letter of Pope Pius XII on the Mystical Body), *Acta Apostolicae Sedis*, 1943, 35, n. 7, 193–248; see 202. For a recent commentary, see the work of K. Rahner cited in bibliography.

ing. The first way would consist in studying belonging in its relation to social cohesion. Deutsch,[46] for example, who has studied to the motivations of belonging, considers belonging from a double point of view which, at the same time, takes into account the group and the individual member. Belonging is for him, therefore, the counterpart of cohesion: the first being an individual attribute, the second a group attribute. The method is appealing and we shall refer to it in our further analyses. In its present form, however, it cannot be used as a general framework of analysis, for it is applicable only to a restricted aspect of behavior, specifically that of the differentiation of various types of adhesion.

Belonging could likewise be compared to a sentiment or to a sense of belonging. Taken in a strict sense, however, the concept of sentiment seems to us too far from the cognitive and dynamic aspects of behavior for us to use it just as it is; it would not be appropriate for the comprehension of all the components of religious behavior. But the word "sentiment" is also used in a more comprehensive sense and in practice is synonymous with attitude. We will willingly accept the word in this latter sense, more especially since the expression "sense of belonging" is being currently used to signify the totality of phenomena which is of interest to us.

Another concept has been employed by certain authors, namely, religious interest.[47] But this notion, as well as that of religious preferences, is too indefinite; both imply psychological content which defies precise analysis.

It will not be denied that religious belonging can be considered as a feeling or as a preference, or interest, but there

[46] See the study of M. Deutsch, "Field Theory in Social Psychology" in G. Lindzey (ed.), *Handbook of Social Psychology* (Cambridge: 1954), 1956, 181–222.

[47] G. E. Lenski, "Social Correlates of Religious Interest" in *Amer. Sociol. Rev.*, 1953, 18, 533–544.

is an obvious advantage in centering the analysis on a concept which is at the same time more comprehensive and better defined operationally. The concept of attitude seems to us to answer these requirements. The theoretical elaboration which has helped to clarify this concept, as much in the United States as in France, keeps us from dwelling at length on the significance that we attribute to the term attitude.[48]

As a reminder, and one which is based on the works of the authors here cited, let us consider the following description. Attitude is a disposition or a structure of dynamic factors positively or negatively orienting behavior with respect to a psychosociological object. It is the dynamic structure preparatory to action. This disposition is the result of a relatively durable organization of perceptive, emotional and motivational processes exerting themselves with regard to a psychological object. One speaks of attitudes with relation to strangers, a political program, a religion, etc.

It is immediately evident how the concept of attitude will be applied to religious behavior. The advantages of its use are to be noted. The concept of attitude is coextensive with all the determinants of behavior and for this reason it encompasses the determinants of religious behavior also; the perceptive and cognitive aspect that we have emphasized makes allowance for the role played by the phenomena of knowledge and belief, which are so important to the understanding of ethicoreligious behavior. Even the notions of disposition or of psychological structure, while indicating the influences which come from the milieu and from psychological experience, leave room for a substratum of personality which could eventually be treated as such by the

[48] See G. W. Allport, "Attitudes" in C. Murchison (ed.), *A Handbook of Social Psychology* (Worcester: 1935), 798–844; J. Stoetzel, "La psychologie sociale et la théorie des attitudes" in *Annales Sociologiques,* 1941, fasc. 4, 1–24.

moralist or the metaphysician. The theologian will consequently see the possibility of reconciling the observations of
psychosociology with his own conception of the factors
which determine religious behavior.

The theologian will likewise note that an analysis based
on attitudes avoids the extremes both of psychologism and
sociologism. There is no longer any need to oppose irre-
ducibly the free individual and the sociological conditioning
to which he is submitted. The dichotomy between sociological conformity and personal autonomy is therefore
overcome, as are the one-sided explanations which used to
constrict the moralists and theologians, accustomed to regard religious behavior in terms of personal responsibility
and socioreligious prescriptions respectively. In an analysis
based on the concept of attitudes one clearly notes the
interaction of the individual and the social as determinants
of behavior. For attitude comprises both the personality
itself and the milieu on which the individual is dependent.
Two sources of our attitudes are thus shown, without confusing them or having their interaction denied. It is *we* who
truly live such an experience within a social framework; it is
we who react in such and such a manner, according to the
influence of the *groups* with which we are identified.[49]

Another point on which psychosociologists are dwelling
more and more deserves to be emphasized, and it is here
that the two notions of attitude and belonging are intimately
joined. The fundamental attitudes of a person are closely
linked with his social relationships. Since the work of Sherif
and Cantril[50] it has become more and more common to
study attitudes in their relationship with the social identifications and with the groups to which the individual belongs.

[49] *Ibid.*, 7, 17.
[50] M. Sherif and H. Cantril, *The Psychology of Ego-involvements:
Social Attitudes and Identifications* (New York: 1947).

55

Thus a solidarity of attitudes and group associations is emphasized, a solidarity we shall here attempt to explain.

Girod[51] remarks that "the values, norms, and patterns of behavior which inspire the attitudes of individuals are generally embodied in groups that practice them, esteem them or symbolize them." In two lengthy chapters on reference groups, Merton[52] has insisted on an important distinction apropos of this matter. Is the reference group a group to which a person is oriented without being a member of it (simple reference groups), or is it rather a group to which he already belongs (membership group)? The membership group is the one which will be of more particular interest to us, but we should note that the simple reference groups, that is, the groups with which one desires to be identified, play a considerable role in the mobility of attitudes and affiliations. We will return to these concepts when we speak of conversions and the variations of religious belonging.[53]

3 RELIGIOUS BELONGING AS THE SOURCE AND AS THE OBJECT OF ATTITUDE

The association of attitudes with social relationships has led us to consider two complementary aspects in the interaction according to which a person identifies himself with his group. From one viewpoint belonging can be considered a source from which attitudes are derived. The fact that one

[51] R. Girod, *Attitudes collectives et relations humaines* (Paris: 1952), 34.

[52] R. K. Merton, *Social Theory and Social Structure* (Chicago: 1957), 279 f.

[53] For an application of these concepts to religious behavior, see our study, "Le rôle des groupes de référence dans l'intégration des attitudes religieuses," an address delivered at the Sixth International Conference of Religious Sociology, Bologna, Sept. 3–6, 1959; see *Social Compass*, 1960, 2, 139–160.

belongs to this or that religious denomination evokes particular attitudes within the order of moral or socioeconomic behavior. Troude[54] has studied from this point of view the moral level of the Norman provinces; the Allinsmiths[55] have analyzed the politico-economic attitudes of the members of eight different religious denominations.

This first aspect of religious belonging, conceived as the generator of attitude, is obviously significant as regards the comprehensive character of religious behavior. "The influence of religious affiliation," writes Stoetzel,[56] "is not without some bearing on attitudes in general;" and relying on the authority of previous research, he adds: "It might even be considerably more important than the influence of sex or intellectual level." We shall have the opportunity to make frequent reference to this first aspect of religious belonging, considered the source of attitudes.

There is a second viewpoint which is more direct in its approach to the phenomenon of religious belonging. This considers belonging itself as an *object* of attitude or, better, as a *specific* attitude. No longer is belonging regarded only as a source of subsequent attitudes, but rather as the fundamental attitude of the member with respect to his group. Belonging therefore is compared to a "psychosociological disposition"; it is conceived as a "stable structure of perceptive, motivational and emotional processes" exerting themselves, on the part of the member, with regard to his group. Thus we encounter that which is most intimate in the psychology of the member conscious of belonging to an organized group. We discover the specific attitude of the

[54] R. Troude, "Le niveau moral de la Normandie selon quatre critères statistiques" in *Etudes Normandes,* 1958, 26, 1–11.

[55] W. Allinsmith and B. Allinsmith, "Religious Affiliation and Politico-Economic Attitude: A Study of Eight Major U. S. Religious Groups" in *Publ. Opin. Quart.,* 1948, 12, 377–389.

[56] *Op. cit.,* 22.

member as such. His belonging is no longer a fact viewed from the exterior, a fact reported to a census-taker, or a religious category; it is a psychosocial reality. The member sees himself as taking part in his group; he identifies himself with it, he participates in it, he receives his motivation from it; in a word, he is in a state or disposition of interaction with the group, which understands, inspires and welcomes him. He belongs to his group and the "psychological structure of his disposition with regard to the group" constitutes his specific attitude of belonging.

4 SPECIFICATION OF BELONGING AND OF RELIGIOUS GROUPS

If the theory of attitudes and group affiliation justifies the preceding propositions it only leads us, however, to the threshold of the real problem, and it tells us very little about the "how."

How are our affiliations formed and transformed? How, specifically, do we become members of a group, and what psychological significance ought we to attribute to our affiliations? It is not certain that the same psychosocial explanations are valid for every category of belonging. Adhesion to a political party, affiliation with a recreation group, belonging to a learned society or to a church: these cannot be combined a priori as one univocal phenomenon.

While starting from the propositions stated earlier, our precise purpose will be to examine the psychosociological implications of religious belonging. Our hypothesis is that the belonging to an organized religion constitutes a specific attitude, probably analogous, under certain aspects, to other forms of affiliation, but comprising unique and irreducible elements, which we must put to further analysis.

It is possible to speak in a general way of belonging to a

58

religion, but in light of what has already been said here our perspective is more precise; we shall concern ourselves with the question of belonging to an organized religion, that is, belonging to a group, a religious body. Apropos of the very concept of religion, we mentioned earlier that we shall not resolve the theoretical question of knowing whether a strictly personal religion is possible; but the very object of our analysis will formally orient us toward some types of religion that are socially organized. It is only incidentally, then, that we shall deal with religious attitudes which are exclusively personal.

A final limitation is imposed on us, both by methodological necessity and by the nature of our documentation and sources. We shall explicitly restrict ourselves to religious groups of Judeo-Christian inspiration. The definition of religion that we have made our own would permit the acceptance of a great many other religious forms as consistent with the very notion of religion, but we believe that it would be rash to attempt at this time to extend our conclusions to every type of belief. We possess at the present time few psychosociological studies about those religions which are not offshoots of the Judeo-Christian tradition. We are, on the contrary, relatively well informed about the Jewish, Protestant and Catholic religions—at least in matters of the western world.

The author, while undertaking his analysis, is himself aware of his own religious affiliation. He recognizes that the group to which he belongs guide his interests and orient his observation; the Catholic structures and behavior are the ones most familiar to him. Both the author's own orientation and the requirement of sound methodology oblige him to avoid confusing the various confessions with one another and to recognize both the elements which they have in common and those by which they are distinguished.

59

The analysis, properly so called, will comprise two principal parts, in which will be considered, in turn, the formation of the religious attitude, and the modes of internal differentiation of religious belonging. In a final section, we will attempt to assemble the elements which constitute the specific nature of the religious attitude.

PART TWO

FORMATION OF THE RELIGIOUS ATTITUDE

CONVERSION AS A MODE OF
RELIGIOUS ADHESION

In the next three chapters, we shall discuss conversion and its socioreligious aspects. Conversion will be considered precisely as one of the forms of affiliation to a religious group. The psychosocial analysis will study conversion insofar as it is the genesis of the bond of religious belonging.

It will be necessary for us to determine the elements of a psychosocial description of conversion (Chapter II). Next, we will see how conversion is distinguished and differentiated according to the very structures of the religious groups which receive the convert. The sects offer in this regard particular patterns (Chapter III). The conversion to a church will suppose a more complex integration on the socioreligious level, as well as the levels of ritual and of psychological adaption (Chapter IV).

Chapter II

The Religious Conversion

1 The religious initiation, formation of the attitude. 2 Preliminary description of conversion. 3 Phenomenology and typology of conversion. 4 Conversion with relation to different religious groups.

1 THE RELIGIOUS INITIATION, FORMATION OF THE ATTITUDE

In a now classic article, Allport proposed to trace the formation of attitudes back to four main processes: integration, which is accomplished by the assimilation of previous experiences; differentiation, or the specification of attitudes which have remained indefinite; crisis, or the dramatic experience, which provides a new and stable orientation; and finally, imitation, or the conforming to attitudes received in a milieu.[1]

Allport's framework will help us distinguish the different ways religious attitudes are formed, but in the course of our analysis, we will regroup our observations under the rather general term of integration. Several reasons prompt us to do this. In one respect, the concept of integration can be applied in a broad and comprehensive sense to

[1] *Op. cit.*, 798–844.

designate "the systematization of individual experiences in a unified 'experience.' "[2]

Moreover, the documentation at our disposal is not too well suited for Allport's framework, for the studies on the genesis of religious attitude have for all practical purposes been neglected by present day sociologists—so much so that if one wished to assemble all the empirical studies devoted to religious initiation he would have to turn to the ethnologists and the specialists in the history of religions. The contributions of religious phenomenology and the history of religions in this area allow us to perceive one of the evident lags of social psychology.

Several years ago Harms[3] expressed the regret that there was so little empirical knowledge about the development of the religious experience in children. In the sciences we have just indicated, these problems were approached for a long time within the perspective of the rites of religious initiation. It is useful to point this out, in passing, before moving on to the works of the psychosociologists; and we could add that a closer relationship between the two types of research is desirable. Religious ethnology, for example, from which Pinard de la Boullaye was able to draw some very enlightening comparisons, offers the sociologists direct or indirect observations which are of help in situating the problems within an empirical perspective, without neglecting, however, the more interior phenomena of the religious conscience.

By perceptive comparisons of one culture with another, by examination of religious symbols, and by the content analysis of religious confidences, one arrives at a description of religious initiation in terms which approximate psycho-

---

[2] See J. Stoetzel, *Théorie des opinions* (Paris: 1943), 296.
[3] E. Harms, "The Development of Religious Experience in Children" in *Amer. Journ. Sociol.*, 1944, 50, 112–122.

sociological language. Cazeneuve,[4] for instance, has treated religious initiation within the context of "archetypal acts," in which concepts the influence of Jung is rather clear. This observation of initiation practices led the author to posit a universal conformation and identification with a sacred archetype, that is, a behavior reproducing symbolically the "repetition of creation." All conduct is consequently sublimated, placed on a special ontological plane; every act, even the most ordinary, is represented as the repetition of archetypal acts; it produces, as it were, a reintegration of the profound personality perfecting itself in relatively identical socioreligious conditions.

On the other hand, some phenomenologists like Van der Leeuw have carefully examined the phenomena of religious conversion and initiation. They have been able to discover, substantiate and over-reach the viewpoint of social psychology. The ritual initiation, for example, will be studied empirically as a "new birth" which one will observe in all its phases.[5] Studies of this kind could eventually furnish the psychosociologists with likely hypotheses of research. Kardiner,[6] who was oriented in this direction, was able to establish a close relationship between the religious elements of a culture and the education of an individual personality. Since his studies have almost exclusive bearing on non-Christian religions, it is difficult to generalize from his conclusions. In any case, eventual collaboration could be possible.

With respect to the Judeo-Christian religions, the most detailed and the most recent studies available are those of

---

[4] J. Cazeneuve, *Les rites et la condition humaine* (Paris: 1958), Chapter 17.

[5] G. Van der Leeuw, *La religion dans son essence et ses manifestations: phénoménologie de la religion* (Paris: 1955), 517 f.

[6] See A. Kardiner, R. Linton, C. Dubois, J. West, *The Psychological Frontiers of Society* (New York: 1945).

Allport, Grensted and Clark. They have attempted an "intuitive" approach to grasp the subjective import of religion for the individual. Let us add that the intuitive method as it is used by experts like Allport is not a form of arbitrary analysis; it is based on a long experience of observation. There exists, besides, a great number of monographs on the motivations or the motives of religious affiliation and on the components of religious attitude. Our purpose, then, will be to draw inspiration from all these studies in order to analyze the formation of religious attitudes. Three modes of integration seem to us more particularly significant in the psychosociological genesis of the religious attitude: conversion, the early stages of education, and religious instruction. These modes of integration do not necessarily exclude one another, but they appear sufficiently distinct at first sight to treat them separately.

2 PRELIMINARY DESCRIPTION OF CONVERSION

We do not intend to present a general psychology of conversion here; we wish to consider conversion simply as one of the forms of affiliation with a religious collectivity. Let us first give a provisory description, and then add some further considerations which will facilitate the socioreligious approach to the phenomenon.

Viewed by the psychosociologist, conversion appears as a total adhesion, sudden and often accompanied with crisis, to values shared by a community; the experience will tend toward the reunification of the personality and toward its social integration. One would not be able to affirm a priori that all conversions are identical. In fact, authors distinguish different types of conversion: political conversion, esthetical conversion, social conversion, religious conversion.[7]

There also exist ideological conversions in which occurs the attraction of an absolute that has suddenly been discovered by the individual. These incidents of sudden illumination are very frequent, and one can encounter several such experiences in the course of his life. However, the extreme fervor sometimes aroused by this type of convention is of interest to religious psychosociology. It is not rare that ideological or humanitarian causes induce a profound and lasting enthusiasm, and that they even come to serve as an absolute substitute for a faith that has been lost. We will return to these phenomena when we treat of the transformations of the religious attitude (Chapter X). For the moment, let us keep to the discussion of conversions which are properly religious.

Even with religious conversions, it will be necessary to consider the significance that the religions themselves attribute to the experience. This would be at the level of patterns and anticipations of behavior, for the conceptions that churches or denominations make of conversion will be determinative. Thus we can anticipate the prime importance of the psychosocial context of conversion; for this very same reason it will be necessary to be careful to situate the phenomenon in its relation to well defined religious groups. The concepts of conversion held by each religious group will form, therefore, the first element for our consideration.

Even the form of the conversion-experience will vary according to whether conversion is conceived by the religious group as an intellectual adhesion—where crises constitute only the first period of a progressive process, or whether the experience is considered much like an emo-

[7] See J. Stoetzel, *Théorie des opinions*, 307.

tional shock—where the sudden sentiment of confidence *forms* the entirety of the conversion. Pinard de la Boullaye has insisted on this methodological precaution.[8] In a study of Protestant conversions in mission countries that remains one of the best analyses on the subject Allier[9] brings out numerous facts that confirm the preceding statement. Even the orientation of preachers will produce conversions of very different types: perhaps a crisis leading to a profound spiritual rebirth, or a brutal shock obtained by the "systematic pursuit of emotion."[10]

The permanent or the ephemeral character of conversions, as well as the very diverse experiences which habitually precede and prepare for them, reveal to us such disparities of behavior that it is impossible to fit them all into one and the same pattern. With Penido[11] we readily agree that it is useless to look for a single general explanation of conversion.

Certain sociologists have shown themselves too hasty in making generalizations here. Misunderstandings originated in part from a false interpretation of the work of Starbuck,[12] who had studied the motives of conversion and had observed that the phenomenon occurred especially during the period of adolescence. These findings were certainly enlightening for those who were looking for motives for conversion derived from social influences. Table 1 summarizes his results.

Starbuck's investigations constituted one of the first attempts to study religious motivation empirically with the help of questionnaires. They had, subsequently, a profound influence on the "psychological explanations" of conversion;

---

[8] *Op. cit.*, II, 338.

[9] R. Allier, *La psychologie de la conversion chez les peuples noncivilisés*, 2 vol., (Paris: 1925).

[10] *Ibid.*, I, 477 f.

[11] M. T.-L. Penido, *La conscience religieuse:* "*Essai systématique suivi d'illustrations*" (Paris: 1935), 45.

[12] See especially E. D. Starbuck, *The Psychology of Religion* (New York: 1899), 1903.

TABLE 1

The motives of 1011 men and 254 women for conversion. Answers
are by percentage.

Fear of death or of hell	14
Remorse	16
Moral ideal	17
Other personal motives	6
Altruistic motives	5
Response to instruction	10
Imitation and example	13
Social pressure	19

Source: Starbuck, 1903, 52.

above all they had the good fortune of being used as basic
material by William James in his writing of *The Varieties
of Religious Experience*.

Today, however, one would not be satisfied with Starbuck's limited research as a basis for formulating general
laws and asserting, as has been done so often, that conversion is essentially a phenomenon occuring around the
sixteenth year, or that one regularly finds in it the motives
shown in table 1. Starbuck himself had been more prudent
by stating that his results, from the very start, referred to
"Protestants living in an American milieu;" he would have
been astonished to see his explanations proposed as universally valid.

If then one wishes to uphold a pluralism which is both
psychological and religious, such as these first findings have
revealed to us, one must be oriented toward the description
of types of conversions rather than toward a general definition of the phenomenon.

3 PHENOMENOLOGY AND TYPOLOGY OF CONVERSION

A typology of conversion, evidently, is only possible after
a vast accumulation of observations the interpretation of

69

which will justify relationships and emphasize differences. To our knowledge there exists no better comparative work on types of conversions than that of Penido.[13] We shall see later how, despite certain differences in terminology, the analyses of Penido agree with more recent studies like those of Baudouin.

From the start Penido avoids all premature simplification: "The more we observe the facts, the more a psychology of *the* conversion seems chimerical to us." An examination of the numerous accounts of conversion which he had collected led him to establish a double typology: one he calls genetic, which explores the causes of conversion; the other structural, which is devoted to pathological and normal phenomena. His genetic typology is of particular interest to us here for it touches upon the collective psychology of religious integration.

If one considers the origins of conversion, there seem to be two principal types which ought to be distinguished: the exogenous conversions and the endogenous conversions, as specified by Penido. The distinction is based on the behavior of the subject with relation to the exterior event, circumstance or particular experience. A relationship between these processes and those which Allport designates as the integration, the differentiation and the crisis might, *mutatis mutandis,* be established.

In exogenous (exterior origin) conversion, it is from the outside that change is induced: a happy or unhappy event will suddenly occur, such as to upset and reorient the fundamental attitude of the subject; the attitude then appears to be dominated by the event.

In endogenous (interior origin) conversion, a minimal

[13] M. T.-L. Penido, *op. cit.;* we refer especially to Chapter Two of this work: "Contribution à la typologie générale de la conversion religieuse chrétienne," 41–131.

importance is accorded to the exterior event, which is reduced to the role of mere occasion; it is within the interior of consciousness that the transformations actively take place. Newman, in his *Apologia,* described a conversion of this second type: "My change did not arise from the shock of exterior influences but it came from the work of my own spirit and the happenings around me."

According to the type of conversion, a more or less defined role is attributed to the exterior event; one will observe nevertheless that this role is "out of proportion with the change which has taken place in the soul of the convert." Conversion comprises a crisis and a phenomenon of resolution whose internal mechanism defies analysis.[14] To speak of the exterior event, of apparent crisis, of the sudden emergence of a new attitude is to dwell on the periphery of an intimate process which transcends observation and which the philosophers or the theologians will explain by other forms of analysis. Penido is aware of these limits and if, as a psychologist, he deals with the phenomena of conversion, he does not wish his conclusions to be extended beyond the scope of empirical observation.

The author likewise has shown how endogenous and exogenous conversions are not categorically opposed. These classifications offer, above all, predominant trends and stable points of reference in the conversions observed. To study the phenomena of conversion is to apply oneself to the observable, to appearances. It is at this level that Penido presents his typology. What interests him, as a psychologist, is the *observable genesis* of the process.

As such, the endogenous–exogenous distinction could be reconciled with the traditional explanations of conversion given by theologians, who customarily consider both the intrinsic elements and the extrinsic elements which pro-

[14] On this point, see J. Stoetzel, *Théorie des opinions,* 306.

duce the spiritual renewal; they also distinguish the two ways of the *vocatio hominis,* the one exterior, such as preaching, the other interior and corresponding to intimate movements of the soul. Penido cites numerous texts of classical theology which are in agreement with the phenomenologists' descriptions.

The distinction between endogenous and exogenous conversion is important in that it provides the elements which will serve to describe the phenomena of conversion empirically. Penido presents the following descriptive account: "A conversion appears to the psychologist as the disintegration, on the religious level, of a mental synthesis and its replacement by another." In every conversion, there is "the elimination of a nonreligious self to the advantage of a religious self." Two processes are at work: a dissolving of the previous psychological structure and the appearance of a new one, but the two processes are manifested differently in the two types of conversion.

Exogenous conversion is characterized by the succession of the two processes of disintegration and restructuring, whereas endogenous conversion reveals on the whole a simultaneity of the processes. In exogenous conversion the disintegration of the nonreligious synthesis is produced first, and only after this does the "new constellation" appear. But in the conversion of the endogenous type the two processes are simultaneous, with the disintegration taking place in some way "by virtue of the reorganization." In short, two cases are clearly enough characterized: "In one instance the nonreligious self recedes and disintegrates under an exterior shock, and it is again from the exterior that there comes the new vitality; in the other, on the contrary, there is an elimination of the nonreligious self, to and in the degree that the religious self becomes established" (see Penido, *op. cit.,* 61).

One can find in Baudouin[15] the use of concepts which types of conversions, the renewal and the quest; and also the explanation of the phenomenon by the substitution of the new self for the old. Speaking, for example, of conversion by renewal, Baudouin writes: "We know, indeed, that in conflicts of this type, the new 'self' which asserts itself is a former 'self' which life has silenced at a given moment and which is awakened and, with difficulty, aroused."

It seems, then, that Penido's guidelines can be used as basic elements for an operational concept of conversion. We shall, however, add another element as indispensable: the community aspect of conversion. Our interest, indeed, is not limited to a conversion which is intimate and conceived as isolated from the sociological universe; we envisage, on the contrary, the conversion to a religious collectivity or, more exactly, *in* a religious collectivity.

These observations concerning the typical forms of conversions found in different religious denominations will help us consider the concept of conversion in its psycho-sociological dimensions. If one envisages conversion in this community perspective, one understands the attempt of sociologists who wish to define conversion according to the theory of social roles or that of socialization. Zetterberg,[16] for example, presents conversion as "the sudden acceptance of a social role proposed by a religious group." We will see in the following chapter the exact significance of this explanation; for the moment we are ready to accept this point of view provided that it is not isolated from more intimate psychological descriptions such as those of Penido.

To these elements we would add a last, one suggested by

[15] C. Baudouin, *Psychanalyse du symbole religieux* (Paris: 1957), see especially 57–75.

[16] H. L. Zetterberg, "The Religious Conversion as a Change of Social Roles" in *Sociology and Social Research*, 1952, 36, 159–166.

a phenomenologist. Van der Leeuw, by way of observation, rejects every description of conversion which would reduce the latter to a "psychic breakthrough" fostered or nurtured more or less unconsciously. There is in conversion more than the total overthrow of a psychology; there is in the convert a spontaneous subordination to a "totally other" perceived as apart, holy. The phenomenologist, as the author has explained, is not able, to the same degree as the theologian, to speak of divine intervention; but the consciousness of the convert whom he observes reveals a behavior which is unintelligible outside of this hypothesis: "We are not able to describe the structure of conversion without taking into account this divine action insofar as it is an element of comprehension."[17] This statement brings out one of the traits of religious conversion to which we will have to return: its absolute character. "It is not man who converts himself," remarks Van der Leeuw, "it is God who converts him, who endows him with a new life . . . conversion is essentially a rebirth." Phenomenology cannot judge the objectivity of the supra-empirical but it can explain the contents of consciousness which, from the subject's viewpoint, motivate his behavior; in this case, the motive consists in a belief in a divine action.

Religious conversion, then, appears to the observer as a complex phenomenon in which psychological factors, collective references and elements of belief interact. From the preceding analyses there finally emerges a specific behavior which one can describe as follows: disintegration of a cognitive and motivational synthesis with a restructuring of the personality on a religious basis; the acceptance of a social

[17] G. Van der Leeuw, op. cit., 522. On the "absolute" character of the intimate experience of the convert, see M. Nédoncelle and R. Girault, J'ai rencontré le Dieu vivant: témoignages avec deux études sur la conversion (Paris: 1952).

74

role prescribed by a religious group; and, as a motive, the consciousness of a call and of a divine action.

4 CONVERSION WITH RELATION TO DIFFERENT RELIGIOUS GROUPS

Having been provided with this descriptive statement, let us examine a little more closely the contribution of present-day research to the psychosociology of conversion. A fundamental observation here demands our attention: almost all studies on religious conversion are placed within the larger framework of a sociology which compares sects and churches. The reason for this is that conversion, or the forms of conversion, have been studied precisely as one of the distinctive criteria of these two types of religious groups.

With reference to what we have said concerning the bearing of the community on conversions, it will be useful to clarify what the sociologists understand by "sect" and "church" and to see how they interpret the behavior that is customarily observed among the members of these two types of groups.

It was Max Weber who suggested to Troeltsch the analysis of this distinction; it has been pursued by several authors such as Becker and Niebuhr and continues to be discussed up to the present. In outline form the distinction offers the following schema: the church is a religious body of which one usually becomes a member at birth; the church reveals a clear institutionalization which expresses itself in a hierarchy, dogmas, discipline, rites and common symbols; the tendency of the church is toward the universal, and the inclusion or the conversion of all; it seeks a *modus vivendi* with the whole of the society, with which it often coincides in its geographical and social dimensions.

The sect appears as a limited group, one which recruits its members on a voluntary basis. Generally there is an insistence on the necessity of a previous experience of personal conversion, and the sect manifests a noticeable opposition to institutionalization, sacramentalism and compromise with the world. The sect members, by isolation and the simplicity of their approach to religion, wish to rediscover the fundamental fervor of the spirit. Following Troeltsch, Wach observed that there exist two rather different sectarian attitudes: one is clearly emotional, revolutionary and radical; the other is more moderate, it is passive and accepts suffering with resignation.[18]

It becomes immediately apparent that conversion will assume a different psychological coloration according to the nature of the religious group which serves as its frame of reference. But at once a question arises: what value should be attached to this dichotomic distinction of religious groups? Are there only two types to consider? The sociologists, in fact, have observed that there exist cases which fall between these two extremes.

Von Wiese and Becker[19] introduce two other types: the denomination and the cult; Pfautz[20] adds the institutionalized sect. Finally, we would have the following typology: church, denomination, institutionalized sect, sect, cult. Dynes[21] believes that it is preferable to return to a more traditional typology in which the sect is conceived as "a community of believers maintaining basic interpersonal relations." In brief, he insists on the criterion of behavior rather than on the criterion of group structure.

[18] *Op. cit.,* 174.

[19] L. von Wiese and H. Becker, *Systematic Sociology* (New York: 1932), 624 f.

[20] H. W. Pfautz, "The Sociology of Secularization: Religious Groups" in *Amer. Journ. Sociol.,* 1955, 61, 121–128.

[21] R. R. Dynes, "The Consequences of Sectarianism for Social Participation" in *Social Forces,* 1957, 35, 331–334.

Johnson[22] in a critique of this typology favors granting the predominant role to another criterion, namely, the institutionalization of the means of salvation: the church is an institutionalized body with a priesthood and the sacramental dispensation of the means of salvation; the sect is only a voluntary association of persons who dedicate themselves to an ethico-religious ideal without seeking salvation and grace through the mediation of an institutional priesthood. Other authors have attempted a differential psychology of the sects themselves. We will return to them when we deal with the cohesion of religious structures.

The debate is still in progress among sociologists. The difficulty of determining how many religious groups must be distinguished will always provide matter for debate, granted the wide variety of cults, beliefs and religious behavior that one generally finds. In practice and under certain conditions, however, we would consider as adequate the two general types of sect and church.

With regard to the church, there is unanimity among the authors in admitting that the institution which is closest to Weber's ideal-type of "church" is the Catholic Church. We possess at later stages of our analysis a point of reference relatively easy to identify. There evidently exists between the sectarian groupings and the Catholic Church a wide range of religious confessions that are frequently designed by the word "denomination." These will not be treated in our analysis. Since at present we are concerned with types of religious behavior or, more exactly, with the concept that religious groups have of conversion, we believe it reasonable to consider the two fundamental types of sect and church. Later we shall see in what sense the concept of church can

[22] B. Johnson, "A Critical Appraisal of the Church-Sect Typology" in *Amer. Sociol. Rev.*, 1957, 22, 88–92. Also consult the critique of H. Desroche, "Autour de la sociologie dite 'des sectes'" in *L'Année Sociologique*, 1955–1956, 3e série, 395–421.

assume a more or less broad content at the level of observation.

The problem is more difficult when one deals with sects, especially when one wishes to make generalizations about them. We shall attempt to avoid the difficulty by carefully mentioning in each case what particular group has been observed; we shall extend our conclusions beyond the group only provisionally or in ways which will indicate the most common tendencies.

Thus we can situate conversion within the community contexts which appear specific. According to the operational concept of conversion, explained above—which serves as a working hypothesis—we assume that there exists a psycho-sociological solidarity between the convert and the religious group which orients and integrates his behavior. In this respect the nature of the religious grouping, i.e., whether it be a sect or a church, seems determinative and permits us to treat each case separately. We shall, then, examine in turn conversion to sects and to a church.

Chapter III

The Conversion to Sects

1 The pattern of religious revival. 2 The problem of sectarian personality and behavior. 3 Socioreligious statuses and roles. 4 Significance of conversion according to the structure of the sects. 5 The apparent religious motivations.

1 THE PATTERN OF RELIGIOUS REVIVAL

To speak of conversion to sects is to recall a pattern of behavior which has been observed many times by sociologists: the religious awakening or "revival." Every joining of a sect does not necessarily take this form, but the conversions produced at "revival meetings" are sufficiently characteristic of the sects for us to treat them first.

Externally, the revival appears as a collective religious manifestation, directed by a leader, and openly encouraging conversion among a certain number of listeners who are said to be touched by the spirit. According to the more intuitive description of Van der Leeuw,[1] the revival corresponds to "a wave of sensibility and religious determination which flows over a community and sweeps along everyone in a strong current of sentiment and decision."

A fundamental point in the consideration of these col-

[1] *Op. cit.*, 599.

lective conversions is the anticipation and representation of the experience in the consciousness of the candidates. Recollection of the personal experiences undergone by the founder of the sect will often play a decisive role. If, for example, in the Methodists' revivals there is insistence on the personal experience of conversion and on the necessity, consequent on conversion, of joining a Christian fraternity, it is because there is an awareness of reproducing and repeating the experience of John Wesley, the founder, who was first transformed by the direct experience of "conversion by faith and without ritual." A model and even an anticipation of the behavior takes place in the psychology of the directors as well as in that of the participants.[2]

In a study of religious assemblies, Alphandéry gives a detailed description of the phases of a revival such as can be observed at the meetings of the Salvation Army. The psychoreligious process is relatively uniform and accepted beforehand by all the members at the meeting. The first predominant feeling, experienced even by the most lukewarm, is the fear of sin and the dread that one suffers when he finds himself morally helpless before God. One knows, on the other hand, that deliverance can be granted by a grace which is wholly individual. The officer who directs the meeting studies the faces of those present, notes those who show the most emotion, and starts, at the right moment, the classic appeal: "There is someone here who is burdened . . . who has a great sin. . . ." A profound feeling grips the participants; each one feels that it is he who has been singled out and he asks himself whether he has not been designated by this call and personally touched by the inter-

---

[2] Several observers of revivals have outlined the following succession of states of the convert's soul: conviction of sin, fear, despair, sense of pardon, joy and peace of soul. The inflexibility of this schema, however, should not be exaggerated nor, above all, should an explanation of "conversion" be sought from it. It is at most only a description.

vention of the spirit. An intense fervor immediately engulfs those who are most disposed, transforms them, converts them and wins them over to the new faith and to the group.[3]

Reduced to its simplest psychological elements, the revival resembles a process which tends to break down previous religious inhibitions while violently insinuating the conviction of sin and evoking in the conscience the obsessive image of the self as sinner. The role of the leader consists, then, in provoking the phase of release and self-surrender; he will appeal to this "hope for a revival" that is more or less conscious and acknowledged by the participants. There is, indeed, a sort of tactic connivance between leaders and participants. The latter, it has been observed, are not simply areligious candidates but have already known, at least during their childhood, some religious experience; the shock will revitalize these forgotten or inhibited sentiments.

Later we will amplify this elementary schema with further nuances. But if one consults the abundant documentation accumulated by Pinard de la Boullaye, Penido, Allier and McLoughlin, he will see that the above description of the revival corresponds, on the whole, to the usual pattern of behavior associated with them.

2 THE PROBLEM OF SECTARIAN PERSONALITY AND BEHAVIOR

Sectarian behavior has always interested the psychosociologists. Since the very general analyses of Sighele,[4]

[3] P. Alphandéry, "Foules historiques: les foules religieuses" in *La Foule* (Paris: 1934), 72. For a study of popular revivals (since 1825), from both an historical and social point of view, see W. G. McLoughlin, *Modern Revivalism* (New York: 1959); consult the classic work of J. Burns, *Revivals, Their Laws and Leaders* (London: 1909); see also the realistic analysis of Ronald Knox, "Some Vagaries of Modern Revivalism," Chapter 22 of his work, *Enthusiasm, A Chapter in the History of Religion* (Oxford: 1950), 1957, 549–577.

[4] S. Sighele, *Psychologie des sectes,* translated from the Italian by L. Brandin, (Paris: 1898); date of the Italian edition is 1895.

numerous studies have kept us informed about the collective psychology of adherents to sects. What type of person is attracted by sects? What is the meaning of their adhesion and their belonging to a sectarian collectivity?

Catton[5] furnishes us with the results of direct observations which answer, in part, the first of our two questions, at least if one considers the simplest form of sectarian behavior. Among the audience of a preacher named Krishna, who called himself "son of God," Catton succeeded in distinguishing two groups of people. One category comprises individuals who are seeking the truth; the other the curious who come merely to observe. With the help of a questionnaire, Catton attempted a psychological investigation of these two categories of listeners, which exceeded four hundred at certain meetings. If one studies the answers of the first group, a general orientation becomes evident. Those who seek—as against those who are curious—do not, for the most part, belong to any church. They read the Bible more frequently than the latter; they think more often of the world beyond, and they feel themselves more isolated socially; also, they are more preoccupied with the threats of war or economic crises. They manifest a profound need of religion but their desire does not find satisfaction from existing institutions. Their credulity is also more striking than that of the curious. Following one of Krishna's statements that he is the son of God, a woman exclaimed in an outburst of ecstatic fervor: "I knew it!" Another characteristic deserves to be stressed: a substantial number of these candidates in quest of truth constitute an unstable religious element that does not join any sect, but rather drifts from one to the other without ever finding any satisfaction. Catton wonders if one could not speak of "sectarian tendency" with

5 W. R. Catton, "What Kind of People Does a Religious Cult Attract?" in *Amer. Sociol. Rev.*, 1957, 22, 561–566.

regard to those who are perpetually dissatisfied, psychologically and religiously. Examination of their socioeconomic condition reveals that they are at levels which range from moderate to poor.

In our opinion, the unstable character of this religious attitude must be noted. Permanent membership in a group becomes impossible for such individuals because of an inability to adapt to the institutionalized forms of the religious life. Park[6] has remarked that this psychological and moral instability is the reason for the multiplication of small sects.

Herbert Stroup,[7] who studied the Jehovah's Witnesses, has noted the same feeling of insecurity among adherents of this group. In it one finds a relatively large number of immigrants, small businessmen and, in general, people who have had difficulties in adjustment. The Witnesses experience a psychological ambivalence with regard to public life, the state, marriage and religious institutions. Cohn[8] has even compared the sect to a proletarian movement.

Similar investigations were conducted by England[9] with reference to Christian Science members. Analyzing a sampling of five hundred "letters of testimony" sent by the members of the sect to the *Christian Science Journal,* the author observes that about half the correspondents were attracted to the movement following such afflictions as sickness, depression, family difficulties or personal handicaps. The majority are city dwellers; women are the most numerous; the greater number suffer from physical or emotional ailments. Their behavior and adhesion are partially explained as response

[6] R. E. Park, "Missions and the Modern World" in *Amer. Journ. Sociol.,* 1944, 50, 177–183.

[7] H. H. Stroup, *The Jehovah's Witnesses* (New York: 1954).

[8] W. C. Cohn, "Jehovah's Witnesses as a Proletarian Movement" in *The American Scholar,* 1955, 24, 281–298.

[9] R. W. England, "Some Aspects of Christian Science as Reflected in Letters of Testimony" in *Amer. Journ. Sociol.,* 1954, 59, 448–453.

to the teaching of Christian Science, in which it is said that the divine spirit will manifest itself by the healing of illness and by the harmonizing of interpersonal relationships. Sickness, poverty, wars are only the illusions produced by mortal spirits. The observer who compares these testimonies of healing with the sect's belief in a God of harmony and well-being will not be surprised to learn of the emotional character of the illnesses reported by the majority of the correspondents. Belief has created predispositions toward cures in a selected group of adherents. The sect, moreover, has its healers or practitioners whose role can be compared to that of psychotherapists.

Let us add to these observations the fact that sectarian conversions will often be ephemeral. Argyle[10] has shown how the evangelical meetings which are most charged with emotion are also those which provoke the largest number of "returns;" but he adds that scarcely 15 per cent of these conversions are permanent.

All these observations point in the same direction; the adherent of the small sect presents a type frequently characterized by unadaptability to existing institutions, instability with relation to fixed reference groups, insecurity and a strong, emotional suggestibility. Certain observers speak of sectarian personality or behavior; it seems, however, that it is necessary to go beyond the strict limits of individual psychology if one wishes to understand conduct leading to affiliation with a sect. In analyzing the concept of conversion in the preceding chapter we distinguished three dimensions of one and the same behavior: psychological restructuring, acceptance of a religious role, and the motivation of a new belief. Admittedly, the elements that we have thus far referred to only clarify the first of these dimensions; one must still be wary of making generalizations, or of inferring at the outset the abnormality

[10] M. Argyle, *Religious Behaviour* (London: 1958), 51–57.

of all sectarian conversion. Conversion, even to sects, is not resolved by an elementary determinism.

3 SOCIORELIGIOUS STATUSES AND ROLES

The person who is converted to a sect should not be considered only in his moral or psychological isolation; it is also necessary to understand how he is involved in an entire context that we would call sociotheological. These sociotheological structures embody the new roles which the convert assumes as well as the theological motivations which the religious collectivity inspires in him.

Certain sociologists have compared conversion to the acceptance of roles which the religious group prescribes. The sect provides for its new members a status which corresponds to a particular form of behavior. The status thus acquired will be examined from two points of view: that of the sect itself and of the environing society. The roles assumed by converts will also be understood according to these two dimensions.

Let us see first how conversion brings about differentiation of statuses and roles within the sect itself. From this point of view Zetterberg[11] has studied about four hundred young members of a Swedish sect. More than two-thirds of them claimed that they had been converted and that they could specify the date and place of the experience. For the majority the event occurred when they were fifteen or sixteen years old and during a revival. But in spite of the sudden character of their conversion, the spiritual experience brought about repercussions which varied a great deal from one individual to another. In some cases the conversion led to a profound transformation and even involved a new philosophy of life. With others the experience of the con-

[11] H. L. Zetterberg, "The Religious Conversion as a Change of Social Roles" in *Sociology and Social Research*, 1952, 36, 159–166.

version was accompanied by practically no change in habits or beliefs.

On examining more closely all of these converts it was discovered that eight out of ten came from families in which the parents were already members of the sect; 81 per cent of these young people were already regularly participating in the sect meetings before their conversion. The experience of the conversion assumes a very different significance, depending on the nature of previous habits. Zetterberg took his information from Clark[12] for an explanation of the observed differentiations. Clark, upon the completion of a study involving 2174 men and women, had concluded that a religious awakening can assume three principal forms: the abrupt awakening, accompanied by crisis; the awakening by emotional stimulation; the gradual awakening. Zetterberg himself divided the conversions he observed into three categories corresponding to the three diverse ways of undertaking a socioreligious role.

The first way is characterized by a *sudden change* of role; it is the case of the convert who, during a crisis, passes abruptly from a "life of sin" to a transformed life.

In the second instance there is a *sudden identification* with a role; the convert, properly speaking, was not "in sin" but, one day, he underwent the decisive experience of total certitude and confidence in the faith. His exterior behavior does not reveal any notable change, but since the date of his "experience" he considers himself a convert and identified with a new role.

Finally, one will have subjects who experience only a *slow assimilation* to a religious role. Brought up religiously they have never known any decisive spiritual experience, but they possess a peaceful assurance of being saved and of belonging to a community of believers.

[12] E. T. Clark, *The Psychology of Religious Awakening* (New York: 1929).

The subjects were questioned to determine what process was responsible for their own conversion. Out of three hundred and seventy-six subjects questioned, 16 per cent fall within the first of these categories; 55.8 per cent within the second; 28.2 per cent within the third. Conversion by sudden change appears to be a relatively rare occurrence; identification is the most frequent case. The second and third categories together show that more than 80 per cent of the conversions in this sect ought to be interpreted, not as absolute beginnings, but rather as partial phases within a broad process of socialization.

The same phenomenon will occur naturally in every sect or in every "revival movement" which persists long enough to welcome a second or a third generation of candidates. Probably there will still be conversions which are brought about by an abrupt change of roles, but a growing number of "revivals" will become, properly speaking, nothing but an identification with or an assimilation to the group and the roles which it prescribes. In the final analysis the statuses acquired within the interior of the community will be similar, but the genesis of belonging will have followed different psychological processes.

The observations of Zetterberg and Clark encourage us to amplify what psychosociologists have postulated concerning sectarian behavior. The second or third generation adolescent who is converted during a revival will probably not reveal the precise traits attributed to the sectarian personality. It will be necessary to discuss further the current affirmation according to which the habitual form of adhesion to sects is conversion. To this is added the fact that the sects themselves often have the tendency to become institutionalized from one generation to another with the result of slowly becoming identified with denominations. It will be noted how these reorientations of structures, experienced by religious groups, bring with them important changes in the behavior of their members. We have already seen that conversion is a phenomenon whose significance cannot be considered univocal. This conforms to and illustrates the methodological question of Pinard de la Boullaye who asks that conversions be clearly distinguished according to the basic orientation of religious groups.

The socioreligious statuses and roles which we have discussed can also be considered in relation to the total sociological situation of the adherents. One may ask therefore, if there does not exist a psychosocial context—for example, situations of unadaptability or of marginality—which favor accession to sects. Without forgetting the personal or community factors studied above, we shall examine the conditions of social integration in which the adherents are found at the moment of their conversion to sects. There are already available the results of investigations which clarify certain aspects of the problem. A few years ago, for example, a study was made of Puerto Ricans living in New York. Here is how their socioreligious assimilation is achieved in their new milieu.

In their native country these Puerto Ricans all belonged at least nominally to the Catholic Church. Once in New York, they are won over by the hundreds to the Pentecostal sects, which multiply among the new arrivals and meet in store-front churches. The Puerto Rican sects recruit their members from their own people and they assist together at meetings conducted in their mother tongue. They read Scripture, they comment on it, they pray for one another. It is not rare that in the midst of prayer the "breath of the Spirit" will suddenly penetrate one or other of those present, who then begin to cry out incoherently in a sort of collective babble. Fervent emotion spreads and each day new candidates are gained. Poblete,[13] who directed

[13] R. Poblete, S.J., *Puerto Rican Sectarianism and the Quest for Community*, unpublished M.A. dissertation presented to Fordham University (New York: 1959).

88

this inquiry while personally taking part in the Pentecostal gatherings, strove to retrace the reasons for such a rapid diffusion of the sect among the Puerto Ricans. In his opinion the most important factors which explain the massive adhesion of Puerto Ricans to the sect can be reduced to a twofold psychosociological reaction.

These reactions correspond to the particular situation in which the immigrant finds himself upon his arrival in a large city. He experiences his first shock when he suddenly becomes aware of his unadaptability, his insecurity, and what the author calls his "state of anomie." A parallel reaction accompanies the first; it expresses a basic need for identification; it is fostered by the kindness of numerous compatriots sharing the same fate and speaking the same language. This experience is described by the author as the "quest for community." The immigrant, arriving without resources and being harshly subjected to contact with a complex culture which seems hostile to him, has the feeling of no longer belonging to anything; he has lost his frame of reference with its natural supports; even the Catholic Church seems a stranger to him. The invitation to join a small religious group where he will meet his fellow countrymen, will pray with them and will be understood, answers his craving for affiliation. The sect informally and in a simple way offers him fraternity, participation in simple rites, and immediate relationship to religious symbols with which he feels at ease and identifies himself; all of this is done outside of established institutions. Several members of the sect confided to the researcher: "No one cares about us . . . here we find brothers, sisters. . . . *They* do not understand us . . . here we pray together, we feel loved, sheltered, helped."

Poblete's results agree with a number of previous studies in which a relationship was demonstrated between the proliferation of sects and the socioeconomic conditions of populations. Holt and Boisen[14] studied these phenomena during the American economic crisis of the 1930's. Insecurity and economic distress had produced at that time great shifts in population, especially in the South. The traditional community structures were disrupted; the newcomers were not welcomed by the religious institutions or by the churches to which they believed, nevertheless, that they belonged. This "cultural shock" was, as the authors tell us, extremely favorable for increasing the ranks of the sects. Figures from religious surveys are significant: in the decade following 1929, the large Protestant denominations showed an 11 per cent decline in membership, while the sects increased their numbers by 50 per cent; a few, like the Pentecostal sects, even tripled their enrollment.[15]

It is necessary to realize, however, that this type of analysis is too general to provide complete assurance as to its conclusions. Hence it is only by way of first approximations to reality that we accept the findings of these studies. We do not deny a priori the influences of socio-economic conditions on the widespread diffusion of sects but, like Wach, we are not willing to grant it a decisive role. It has already been shown that the religious psychology and behavior of the convert are far more complex than this.

It is with the same reservation that we accept the conclusions of Pope[16] for whom the small sects represent a religious form of protest against social exclusion, as well as a pattern of compensation destined to restore social status and to redefine, in a religious context, class differences.

[14] J. B. Holt, "Holiness Religion, Cultural Shock, and Social Reorganization" in *Amer. Sociol. Rev.,* 1940, 5, 740–747; A. T. Boisen, "Economic Distress and Religious Experience: A Study of the Holy Rollers" in *Psychiatry,* 1939, 2, 185–194; see also the latter author's *Religion in Crisis and Custom: A Sociological and Psychological Study* (New York: 1955).

[15] See Boisen, *Religion in Crisis,* 71–72.

[16] L. Pope, "Religion and the Class Structure" in *Annals of the Amer. Academy of Political and Economic Science,* 1948, 256, 84–91.

4 SIGNIFICANCE OF CONVERSION ACCORDING TO THE STRUCTURE OF THE SECTS

We agree with Penido that it is necessary to concede a role to the element of compensation in conversions to sects, even in "normal" conversions. But how this influence acts is not explained in the socioeconomic studies just cited. The explanations would no doubt be facilitated if one were to add to the socioeconomic observations an analysis of differential psychology according to sects. The work of Pfautz,[17] who examined the phenomenon of the institutionalization of sects, helps us to understand that religious conversion and belonging assume a significance proper to each stage in the institutionalization process.

Consider, for example, the three following forms in the development of one of these religious groups: the cult, the sect, the institutionalized sect. The simplest group, the cult, presents a solidarity which is elementary and quite affective; it is made up of a restricted number of isolated members who are subjected to an influence that is locally limited. The norms of the group are implicit, with no structure being differentiated. The survival of the group and the feeling of belonging itself are rather precarious. The group affords scant security for the convert who, more or less consciously, is seeking a compensating social status.

The sect, properly speaking, already has started the process of differentiation; norms are defined, authority is asserted, one is protected against exterior conflicts and persecutions. The environing society, however, considers these sect members outcasts. The group does not yet have an accepted place in society; to adhere to such an association provides little social prestige.

[17] H. W. Pfautz, "The Sociology of Secularization: Religious Groups" in *Amer. Journ. Sociol.*, 1955, 61, 121–128.

The institutionalized sect exhibits evidence of legal and liturgical forms; conflicts are resolved according to established procedures. The group is viable and can continue from one generation to another. Traditional membership, then takes on a meaning; membership even becomes respectable.

Pfautz[18] retraces the stages that we have just described in his account of Christian Science. He states that the members' motivations are less characterized by emotion, that the members' behavior appears more rational to the degree that the group matures, and that the group becomes more heterogenous with more structual differentiations. The work of England[19] concerning Christian Scientists will be completed, then, by Pfautz's observations. These analyses show us that the psychosociology of conversion to sects will have to take into equal account the convert's condition and the state of the group which receives him. If conversion is motivated at times by a secret desire for compensation, this motivation should be interpreted not only in terms of the subject's dispositions and insecurities, but also in terms of the special and tangible advantages offered by the group itself.

5 THE APPARENT RELIGIOUS MOTIVATIONS

We spoke earlier of the socioreligious context which can color the psychology of the convert to a sect. We have attempted to distinguish and appraise, according to their relative value, the multiple concomitants of conversion;

[18] H. W. Pfautz, "Christian Science: A Case Study of the Social Psychological Aspect of Secularization" in *Social Forces*, 1956, 34, 246–251.

[19] See R. W. England, "Some Aspects of Christian Science as Reflected in Letters of Testimony" in *Amer. Journ. Sociol.*, 1954, 59, 448–453.

but we have scarcely touched upon religious motivation, properly so called. While recalling what we explained in the preceding chapter concerning the empirically inaccessible character of the spiritual experience itself we should still point out what formal sociology teaches us about the religious motivations of adherence to a sect.

Mensching[20] suggests that the following be considered separately: "dogmatic" sects, where belonging assumes a doctrinal significance; and sects of "practical piety," which promise the experience of personal fervor without any special attention to dogmatic differentiation.

In any event, a convert joints a "holy community, "one without a sacramental system. If one adheres to an aggressive sect or to a passive sect conversion will be tantamount either to an act of religious radicalism or to the acceptance of a role which is resigned and tolerant with regard to outsiders considers as heathens and often persecutors. But the emphasis will always be placed on the individual meaning of the religious action; the group here is only a community of brothers, not a holy institution in itself, as is a church. "The essence of the sect," according to Troeltsch,[21] "is the holy, conscious and mature community whose sanctity resides in a practical religious effort and not in the divinity of the institution and its treasures of grace. . . . The organizations of the community are so structured as to accept only conscious Christians."

If a comprehensive conclusion emerges from these diverse analyses it is not in the form of a unique, all-encompassing explanation. The behavior of converts to sects depends on too many influences and motivations to be reduced to a single combination of factors. The operational framework postulated for the study of conversions has permitted us to

[20] G. Mensching, *Sociologie religieuse* (Paris: 1951), 216.
[21] E. Troeltsch, *Protestantism and Progress* (New York: 1912), 149.

distinguish empirically between the different orders of factors: psychological, communital, sociotheological.

In concluding this chapter, we see the first confirmation of the working hypothesis that we had stated earlier as a psychosocial definition of conversion. We have seen that conversion to sects involves a dynamic process. In it the observer perceives an individual psychology exercising itself in and through a collectivity which symbolizes and extols absolute values and norms. These socioreligious norms determine the status and the role which are proper to the convert; and it can be said that, when conversion is complete, the values of the group have become the object of new perceptive, emotional and motivational processes. Conversion corresponds to the genesis of a fundamental attitude which orients the neophyte in relation to the world and to God.

Chapter IV

Conversion to a Church

1 The church as a specific group. 2 Phases of conversion: resolution of crisis: (a) the integrated personality; (b) the convert's behavior, his conviction. 3 Identification with the church: (a) the institutional referent of conversion; (b) ritual and psychological integration.

1 THE CHURCH AS A SPECIFIC GROUP

It is in a sense easier to analyze sectarian behavior than the conduct of the church member. The church, as sociologists have noted, presents one of the most complex forms of institutionalization. Hughes[1] has stated, for example, apropos the Catholic Church, that "sociologically speaking, everything has happened to it." Elements which deal with the history of origins, with beliefs, with rites, with norms of behavior, and with the world of symbols are integrated into a dynamic synthesis which for the most part eludes empirical analysis. As Van der Leeuw observed, "such as she lives in the consciousness of the believer, the Church does not fall within the scope of phenomenology;" and apropos

[1] E. C. Hughes, "The Early and Contemporary Study of Religion" in *Amer. Journ. Sociol.*, 1955, 60, I–IV.

this reality which "escapes all comprehension," he added: "She is the one that all comprehension presupposes."[2]

It is important to specify the sociological meaning that one intends to give to the concept of the church. The Catholic Church was the point of reference of the first sociologists who defined the church type,[3] and it is still the customary perspective of studies which treat the church as a specific group. Such will also be our express preoccupation. We will not ignore, however, the other large denominations that are usually referred to as churches: Orthodox, Anglican, Episcopalian, etc. We will also take into account the broader acceptance of the word church as it is currently used when one speaks, for example, of the diversity or the unity of churches.

In one sense the word church does not exclude plurality, but Wach is well aware that the strict concept is not "purely descriptive. "It also carries a normative significance, one "implying a well defined content," and thus "there can be only one Church."[4] Only theology can debate the questions which go beyond these observations; but, at this first level, a specific institutional structure is already delineated and the affirmations that the church makes of herself are specified. And these are the very traits that it will present to the candidate who is confronted with the question of conversion.

From the start, let us note the relative place of conversion among the ways of becoming a member of a church. Affiliation to the church assumes more than one form; here, hereditary membership and religious instruction take on an importance which is not found in the sects. Also, what we shall see with regard to church conversion will be supplemented by the observations that we will subsequently make

[2] *Op. cit.,* 263.
[3] See, for example, the works of Max Weber, Troeltsch, von Wiese, Becker, etc.
[4] *Op. cit.,* 130.

about religious education and instruction.[5] In the case of the church, conversion no longer appears as the unique mode of affiliation with the Christian community. Once the church is well established, the baptism of children becomes the most common method of acquiring new members. The fact remains, however, that conversion presents itself as a constant phenomenon in the church and it deserves to be studied in itself.

Without claiming to enter into all the details of a psychology of conversion to the church—an analysis which extends beyond our present concern—we will examine the fact of conversion simply as the genesis of belonging. Here, two subjects are of more specific interest to us: the problem of phases of conversion, and the question of identification with the church.

2 PHASES OF CONVERSION: RESOLUTION OF CRISIS

The first problem could be formulated as follows: if it is admitted that conversion is one form of integration of the religious attitude, is there any reason to conceive this as a sudden or as a gradual process? The question is again raised as to what role ought to be attributed to crisis in conversion. Does it effect an immediate resolution and integration? Is it only one stage in a slower restructuring of attitudes. Specifically, it is a question of determining whether the convert suddenly becomes a member of the church (on the psychosociological level) or whether his belonging is not rather formed gradually and by successive stages.

What is meant when one speaks of a convert's religious crisis? The convert's intimate experience, as we have said, is only known to us in an indirect manner; and it should be

---

[5] See especially Chapters V and VI.

recalled here that "the psychology of conversion," as Stoetzel emphasized, "collides with the pure event." Lacking
direct observations one can, however, consult works which
have analyzed converts' testimony, thanks to which diverse
"contents of conscience" have been rather closely studied.
According to these confidences the psychoreligious crisis
appears as a state of disconcerting tension, as an unstable
and painful situation in which the individual feels himself
torn in a sort of interior conflict; he is aware of an intimate
and agonizing disunity which suddenly brings into question
the "moral certificates" around which his personality was
more or less clearly unified. Would there not be found at the
root of this anxiety the two poles of religious experience
which the authors have often noted while studying conversion: on the one hand the renunciation, the rejection of
one's past (contrition), and on the other the tension toward
the Other, toward the new Life, toward adoration?

The psychosocial dimension of religious crisis also leads
us to suspect that one of the causes of anxiety experienced
by the convert is the ambivalence of his feeling with regard
to the spiritual community. His disturbing indecision, his
interior debates bring to light an inborn conflict of the still
half-expressed desire to belong to the church and of the
rejection soon regretted, of this inclination to religious
affiliation. To accept or to refuse belonging to the community of the faithful constitutes the very basis of his psychosocial instability.

This first description of religious crisis permits us to
situate the phenomenon within a perspective which is
at the same time psychological, social and spiritual: the
three dimensions we keep finding when we analyze the
different forms according to which the convert's intimate
crisis is resolved. We will see how, in instances of genuine
conversion, the solution of the spiritual conflict leads to a

reintegration of the personality, as well as an institutional and ritual identification with the church.

The forms of the personality's religious reintegration have been often studied by psychologists interested in conversion; they have always devoted a great deal of attention to the religious crisis in the intimate transformation of the adult neophyte. Let us examine what their studies reveal. It will remain for us, however, to interpret these observations within the content of adhesion to a firmly structured church. Indeed, it is not so much conversion in itself that interests us here as its consideration as a form of adhesion to a church.

When studying the phases of conversion, early psychologists were struck by two types of conversion, the one sudden and almost instantaneous, the other more gradual. In the first case, there develops a dramatic crisis which involves an abrupt transformation of attitudes; in the other there is, in fact, a crisis but it is only by stages that it is resolved in a new synthesis.

Starbuck[6] introduces by way of explanation a distinction between the active convert who works his way to faith and the passive one who abandons himself to the forces operating on him. Conversion, as he observes, always remains associated with a crisis, a crisis which even constitutes its specific element. Starbuck adds that in its dramatic form conversion is a phenomenon of growth which occurs when normal development has been hindered. This, as is evident, gives to crisis a capital role in conversion.

The Italian psychologist De Sanctis[7] has objected to this interpretation. For him crisis is only one element among others and, at that, a secondary element whose significance

---

[6] *Op. cit.*, Chapters 12 and 13.
[7] S. De Sanctis, *La conversione religiosa: studio bio-psicologico* (Bologna: 1924), Chapter 3.

will have value only if it induces a durable transformation of religious conceptions and moral behavior.

For us it seems preferable to choose with Penido[8] an explanation less radical than the preceding ones. That certain conversions are consciously preceded by a preparation, from which a "crisis" arises at a certain point— dramatic to be sure, but on the whole accessory—is a fact that cannot be denied. There are numerous cases of those who have considered entering a church and who had sought, consulted, meditated before definitely committing themselves. One will also be ready to dismiss as a genuine conversion the simple, emotional shock comprising, in fact, a crisis, but not leading to adhesion to the Christian community. One could not, in that case, speak of "conversion to a church." On this point, De Sanctis is correct in not confusing crisis and conversion.

But on the other hand it must be acknowledged that in certain cases crisis alone constitutes the decisive point in the process of conversion; crisis disrupts, in dramatic fashion, the existing cognitive and emotional pattern, and it accompanies the definitive consent which will change all subsequent behavior. Of course, there will be in every conversion a later phase of adaptation, but it would be most precise to speak of this as one of the effects of conversion.

This does not necessarily lead us to identify conversion with crisis itself. Admitting the decisive character of certain crises should not keep the psychologist from carefully examining the antecedents and the effects of conversion. Some examples will clarify this last point.

Penido studied the testimony of Claudel: converted in an instant in the Cathedral of Notre Dame, he required four years to complete his moral transformation. He was truly converted in a moment of crisis, even if the total renovation was not yet realized. Forty years after the event, Claudel

[8] *Op. cit.*, 41–133.

100

tells of the progressive transformation "that I have tried to accomplish since the day on which I was converted." It happens, then, that crisis appears like "a source from which the rest flows." Penido's conclusion restates what Grensted affirmed concerning the extraordinarily durable effects of certain conversions which alter, in one dramatic moment, the whole course of a life.[9]

But even regarding the conversions that are apparently sudden it is useful to examine the psychological antecedents that have gradually sensitized the subject for the interior call or for the decisive event. Baudouin[10] distinguishes two typical cases. In one there is an interior self "held in check . . . which protests;" in the other there is a "maturation" or "new growth" of a self until then unknown. As Baudouin states: "In the one case, we find the reappearance of something repressed, a regret and a discovery; in the other, there is an effort to adapt oneself to new condition, there is a seeking and a quest." In this perspective, the author has studied at length the conversions of Racine and Pascal, which seem to him characteristic of both spiritual approaches. Here is how he summarizes his general hypothesis:

Both experienced a religious crisis which ended in a remarkable conversion. In both, conversion manifested itself in the same atmosphere of Port-Royal. However, if we study the subconscious steps which, in these two famous, and almost identical, cases, prepared the event, we will see that they do not proceed from similar impulses and that, in each case, the "ways of God" are, in different ways, unpredictable. It seems to me that these two conversions would correspond respectively to the two types of which we spoke: that of renewal and that of quest.

Remembering Penido's distinctions concerning the central or marginal role played by the element of crisis, in dif-

[9] L. W. Grensted, *The Psychology of Religion* (New York: 1952), 73; see also W. H. Clark, *The Psychology of Religion* (New York: 1958), Chapter 9: "Conversion," 188–218.
[10] C. Baudouin, *op. cit.,* 57–75; the citation is from 59.

ferent conversions, and keeping in mind Baudouin's explanations, we are led to examine another dimension: that of the religious personality which seeks itself or finds itself again. Let us consider for a moment this problem of personal integration.

(a) The Integrated Personality

Not every conversion is necessarily overwhelming. To overemphasize the role of "crisis" is to run the risk of oversimplifying the convert's behavior. The formation of a new and enduring attitude supposes a profound psychosociological reorganization; in this case it will involve the integration into the personality of the sense of belonging to the church. The dramatic experience will often serve as a decisive mechanism in this process, but we must not forget that this mechanism operates in a personality already oriented cognitively and motivationally.

In this regard the observations of Iisager[11] can be cited. After examining the political or religious changes undergone by seventy-six persons the author notes that for religious conversion the most important and most frequent factor is not the dramatic incident, but personal reflection. This is not to deny that there may be crisis, but it emphasizes that crisis is not to be conceived in every case as an objective, isolated and decisive element. Crisis, to use Baudouin's categories, is undergone by a personality which is seeking itself or which is finding itself again. For this reason crisis will appear as an ambivalent process in conversion.

Stoetzel has lucidly described this ambivalent character of crisis. If it succeeds in effecting conversion it will pro-

[11] H. Iisager, "Factors Influencing the Formation and Change of Political and Religious Attitudes" in *Journ. Soc. Psychol.*, 1949, 29, 253–265.

duce "the total unification of the personality;" however, it is not resolved in all cases by "a definitive blossoming of the individual." The cases which are happily resolved will bring peaceful illumination and certitude. But crisis can endure and the painful experience will find relief only in a compensatory reaction. Radicalism is often an unconscious expression of this need for compensation.[12]

At this point we need not enter into the properly psychological explanations of the integration of the religious personality; but for our general perspective it will be useful to emphasize briefly this integrating function of conversion or, rather, of crisis which results in an adhesion to the church.

(b) The Convert's Behavior: His Conviction

Another aspect of crisis deserves to be examined: its unstable and distressing character. The candidate cannot remain indefinitely suspended between the alternatives to which he is drawn. If crisis is deeply rooted, then simple rejection is impossible; certitude is imposed in one way or another. Thouless[13] has carefully studied this problem. He shows that, in religious questions, one rarely remains in an attitude of complete skepticism. Since religious belief is not usually considered as an object for speculation only, but rather as practical principles of behavior, one is led to form his convictions along one set of lines or another. Thouless systematically questioned one hundred and thirty-eight university students who were 20 or more years old. Some questions dealt with themes of religious faith, some with beliefs which are secular and devoid of emotional association, others, finally, with political views. A scale of attitudes with three positive and three negative degrees permitted the sub-

[12] See J. Stoetzel, *Théorie des opinions,* 308 f.

[13] R. H. Thouless, "The Tendency to Certainty in Religious Belief" in *British Journal of Psychology* (General Section), 1935, 26, 16–31.

FIGURE 1

Distribution of answers given by 138 students to the question: "Does a personal God exist?" Answers are classified according to the degree of certitude.

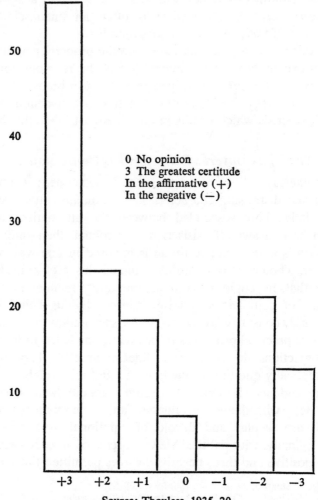

0 No opinion
3 The greatest certitude
In the affirmative (+)
In the negative (−)

Source: Thouless, 1935, 20.

FIGURE 2

Distribution of answers given by 138 students to the question: "Is Jesus Christ the Son of God?" Answers are classified according to the degree of certitude.

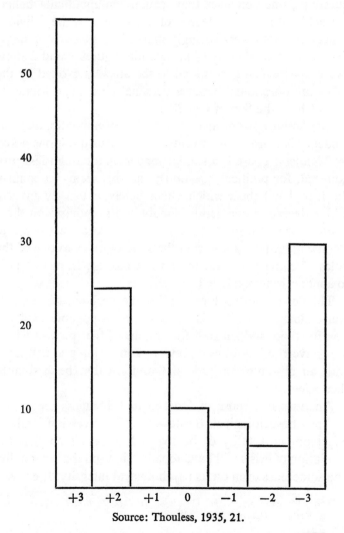

Source: Thouless, 1935, 21.

105

jects to record the degree of their conviction, favorable or unfavorable, with regard to each proposition. The zero point indicated lack of preference or total uncertainty. If one compares the answers received for the different categories of questions, one perceives that secular (nonpolitical) beliefs are held with a weak degree of conviction; while religious beliefs incite answers strongly marked by positive or negative conviction. By way of illustration, figures 1 and 2 show two graphs which correspond to the answers evoked by the following questions: "Does a personal God exist?" and "Is Jesus Christ the Son of God?"

Convictions, for or against, are clearly emphatic, and this tendency is constant for twenty-six religious questions asked by Thouless. There is a similar tendency, although less pronounced, for political questions; and this seems to confirm the fact that beliefs which effect behavior usually involve a high degree of conviction. Doubt and skepticism on these matters being unstable attitudes, the subject must come to a conviction. He passes from the state of crisis to one of the poles of conviction. But the abrupt passage from one pole to another is not excluded.

Thouless, who has long studied the problem of religious conversions,[14] sees in this phenomenon a possible explanation for those sudden transformations of the spirit in which the convert relinquishes a previous conviction and embraces with an absolute certitude the position that he had until then rejected.

Analyses like those of Stoetzel and Thouless emphasize the psychosociological framework of conversion and its effect on the totality of behavior. We have seen that the resolution of crisis will have repercussions on the personality and sometimes even on its psychological integrity. If conver-

[14] See, for example, R. H. Thouless, *An Introduction to the Psychology of Religion* (Cambridge: 1928).

106

sion contributes to the reunification of the individual's psychology, it prolongs its effects in a redefinition of practical behavior; from this comes the "conviction" which tends to attach to the values embraced by the convert. He is, henceforth, personally involved because of the motives that he considers absolute and proper for directing the new orientation of his conduct.

In addition to its relationship with the person's psychological integration and behavior, church conversion also comprises some institutional aspects which we must clarify.

3 IDENTIFICATION WITH THE CHURCH

The treatment of the institutional aspects of conversion raises the rather general problem of religious identification. Since the phenomena of identification are not restricted to the process of conversion, we will consider at this moment of our analysis only two points which are of immediate interest: reference to the religious institution and ritual integration with the church.

(a) The Institutional Referent of Conversion

While observing in conversion an element of identification, one is led to ask how, in the course of the formation of the new attitude, the relation between the candidate and the church is established. In fact, the church ought to be perceived and known, at least as a simple reference group, according to the distinction made in our first chapter.

If in the experience of the candidate the church appears as a group to which he desires to have access, the institutional reference of which we spoke is verified, and his behavior is relatively easy to understand. But converts' autobiographical accounts reveal some cases in which the church seemed to be absent from the sphere of consciousness, and no institutional reference was apparent in the psychology of the subject. The church appeared neither as a possible group of belonging nor even as a simple reference group. One notices, however, that there was an abrupt conversion to the church. In this case, how is the sudden identification with the church explained?

Sociologists have noted that side by side with an individual's indifferent attitude there can exist a complex of institutional influences which, often without his being aware of it, condition his behavior. In a study of religious "marginality," Cuber[15] succeeded in showing that the cultural impact of the church is not reduced to a dichotomy: real influence or no influence. To say that someone is on the fringe of church culture does not mean that his participation in this culture is nonexistent. Marginal participation itself remains a form of participation.

Merton goes further and affirms that the influence of religious values can continue to be felt with an astonishing persistence even in a milieu in which the theological bases which logically justify this order of values have been rejected. In this regard he cites Troeltsch's statement: "The present-day world does not live by logical consistency, any more than any other; spiritual forces can exercise a dominant influence even where they are avowedly repudiated."[16]

It is cultural sociology which must determine the zones of collective psychology in which the influence of these values is exercised; but the analysis of individual behavior already reveals some traces of this influence. Penido cites this testimony of an English convert in which the effect of marginality clearly appears: "My liberal Protestant tenden-

[15] J. F. Cuber, "Marginal Church Participants" in *Sociology and Social Research*, 1940, 25, 57–62.

[16] See R. K. Merton, *op. cit.*, 583; see E. Troeltsch, *op. cit.*, 38.

cies, which the Anglican influence *secretly undermined, but without my knowledge,* again became pronounced together with my hostility toward Rome. Without doubt, I *unconsciously* experienced the need of defending myself against the Catholicism which was drawing me by certain of its aspects ever since I knew the Anglicans. This is the time that I wrote in the *London Signal* some articles, very hostile to the Church, which I never would have written if Catholicism had left me indifferent."[17]

This example brings to light the phenomenon of cultural marginality. The observer should keep this in mind when he looks for institutional referents of conversions. One can see that the influence of values is sometimes exercised in reverse. Merton refers to this as a "dysfunction." An institution—in this case, a church—will be present to a person who is hostile and sometimes even to the indifferent. According to Jung, radicalism and fanaticism represent overcompensation for innermost doubts and uncertainties.

The abrupt conversions described by Thouless[18] can be better understood if one takes into consideration the institutional context in which they occur. It seems, in certain cases, that no explicit relation exists between a convert and the church; but it cannot be denied that being on the fringe of the church already implies a certain form of participation, negative perhaps, but real, with the religious culture diffused within a milieu. This point will be clear if one examines the process contrary to identification, which is called projection and which consists in rationalizing one's behavior by attributing to "the other" one's own characteristics, especially those which are less favorable. Stoetzel has remarked that projection is directly connected with ignorance of self. If projection is practiced with regard to a

17 Testimony quoted in M. T.-L. Penido, *La conscience religieuse,* 69.
18 See above 103–107.

church, one can explain why, in an abrupt conversion, the spiritual reunification of the personality is accompanied by a sudden change from projection to identification. The convert discovers himself by discovering the church. An intimate resemblance is made apparent to him. Allport defines identification as affective imitation. The convert knows himself and adheres to the church. He accepts the new status and role which the religious institution, to which his behavior will be referred henceforth, offers him.

(b) Ritual and Psychological Integration

Sociologists have attached several meanings to the concept of institutional behavior. Used in a rather restricted sense the concept designates a type of conduct inspired by the norms of an organized group. Thus conceived the term institutional behavior will serve to describe an important aspect of church conversion.

The resolution of crisis, while reorienting the personality in the direction of the church, de facto furnishes the convert with models of behavior which are clearly institutionalized. His intimate experience is in keeping with institutional life itself. Certain sociologists have, in our opinion, exaggerated the inflexibility of the two aspects of religious life. Their distinction between personal religion and sociological religion seems to us to be rather arbitrary when one is considering the behavior of a church member.

Conversion itself, at first sight a strictly individual act, involves some social aspects. And religious integration, initiated by the decision to become a church member, will find its religious and psychosociological fulfillment only in the integrating process par excellence which is the church rite.

We shall consider explicitly the adult convert who comes

to the church for the first time. His specific attitude as a church member will be perfectly integrated only at the completion of the baptismal rites. Ritual integration will complete his institutional behavior. In phenomenological terms, one would say, with Van der Leeuw,[19] that "behavior becomes a celebration." The author protests against the overly logical distinctions that are sometimes made between a strictly psychological aspect of behavior and a ritual aspect. Conversion and baptism, as he says, are not realities that should be opposed; they are the two moments of a unique transformation which is new birth.

Studies on the sociology of rites clearly bring out the integrating role of ritual acts. Durkheim thought they were so important that he devoted a third of his work, *Les Formes élémentaires de la vie religieuse*, to ritual attitudes. In a review of the question, George[20] shows that the rite can be considered a form of symbolic communication. It is a pattern of ceremonial conduct expressing the religious life of communities and establishing a relationship with a reality which transcends deeds and words. The rite has a unifying effect. It counteracts tendencies toward anomie for it creates a "we feeling" and has the power of identifying the individual with the group. In addition to the theological functions attributed to the rite, the author sees a latent sociological function: integration within a social structure as well as differentiation of statuses and roles within the community of the faithful.

Analysis of ritual initiation brings us back, therefore, to the psychosociological data presented by Zetterberg.[21] If the transformation of the convert's attitudes were compared to

[19] *Op. cit.*, 333, 518.
[20] G. George, S. J., "The Sociology of Ritual" in *Amer. Cath. Sociol. Rev.*, 1956, 17, 117–130.
[21] H. L. Zetterberg, "The Religious Conversion as a Change of Social Roles" in *Sociology and Social Research*, 1952, 36, 159–166.

a change of socioreligious roles, one would understand that the baptismal rite plays an important function in sacramentally integrating the candidate within the church structure and in assigning to him definitive Christian status.

Certainly, more discerning studies would permit us to advance the psychosociological analysis of conversion further. The phenomenon of religious belonging has revealed itself to us in the perspective of identification. In insisting on the church as a reference group, then on its structure and its rites, one does not, nevertheless, deny the immediate process of affiliation.

After Spranger, the psychologists Vernon and Allport[22] insisted on the fact that religious behavior has as a motive the at least implicit unification of the world of values. Religious interest, as they stress, appears as the best defined and the best organized of feelings; it "colors the whole of life."

A single word can summarize the desire for participation and search for religious affiliation: love. Phenomenologists, as well as psychologists, today agree on a reorientation of their studies in this direction—a direction an overconcern for "objectivity" had made them avoid. Van der Leeuw concurs with Lévy-Bruhl's penetrating observation that "the need for participation remains assuredly more pressing and more intense, even in our societies, than the need for knowing or for conforming to logical exigencies. It is deeper, it comes from the depths." The convert's attitude toward the church seems inexplicable to us except in terms of the sentiment of love which motivates it. In our hypothesis we are dealing with affiliation to a well defined church, the Christian church; and for Van der Leeuw, "a single word suffices to characterize the typology of Christianity: love."[23]

On the psychologists' part, an analogous effort has been

22 P. E. Vernon and G. W. Allport, "A Test for Personal Values" in *Journ. Abn. Soc. Psychol.*, 1931, 26, 231–248.
23 *Op. cit.*, 528, 630.

made to reinterpret the religious attitude within the framework of affective motivations. Regretting the lag of his discipline in this area, Allport endeavored to discover the principal traits of a psychosociology of love. His study is included in a collective work directed by Sorokin[24] and published as symposium on "altruistic love." Allport affirms that one of the failings of modern psychology is the incapacity to comprehend the human being's desires for affiliation; present-day methods, he says, are better adapted for the analysis of conflicts, prejudices and dissensions. Allport, elsewhere, has tried to explore the problem of love and the need for participation. These concepts, in fact, seem to him indispensable if we are to have an adequate theory of personality.[25] In his work on religious psychosociology, he overcomes what he terms the "taboo of tenderness," and expresses his belief that a new orientation disposes psychologists to taken into account the "pressing desire for affiliation" which directs all behavior; a "cosmic feeling of belonging" seems indispensable for all; but, ultimately, the "love of God will be necessary to make life complete, intelligible, properly oriented."[26]

Grensted also wrote on the problem of the personality's integration with relation to the object of the sentiment of love. The only feeling which truly succeeds in integrating the totality of the personality, as he explains, is "the love of God," which he calls the "master sentiment." At this point, says Grensted, the analysis can advance no further, for "psychology offers no answer here, but neither can it close the door."[27]

24 P. A. Sorokin (ed.), *Explorations in Altruistic Love and Behavior: A Symposium* (Boston: 1950); see G. W. Allport's chapter on "A Psychological Approach to the Study of Love and Hate," 145–164.
25 G. W. Allport, "The Psychology of Participation" in *Psychol. Rev.*, 1945, 52, 117–132.
26 See G. W. Allport, *The Individual and His Religion: A Psychological Interpretation*, 91.
27 See L. W. Grensted, *op. cit.*, 82.

These observations, when referred to the feeling of belonging that we have studied in the convert, allow us to
understand how conversion is a complex identification, em-
bracing both the church-institution and God himself. If at
this stage of the analysis social psychology is unable to
advance further without going into theology, one can bor-
row from phenomenology a final observation which will
help clarify the complex object of the convert's identification and affiliation. We see that God and the church do not
form a duality in his consciousness; and, to use Van der
Leeuw's words, "the love responding to God's love assumes
a form: the Church, which shows its irreducible unity with
love . . . ."[28]

This last statement shows how ambiguous is the idea of
assimilating, without reservation, the simple desire for participation with the striving for charity. Charity supposes
a great deal more than an undifferentiated adhesion to
religious values. It produces an eminently personalized
identification, and an acceptance from within of all that is
associated with the sacred community. The symbols of
fraternity and of the family convey most adequately the
quality of this identification.[29] Chapter IX will show how in
the psychology of the faithful the church appears particularly apt for simultaneously satisfying the needs for participation, identification and charity.

As a phenomenon of personality unification and socioreligious identification, conversion includes also from the
theologian's viewpoint a basic element: the adhesion to a
belief, that is, to a faith professed by the church. "Do you

[28] *Op. cit.,* 633.
[29] Phenomenology itself points out the frontiers which separate the
simple psychological participation from personalized charity. Freud himself, whose remarks we shall later comment on, wrote on this point: "It is
incontestable that the bond which attaches each individual to Christ is
the cause of the bond which attaches each individual to all others." See 228.

114

believe . . . ?" will be one of the last questions that the candidate is asked before baptism. We will treat this problem more directly when we discuss the question of religious education and that of the relationships between belief and behavior. Let us note here that the convert's identification with the church includes the totality of behavior in its cognitive and motivational aspects. Both preparatory and subsequent phases of the convert's decision will involve an initiation into the church's doctrine. His will to belong to the church constitutes not only a desire for social affiliation, but also an affective and intellectual participation in all that the church symbolizes and teaches.

Since, in our restricted perspective, we need not analyze the phenomenology and the content of the act of faith, we only note that the identification achieved by the convert between the church–institution and Divine Authority supposes adhesion to an absolute belief. Psychology cannot verify the fact directly; the act is interior and is supposed as an indispensable explanatory element. One would wish, however, that a "psychology of the act" would further extend the analysis. The expert on religious questions will hardly be satisfied with the explanations obtained through observation of exterior behavior. He will favor this "psychology of the act" whose "evident superiority" for the study of religious behavior, "in which the subject's interior drive is quite important and in which the exterior behavior is a great deal less revealing,"[30] was demonstrated by Allport.

[30] See G. W. Allport, *The Individual and His Religion,* 142 f.

Section 2

Religious Education

Subjectively, religious education is an experience which the faithful member undergoes continuously. For its analysis, however, one can distinguish diverse stages in this slow process of spiritual formation: one which corresponds to the child's religious initiation, one which later comes to strengthen the adolescent's spiritual attitude, and one which aids the adult in establishing a relationship with his culture and his socioreligious milieu.

From our viewpoint, religious education and instruction will appear as processes of apprenticeship and acculturation which lead to the member's identification with his group and which strengthen his integration within the religious institution. It is possible to distinguish between early education, formal instruction and the diffusion of doctrine by the more general way of preaching. These processes will be treated in the two following chapters: one on the child's religious education and his "discovery" of the church (Chapter V), the other on religious instruction at school and post-school age (Chapter VI); this last chapter will also examine the particular role of preaching in the strengthening of religious affiliation.

EARLY EDUCATION

1 Identification with the religion of parents. 2 Early awakening of religious attitudes. 3 The immediate cultural environment. 4 The child's discovery of the religious institution.

1 IDENTIFICATION WITH THE RELIGION OF PARENTS

In the most diverse culture, sociologists have observed close relationships which link an adult's religious feelings with the first experiences he has known within his family and his primary milieu in general.[1] Between the family and the church Boisen sees bonds which are completely distinctive and are not to be found between any other two institutions.[2] Family life and religious life, indeed, offer a striking analogy in behavior and symbols; and this suggests to us that the family is not only an institution which parallels religion, but that its structure makes it eminently suitable for the task of the religious socialization of the child in whom a sort of symbiosis of familial and spiritual affiliations is realized. For Murphy,[3] the structure of the family is

[1] See J. Wach, *op. cit.*, 26 f.
[2] A. T. Boisen, *op. cit.*, 35 f.
[3] See G. Murphy, "Social Motivation" in G. Lindzey (ed.), *Handbook of Social Psychology* (Cambridge: 1954), 1956, 601–633; see in particular 615–616.

117

virtually religious, and religion is "saturated with familial psychology."

It is common, in Western society, to attribute great importance to the parents' example in the religious formation of the young. But how does one analyze this complex reality of example? Mensching has attempted to grasp its general meaning from the perspective of religious imitation.[4] In the present case psychosociologists will speak rather of identification with the parents' religion.

The process of identification has unlimited implications. We shall consider here only those aspects having direct bearing on identification with a community. Like Dewey and Humber,[5] we retain the two primary traits which to us seem particularly significant for our analysis: the double bond which exists (a) between the identification with and the acceptance of collective values and (b) between participation in these values and loyalty to the group. From this viewpoint, one will say that to identify oneself is to assume the values of another; and to share group values is to manifest one's loyalty to the group itself. There are certain authors, among them Gerard,[6] who, when they describe this phenomenon, state that the attitudes are essentially anchored in the group. The esteem that a member will have for the group to which he belongs will be reflected in his attitude toward the values inherent in the group. Kelley has applied this analytic schema to religious belonging. We shall return to this point shortly.

Another aspect of identification which we shall retain here is its dynamic character. This aspect has been emphasized by Lagache,[7] who has shown the progression from

[4] *Op. cit.*, 258 f.

[5] R. Dewey and W. J. Humber, *The Development of Human Behavior* (New York: 1951), 1954, 155.

[6] H. B. Gerard, "The Anchorage of Opinions in Reference Groups" in *American Psychologist*, 1952, 7, 328 (abstract).

[7] D. Lagache, "Quelques aspects de l'identification" in *Bulletin Intern. des Sciences Sociales*. 1955, 7, 37–46.

identification to *objectivation*—a progression that is found in both cultural development and personality formation. Identification (the act of becoming identified with the object) is conceived as the assimilation or the attribution of a role, and can assume two forms: the subject plays another's role or represents another as playing his role. Identification is not a cognitive process but a total participation. Objectivation (the act of identifying an object) is, on the contrary, a process of knowledge affectively freeing the knowing subject from the object known. We will use this conceptual framework when we examine adult affiliation.

In brief, three aspects of identification are of special interest to us: the values that are involved in the process of identification, the relationship of identification to primary loyalties, and the eventual objectivation of the bond of belonging.

Bossard,[8] in studying documentation on some four hundred families, has observed the intimate interdependence of religious behavior and family structures. The religious actions, rites, prayers, celebration of holy days, etc., give cohesion to the family group; and, in turn, ritual actions are given value by collective participation. The author cites numerous accounts of adults who can recall the details of the family rituals of their childhood. Identification acquired in childhood has left its trace on the adult's personality; his sentiment of religious belonging remains marked by it.

Allport[9] has described the method by which the child conforms to his parents' religion. To perform the religious acts that his parents suggest is, for the child, "a confirmation of his identification with those who provide him with security, affection, approbation"; the in-group is normative and deeply personal; it gives value to religious behavior. But one can question whether these primary identifications can

[8] J. H. S. Bossard, *The Sociology of Child Development,* revised edition (New York: 1954), Chapter 14.
[9] G. W. Allport, *The Individual and His Religion,* 27 f.

119

be considered really religious. Allport affirms that the first apparently religious reactions of the child have nothing religious about them at all; they have only a social character. It is difficult, on the level of psychosocial behavior, to resolve the question. Allport's conclusion is not universally shared. Harms,[10] a specialist on the psychosociology of children, observed the religious behavior of several hundred children, three or more years old. He notes, in all the children, a characteristic reaction of wonder, reserve and reverential fear when a religious subject is mentioned before them or when their answers are prompted by a simple drawing. He thus concludes from his numerous observations that children possess a "capacity for the experience of the divine" and that the latter manifests itself upon the awakening of consciousness.

Further research will be necessary before the young child's psychoreligious apprenticeship can be described exactly. The studies of Wallon and Piaget only indirectly elucidate our particular problem; it was precisely their respective treatments of the "sociology of education" which stirred up a bitter dispute between them.[11] To facilitate research it might be well to follow Grensted's[12] suggestion. It is, as he explains, by studying the child's prayer that one can best observe the awakening of his religious feeling; this prayer should not, however, be considered a simple verbal reaction but a total behavior in which actions, expressions and imaginative representations concur. Here, learning of prayer serves as a guide for analyzing, at different periods of

[10] E. Harms, "The Development of Religious Experience In Children" in *Amer. Journ. Sociol.*, 1944, 50, 112–122.

[11] For their works, see bibliography.

[12] L. W. Grensted, *op. cit.*, 35. Let us cite also Mailhiot's fruitful study on children, aged 4 and 5, who were observed at their prayers and their pastimes; the author states that, in order to emerge from the simplicity of their first religious identifications, the children need to be awakened, gradually and according to their capabilities, to the objectivation of their faith. See B. Mailhiot, O.P., "L'univers religieux de l'enfant d'âge préscolaire" in *Revue Dominicaine*, 1958, 64, 131–143.

growth, the place which religion holds in the normal child's development.

2 EARLY AWAKENING OF RELIGIOUS ATTITUDES

For want of more systematic information on the form of the first psychoreligious awakening, we shall refer to a connected phenomenon which has been quite thoroughly studied: the relatively early development of religious attitudes. Upon investigation this procociousness of the religious is brought to light by a double series of observations: the age from which the subjects trace the first formation of their religious attitude, and the influence that they attribute to their parents in acquiring their religious feelings.

Following a survey of Danish students, Iisager[13] drew a striking parallel between the formation of the first religious attitudes and the first political opinions. Political attitudes are usually formed toward the end of adolescence, while the religious attitude goes back to childhood. For the majority of students the awakening of religious feelings takes place between the ages of 7 and 14, and their political attitudes first become definite between the ages of 15 and 18.[14] Among the factors stated by the students as influencing religion, one finds in order of importance: parents, personal

[13] H. Iisager, "Factors Influencing the Formation and Change of Political and Religious Attitudes" in *Journ. Soc. Psychol.*, 1949, 29, 253–265.

[14] All that we wish to retain from this comparison is the rather great precocity of the religious attitude in relation to political attitudes. One would not infer from these facts that the religious feeling is nonexistent in the child before the age of 7. Here we are dealing only with a particular statistical result; some will become aware of the spiritual life before the age of 7, others after the age of 14. Let us note, besides, that the students questioned are speaking from their reminiscences; their answers reveal the present state of their religious memories rather than the real attitudes of their first years. These answers, thus interpreted, in no way contradict the observances of child psychologists concerning the very precocious awakening of moral and spiritual feel-

121

reflection, school. The formation of political attitudes is mainly due to reflection, discussions, reading and, finally, the influence of relations and friends.

Allport and his associates[15] observed the same "pre-eminence of parental influence" in the religious formation of some five hundred American college students questioned. Using an "inventory of attitudes," they attempted to evaluate the religious needs of the students and to analyze the religious influence which the latter claimed to have experienced during their childhood. The answers indicate that present religious needs have a direct relationship to the "intensity" attributed to previous religious education. For example, here is what a survey of the boys reveals: a firmly declared religious need is found in 82 per cent of those who had an "outstanding" religious education during their childhood; in 78 per cent of those who received an "ordinary" religious education; in 52 per cent of those who described their religious education as "superficial;" in 32 per cent of those who received no religious education. The authors of this investigation would conclude that, in the majority of cases, early education decisively influences future religious attitudes.

The same survey furnishes us with the opinion the students have of their parents' religious attitudes. Let us recall that eighty-six of the five hundred students are girls; that the majority of these five hundred students are Protestants; that about 17 per cent belong to the Jewish religion; and that 15 per cent are Catholic. Table 2 gives the results in detail.

---

ings in the child. On this subject see A. Gesell and F. L. Ilg, *The Child from 5 to 10* (New York: 1946): from the age of 3 or 4 there can be a "noticeable interest in God," an awakening to religious things, the repetition of prayers, etc.

[15] G. W. Allport, J. M. Gillespie and J. Young, "The Religion of the Post-War College Student" in *Journ. of Psychol.*, 1948, 25, 3–33.

This kind of comparison provides us with a sketchy view of the parents' objective faith, but it reveals the image that the younger generation have of their fathers' and mothers' religion. Rarely do the students consider themselves more religious than their parents; they portray the faith of their mother as firmer than that of their father. There is perhaps in these data an indication of a decline in faith from one generation to another, but the difference does not seem attributable to this fact alone (only 12 per cent of the students are atheists). To the students, their parents' religious influence on them seems basically important. The same opinion has been expressed in responses to another question which asked the males of the same group to indicate the factors that notably influenced them in the religious sphere. Most frequently noted was the influence of parents. This influence seems slightly stronger in boys than in girls. The latter attribute greater importance to personal sentiments and to motives of gratitude. Iisager[16] noted, however, that the parents' influence was more noticeable in girls than in boys. On this last point no final conclusion can be drawn from these surveys. Nonetheless, let us keep in mind the central idea of the parents' privileged role in the formation of durable religious attitudes. There is a continuity between the religious attitudes of the parents and those of the children that is clearly shown in the testimonies revealed in the surveys.

The same continuity has been observed in a poll conducted by the Institut Français d'Opinion Publique[17] on a sampling of French youth from the ages of 18 to 30. Table 3 shows a very distinct correlation between "family con-

[16] H. Iisager, "Factors Influencing the Formation and Change of Political and Religious Attitudes" in *Journ. Soc. Psychol.*, 1949, 29, 253–265.

[17] "La nouvelle vague croit-elle en Dieu?" (Enquête de I.F.O.P.), in *Informations Catholiques Internationales*, 1958, 86, 11–20.

TABLE 2

Comparison made by students between their faith and that of their parents. The numbers indicate the percentage of students who made each of the comparisons.

	Faith of the male student compared with his mother's	Faith of the male student compared with his father's
More firm . . .	7	16
Less firm . . .	51	27
Similar . . .	32	36
Don't know . . .	10	21
	Faith of the female student compared with her mother's	Faith of the female student compared with her father's
More firm . . .	14	23
Less firm . . .	41	27
Similar . . .	27	24
Don't know . . .	18	26

Source: Allport, Gillespie and Young, 1948, 15.

TABLE 3

Comparison between the religious attitude of French youth (18 to 30 years of age) and that of their parents. Answers are by percentage.

The Children's Religious Attitude	The Parents' Religious Attitude						
	Believers			Practitioners			
	Both	One	Neither	Both	Father	Mother	Neither
Practicing Catholic . .	88	10	2	64	2	27	7
Nonpracticing Catholic .	68	22	10	20	2	40	36
Others . . .	75	20	5	47	5	31	15
Deists . . .	64	31	5	22	4	31	39
Atheists (uncertain). .	19	49	32	4	3	31	57
Atheists (certain) . .	18	33	49	8	—	15	67

Source: *Information Catholiques Internationales*, Dec. 15, 1958; 13 (survey of the I.F.O.P.).

ditioning" and the youths' religious attitudes. The extreme figures are particularly significant. For the large majority the practicing Catholics come from families in which the father and mother were themselves practicing Catholics (64 per cent). Nonpracticing youth frequently come from homes in which the mother alone practiced her faith (40 per cent), a fact which indicates the importance of the paternal role in the religious education of Catholic youth. The survey also brings out that convinced "atheists" are occasionally produced in families where both parents were believers (18 per cent); but, for the most part, they come from families in which neither parent was a practicing member (67 per cent).

Evidently the family is not the only milieu which contributes to the formation of the bond of religious belonging, but it is noteworthy that in examining the parents' influence, one can observe such a convergence in the surveys made: the studies comparing the parents' religious situation and that of their children, the studies on youth's opinion with regard to the religion of their parents—all these strengthen the evidence. Education within the family appears to be an important factor in the formation of religious attitudes, and the influence seems more pronounced in this domain than in other forms of institutional behavior, for example, in the formation of political attitudes.

Those surveys illuminate the continuity of generations. The adolescent becomes aware very soon of the religious identities which bind him to his parents and the wider family group. We are confronted here with solidarities which are in some way spontaneous: religious solidarities and family solidarities. Multiple loyalties become evident in which the values both uniting and distinguishing them remain imperceptible. We shall move a step further in this area by examining the influences of the cultural milieu.

3 THE IMMEDIATE CULTURAL ENVIRONMENT

The influence of parents does not operate in a vacuum; it is found within the framework of a larger primary milieu. Here intermingle the customs, traditions and practices of an ethnic group as well as the many other factors which we shall consider in our analysis of the cohesive force of the religious attitude. Let us for a moment examine the culture of this larger but immediate group; its role should not be overlooked in the formation of the religious attitude. The parents themselves are represenative of the cultural values which they transmit to their children. Therefore, in speaking of the culture of the group, we shall not ignore the role of the family; it remains an integral part of our analysis, but as a group embodying a culture and transmitting its values from generation to generation.

From our point of view how should culture be understood? Diverse orientations would be possible. If we were to follow Ruth Benedict we would insist rather on the function of custom as the primordial element of culture. "There is no social problem it is more incumbent upon us to understand than this of the role of custom. Until we are intelligent as to its laws and varieties, the main complicating facts of human life must remain unintelligible."[18] If we were to agree with Kardiner, however, we would emphasize the more specifically psychological elements of culture. We shall not neglect these two approaches, but we will fix our attention on a concept of culture which leads us in the direction of total behavior. The concept of culture, as Kluckhohn notes, stems from behavior and terminates in behavior. For Kluckhohn,[19] culture consists of behavioral

[18] R. Benedict, *Patterns of Culture* (New York), second edition.
[19] C. Kluckhohn, "Culture and Behavior" in G. Lindzey (ed.), *Handbook of Social Psychology* (Cambridge: 1954), 1956, 923.

patterns, acquired or transmitted by the means of symbols; culture is the distinctive product of human groups; the essential basis of culture comprises traditional themes and especially the values which are attached to them. We shall be content with this definition of Kluckhohn, adding only one comment.

Whatever definition of culture one accepts methodologically, one will always encounter an element that ethnologists and sociologists consider as basic: the world of values. In a milieu where religion remains vital it is the religious values which will become the principal agent for integrating culture as well as the social structure. This aspect is well brought out in Yinger's analyses[20] and in those of Lévi-Strauss.[21] For the latter religion appears as one of the most revealing elements of a social structure.

If we were to explain the relationship that exists between the world of values and the transmission of culture from one generation to another, we would enter into a perspective familiar to psychosociologists. Like Newcomb, we shall consider the processes of cultural transmission as inseparable from early education. He explains the child's experiences as "a link in the chain which joins the culture of a milieu and the personality of the younger generation.[22]

In this perspective the child's religious education takes the form of apprenticeship or formation of a religious personality by the assimilation of supreme values from the surrounding culture. According to Allport's observation, conformity to culture, especially in the child, is a fundamental form of religious development. The child, by the

[20] J. M. Yinger, *Religion, Society and the Individual: An Introduction to the Sociology of Religion* (New York: 1957), 60 f.

[21] C. Lévi-Strauss, "Social Structure" in A. L. Kroeber (ed.), *Anthropology Today* (Chicago: 1953), 524–553.

[22] T. M. Newcomb, *Social Psychology* (New York: 1950), 1958, 448.

127

mere fact that he participates in the security and the protection of the family group, learns to esteem and reverence what his parents most deeply cherish. That which is beyond parental affection itself assumes absolute value in his eyes. Little by little he discovers the complex of allegiances owed by his natural group. The love of his parents, the benefits of security, the common norms and the religious acts that they prescribe are all connected with mysterious relationships which he learns to name in his simple prayers. Gradually there is born within him the feeling that the most respected realities of his environment extend beyond the immediate advantages that he enjoys. Between the child and his parents, then, a spiritual community is established which achieves both the psychological unification of the individuals and the cohesion of the group. Wach has remarked: "More than any other group, the family finds its integration in the community of worship."[26]

The transmission of religious culture is not, as one would think at first sight, a one-way process which affects only children. Parents also are affected by this process; the arrival of a child will prompt the married couple to redefine their status with relation to the familial group and the cultural milieu. A number of investigations into religious behavior of families leads us to believe that the feeling of religious belonging is particularly aroused in the parents when, at the arrival of their child, they suddenly become aware of the values that they have to transmit.

Reviewing the existing research on religion and the family, Reuss[24] noted that one of the most frequent conclusions in this type of inquiry was that the presence of children in a

[23] *Op. cit.,* 58.
[24] C. E. Reuss, "Research Findings on the Effects of Modern–Day Religion on Family" in *Marriage and Family Living,* 1954, 16, 221–225.

family gives the parents a renewed interest in religious participation. Sarah[25] stated that this fact is particularly noticeable when the children are younger. Telford[26] makes the same observation.

Another sociologist, Lenski,[27] has pushed his observations further. Using a select sample of eight hundred and sixty families, each comparable as regards age of husband and wife, duration of marriage, education, religion (Protestant), etc., the author has attempted to interpret the religious interest of the married couple in relation to the presence or absence of children in the home. A scale of attitudes was offered to the husband and wife separately. Table 4 summarizes the results obtained by the comparison.

TABLE 4

The degree of religious interest since the time of marriage, according to the composition of the family group.

Composition of the Family Group	Religious Interest			
	Weak	Average	Strong	Total
No children[1] . . .	35.9	42.4	21.7	100.0
One child or more . .	25.5	42.1	32.3	99.9

[1] The sampling was taken in such a way that the absence of children was due to the wish of the married couple. Source: Lenski, 1953, 536.

Let us examine this table. Comparing the two categories of couples, those without children and those with children, we find that religious interest is stronger among those who

[25] A. Sarah, "Religious Behavior of Church Families" in *Marriage and Family Living*, 1955, 17, 54–57.

[26] C. W. Telford, "A Study of Religious Attitudes" in *Journ. Soc. Psychol.*, 1950, 31, 217–230.

[27] G. E. Lenski, "Social Correlates of Religious Interest" in *Amer. Sociol. Rev.*, 1953, 18, 533–544.

do have children. Almost one-third of the families with children, but only slightly more than one-fifth of those without children, are strongly religious. Lenski observes that the two factors, presence of children and religious interest, can mutually influence each other. In the present instance, however, he believes in the influence of the former factor on the latter. "The arrival of the child," he writes, "causes a renewal of religious interest in the new parents; the phenomenon is brought about especially at the time when the parents must think of transmitting to their children 'the cultural heritage.' "

We would distort the meaning and conclusions of these authors if we were to assign to religion the simple role only of a vehicle for the transmission of cultural values. Nor, on the other hand, does it follow that religious formation can be subsumed entirely under the rubric "transmission of culture." This type of study in no way prejudices the specific character of religious formation. Instead, it draws attention to the relationships which, in the concrete case, link membership in a family with membership in a religious group.

Some other aspects of identification should be noted. That there is in religious identification both a spontaneous and a passive role should not, as we noted above, be particularly surprising. But we should also mention another consideration which the researches of Lenski and his colleagues have brought out. Cultural identification is explicable not only by the child's receptivity, but also by the parents' active role. Identification is selectively received on the child's part, but it is directed and oriented by the father and mother who, from the day on which they become parents, see their status redefined with relation to the whole of socioreligious culture. Identification in some way presupposes that the patterns of behavior are complementary.

130

4 THE CHILD'S DISCOVERY OF THE RELIGIOUS INSTITUTION

By considering phenomena of identification only, one would be led to believe that religious and familial affiliations remain more or less confused. Religious belonging, then, would be viewed as a general and indistinct attitude. In the child, a new development occurs to make specific the significance of his spiritual belonging, namely, the discovery of the religious *institution*. This discovery can be conceived as a further phase of the socialization process.

Piaget[28] has pointed out how the child's "sociocentric" thought (or attitude) gradually is differentiated. If socialization is operative at all stages of psychological development, the respective dynamisms of the social and the individual elements afford rather different stabilizing influences which vary according to the child's age. Before the age of 7 or 8, there is confusion and indifferentiation of the individual and the interpersonal in the child's psychology. "The social and the individual, then, are not at all inseparable, but simply undifferentiated in the consciousness of the individual who confuses them." It is only gradually that the "autonomy of the person" is acquired by the assimilation of social influences and by the differentiation of phenomena of coordination and reciprocity or, in other terms, by the discernment of the individual and the interpersonal. There would then be as the two terms of the process of socialization an initial phase, comprising the indifferentiation of the social (egocentric phase) and a final phase in which the social is then perceived and distinguished (sociocentric phase).

Life Murray,[29] we shall go further and examine the rela-

[28] J. Piaget, "Pensée égocentrique et pensée sociocentrique" in *Cahiers Intern. Sociol.*, 1951, 6, 34–49.
[29] H. A. Murray, *Explorations in Personality: A Clinical and Experimental Study of 50 Men of College Age* (New York: 1954).

tions which exist between sociocentrism and institutions. Sociocentrism, he explains, is characterized by a triple form of social participation: acceptance of interests or common values (e.g., a creed), cooperation with other members, submission to a leader. One or the other of these three elements can be prevalent in the incipient phase of belonging. A personal bond links the member to *his group*. A transference takes place and the group's cause becomes his own cause. According to Murray's description, the member's energies are channeled by his belonging: he lives for his group; he "is delighted and feels proud when it succeeds; he is depressed and feels dejected when it fails; he is hurt or annoyed when it is criticized; he does not appreciate any joking at its expense; and he is ready to attack other groups which oppose his. Sometimes, his very existence becomes involved in the cause. In extreme cases, he will even sacrifice his life for it."[30]

It is evident that the bonds of belonging between the child and his group are strengthened only by stages; but, according to Piaget, the sociocentric attitude becomes apparent fairly early in the course of the child's development: starting at the age of 7 or 8 and becoming stronger at the age of 11 or 12. In the religious sphere we are fortunate to have at our disposal several works of research which will permit us to verify the general explanations sketched above.

In his *Sociology of Child Development,* Bossard[31] emphasized the function of the family rituals in the socialization of the young. Family ritual assumes a rather broad meaning for this author.[32] He sees it as a generic process of interaction which embraces practically all collective values. Special

[30] *Ibid.*

[31] J. H. Bossard, *op. cit.,* confer Chapter 14, "Family Rituals and Child Development," 290–314.

[32] See J. H. S. Bossard and E. S. Boll, "Ritual in Family Living" in *Amer. Sociol. Rev.,* 1949, 14, 463–469; and also by the same authors, *Ritual in Family Living* (Philadelphia: 1950).

attention, however, is given to religious rites. The children's participation in rituals (holy days, celebrations, etc.), develops in them a sense of communion and solidarity with the past. The rite transmits the norms and values of the group; it ensures moral security and develops the sense of individual responsibility.

We should point out that certain rites such as the celebration of religious holy days have a double significance. Christmas, for example, is both a religious and a familial holy day. Barnett[33] emphasizes the principal cultural traits associated with the celebration of Christmas, and he has shown how almost all of these traits are related to two institutions: the family and the church. Some analogous conclusions were suggested upon completion of a study on the feast of Easter.[34] We are able to see how, in children who take part in these feasts, familial solidarities can be strengthened and the feeling of belonging to a church-institution developed.

From one milieu to another, however, some notable differences will appear with regard to the manner of celebrating these holy days and with regard to the real social participation that each involves. Studies conducted in France indicate that it would be imprudent to make generalizations in this matter.[35] It is enough to note here the role played by rites and celebrations in the religious socialization of the child, and to observe to what extent holy day participation is apt to facilitate the institutional transfer of which we have spoken.[36]

[33] J. H. Barnett, "Christmas in American Culture" in *Psychiatry*, 1946, 9, 51–65.

[34] J. H. Barnett, "The Easter Festival: A Study in Cultural Change" in *Amer. Sociol. Rev.*, 1949, 14, 62–70.

[35] "Les Fêtes" in *Sondages* (numéro spécial), January, 1949, 11, 1–12.

[36] It is evident that mere participation in holy days is not of itself sufficient to make the child become a part of the religious institution. In certain circumstances, it even happens that ceremonies like First Communion, Profession of Faith and Confirmation, mark the end of

133

Harms' observations[37] are in closer agreement with the explanations of Piaget and Murray. We have already cited his research on child psychosociology which confirms Piaget's general principle that the child's sociocentric tendency becomes more pronounced after the age of 7 or 8. Harms, after having made several hundred observations, affirms, in effect, that the discovery of the religious institution usually occurs between the ages of 7 and 12. The school-age child who has received religious training will exhibit a characteristic form of behavior. Here we shall outline the principal traits the author mentions. In the child of this age religious convictions appear firmly established; he becomes capable of personal religious decisions. The child is impressed by the attitude of adults, especially by the seriousness with which they regard religious matters, and by the sincerity which spiritual leaders manifest. For him the church and the catechism disclose the organized, institutional aspect of religion. More than at any other age he seems ready to adapt himself to institutionalized religion and to welcome the teaching provided by the church. It is a period during which he becomes aware of God's reality. Like Smith,[38] Harms here remarks that the child of this age experiences a rapid development in his feelings and emotions

close contact with the Church. For the child, holy days most frequently will derive their socioreligious signification from the spiritual atmosphere of the family itself. Despite the occasional worldly or profane character of certain of these feasts, we should not, however, consider their effect on the child as negligible. These experiences, which are both familial and religious, will, perhaps, not succeed in evoking a lasting institutional transfer toward the church, but the fact remains that, for each of the children considered individually, the feelings experienced during this time constitute, in the majority of cases, an emotional factor whose repercussion and remembrance will persist for many years.

[37] E. Harms, "The Development of Religious Experience in Children" in *Amer. Journ. Sociol.*, 1944, 50, 112–122.

[38] J. J. Smith, "Religious Development in Children" in B. F. Skinner and P. L. Harriman (ed.), *Child Psychology* (New York: 1941).

and that this growth is directly related to his religious experiences.

According to Harms, this age is also a period during which the ethical aspect of the religious sentiment emerges. Moreover, symbols (e.g., crucifixes, statues), seem to exert a veritable fascination on his spirit. In brief, the child by his new experience discovers the religious institution: he has a receptive attitude with regard to its norms and its teachings, and he perceives and associates symbols with invisible realities. He becomes institutionally oriented with reference to his religious group and his spiritual leaders. It is a time when the bonds of affiliation, which make him a member who is aware of belonging to the church, are engraved on his consciousness. Harms calls this period the realistic stage of religious development.

In the child's discovery of the religious institution, it would be easy enough to retrace the elements of socio-centric experience as previously described by Murray: conscious participation in a religious creed, cooperation with other members of the faith, and acceptance of a spiritual leader. The process results in a redefinition of religious affiliation. Belonging to his parents' religion assumes a new, broadened dimension, which corresponds to the institutional structure of the ecclesiastical community. He is henceforth identified with his religious group, he embraces its cause. In certain cases it is not impossible that some very young children give their lives to remain faithful to their church.

There should not, however, be any misunderstanding concerning the significance of religious belonging nor should there be any desire to reduce all the religion of the child to this unique phenomenon. Just as we shall deny the validity of the position of those sociologists who, as Murray[39] mentions, claim that personality is the sum of social affilia-

[39] H. A. Murray, op. cit., 712.

tions, so too must we refuse to identify total religious behavior with the mere sentiment of belonging to the church. It
will become clear that socialization cannot be defined as a
process of simple conformity to culture or to the group.
Wallon[40] emphasized the essentially ambivalent character
of the child's socialization. The process involves two developments: an assimilation into the group together with a
deepening of self-awareness. Indeed, there is observed in
the child the simultaneous emergence of the consciousness
of self, and the discovery of the surrounding social milieu.
"Their differentiation," writes Wallon, "is mutual and
interdependent. . . . All progress in self-awareness leads
to concomitant progress in the aptitude for discerning society."

If the fact of belonging to groups does not explain the
totality of the self it does, however, furnish experiences
which enrich the personality and contribute to its originality.
In this perspective the child's discovery of the religious
institution will eventually perfect in him his previous religious feeling. It is precisely in the sense of a progressive
personalization of the religious feeling that the child's development as a church member occurs. Harms implies that
at the first realistic stage there is in the child a noticeable
tendency toward a more individualized religion. Adolescence and post-adolescence will be strongly marked by it.
As Harms notes in his study cited earlier, it is a critical
period for religious education, for the young church member
must learn to reconcile interiorly the meaning of his liberty
with his religious belonging. For the first time he is confronted with this apparent antinomy; institutionalized and
personal religion. By studying the adult's religion we shall

[40] H. Wallon, "L'étude psychologique et sociologique de l'enfant" in
Cahiers Intern. Sociol., 1947, 3, 3–23.

attempt to understand the implications of this difficult problem. More immediately, at the child's level, a new integration of religious attitude will take place. This is a further stage in the formation of his feeling of church belonging. Religious instruction will be the solution to this new need.

Chapter VI

Religious Instruction

I The Integrating Role of Doctrine. II Religious Training of Youth. 1 Research on the religious life of youth. 2 Religious instruction and religious adhesion. 3 Differential integration of the religious attitude. III Preaching in its Social Context: 1 The preacher and his milieu. 2 Reorientation of collective attitudes. 3 Preaching and socioreligious identification.

I The Integrating Role of Doctrine

No one would think of minimizing the role of religious instruction in the formation and stability of the bond of church belonging. On this point sociologists as well as spiritual leaders are in complete accord. The evidence is quite clear. Fichter's[1] investigations, for example, reveal that of the Catholics who no longer participate in the activity of their Church more than 75 per cent received no religious instruction. Churches are aware of the intimate relation that exists between doctrinal instruction and religious fidelity. In one of his studies Coughenour[2] vividly portrayed the care which

[1] J. H. Fichter, S. J., *Social Relations in the Urban Parish* (Chicago: 1954), 75 f.
[2] C. M. Coughenour, "An Application of Scale Analysis to the Study of Religious Groups" in *Rural Sociology*, 1955, 20, 197–211.

the churches devote to the instruction of their members. Comparing subgroups and services in five hundred and five rural parishes or churches (Protestants and Catholics), he found that catechism instruction is the most frequently observed form of service (observed in 95 per cent of the cases).

The transmission of doctrine is for a religious group the very condition of its survival; it is not only an educative function that it performs along with other services—it is a way of integrating and rooting the faithful within the community. Van der Leeuw's explanation makes one realize the great importance of doctrinal instruction. For him it consists, in a word, in a transmission of the "sacred possessed in common." In effect, participation in the sacred is the source of social cohesion. "The sacred common good," notes the same author, "is not sacred because it is common but it is common because it is sacred. By worshiping God, humanity does not worship itself, but it worships God by assembling together."[3]

It is not for the sociologist as such to judge the value or validity of religious doctrines, but he cannot ignore their integrating role at the core of a community of worship. An examination of the doctrines reveals, in effect, the patterns of behavior and cultural models of a religious group. By means of representations, symbols and sacred writings, one discovers the ultimate values which unite religious groups. If we did not take into account religious training, doctrines and dogmas, we would be neglecting one of the most significant ways of analyzing collective religious behavior.

Years ago, Pinard de la Boullaye stated his regret that psychoreligious studies paid so little attention to religious instruction and writing. Are they not both a reflection of a milieu and a source of an era's cultural inspiration? In be-

[3] *Op. cit.*, 265, 435.

coming involved with their milieu, preachers and spiritual writers are answering certain desires and needs. Their works and writings "would not have met with such success if they were not, in large measure, satisfying to the intimate yearnings of numerous souls." Acknowledging the spiritual originality of the great religious founders, the author notes that they are, in some way, products of their contemporary culture; on the other hand, one can observe the effect of their message on the behavior of the masses: "For one finds in every milieu the echo of principles inculcated by preaching, a mentality developed by leaders of sects or religious groups."[4]

Perhaps social psychology will one day have researchers who will use the approach suggested by Pinard de la Boullaye, and who will provide us with a psychosocial study of religious sentiment which would be a counterpart to Bremond's literary work. For the moment let us recognize that very few generalizations are yet possible, even on the restricted theme to which we have limited our analysis, that is, on the immediate integrating role of religious doctrine. Wach[5] nevertheless has treated this problem and his brief study will serve as an introduction to the detailed analysis which we will undertake.

Wach begins by recalling that the official credo of a group of believers should be considered "the formulation of its fundamental religious experience." This summary explanation should not deter the psychologist from attempting to verify facts, nor from seeking for latent motivations or the

[4] *Op. cit.,* II, 318.

[5] *Op. cit.,* 35 f; let us keep in mind that, in relation to the general problem of sociocultural integration, *religion* should be considered in its positive functions as in its dysfunctions; on this question, see J. H. Fichter, S. J., "Religion: Integrator of Culture?" in *Thought,* 1958, 33, 361–362; F. Houtart, "Les variables qui affectent le rôle intégrateur de la religion" in *Social Compass,* 1960, 1, 21–38.

symbolic meanings of the doctrinal forms (e.g., in the founders of the sects). The sociologist will devote his attention, then, to the symbols which reflect a specific religious experience and he will observe how this experience, indirectly perceived, "integrates a religious group and, at the same time, separates it from the exterior world in order to make it a sociological unity." Religious doctrine tends to gather together the initiated and to segregate them from those who do not share the same faith. The integrating power of doctrine becomes a part of a complex phenomenon in which one discerns communion with one and the same religious experience; initiation or symbolic communication of the experience; and the sociological effects of the common doctrine. Whenever a sacred tradition exists one can observe the same social consequences. A message proclaims the experience of the sacred; those who understand and are beneficiaries of the experience associate with one another, and they consider themselves distinct from others. One witnesses, then, a progressive determination of the teaching forms and of doctrinal transmission. "The religious society," continues Wach, "achieves, during the course of time, the consolidation of its unity by the formulation of symbols of faith and creeds destined to express and encourage the solidarity of those whom the identical or analogous experiences influence and inspire."[6]

These propositions remain general, but they are sufficiently coherent to enable us to make extensive references to them in our analysis of the development of the religious attitude. We shall consider, therefore, religious instruction as one of the means whereby the religious attitude is integrated. We shall examine some particular forms of religious instruction, notably that which is provided for the young-

[6] *Op. cit.*, 37.

sters of school age. Finally, we shall treat the broader problem of religious preaching, and discuss the different forms of doctrinal transmission.

II Religious Training of Youth

1 RESEARCH ON THE RELIGIOUS LIFE OF YOUTH

The preceding propositions remind us that the transmission of doctrine is an ordinary way of integrating new members with a religious group. With this in mind, we now propose to analyze the doctrinal education of the young members of a Christian community, where we shall find the opportunity of observing the development of the religious attitude more closely.

A methodological remark should first be made: it will clarify the perspective of our analysis and will indicate the limitations which are imposed upon us by the present state of research. If we are relatively well informed concerning the child's identifications with his primary group, we must admit that for the most part the sociology of adolescence remains incomplete. But with regard to young people who are 16 years old or more, as well as those who are of university age, the documentation is more abundant. This, therefore, allows us to bypass the difficulty and to take up the study of the behavior of younger youth as reflected in their later recollections. Indeed, the more thorough studies on 20-year-olds permit an indirect but enlightening observation of the process of formation and maturation of the religious attitudes. This fact will explain the indirect character of the analysis which follows. Being aware of gaps in the evidence, we shall try to make up for this deficiency by analyzing the young people's confidential discussions of their past religious experiences, and we shall attempt, to the degree that it is possible and with as much care as is required, to evaluate their previous religious formation through their differential behavior of today.

2 RELIGIOUS INSTRUCTION AND RELIGIOUS ADHESION

At first sight the facts seem simple and easy to analyze: a good religious instruction will assure the solidity of the bond of belonging and fidelity to the church. Here are, for example, some figures which we have taken from "Youth and Religion,"[7] derived from a survey conducted among English Catholic youth between the age of 15 and 24. The authors of this inquiry believe that sufficient data have been obtained for the first time on a problem which has long been discussed, namely, the relationships between religious education and later religious participation. Based on a nationwide sample, the results indicate a very clear tendency toward religious abstention in proportion to the decrease in the level of religious instruction. Table 5 shows the most important figures. One notices that weekly participation varies from 86 to 25 per cent, as religious instruction decreases, while complete abstention increases from 5 to 42 per cent. A study of the statistics will bring out that weekly participation declines from 86 to 16 per cent with regard to boys and from 86 to 36 per cent with regard to girls, depending on whether their religious instruction was thorough or superficial. Complete abstention, on the other hand, in-

[7] "Youth and Religion: A Scientific Inquiry into the Religious Attitudes, Beliefs and Practices of Urban Youth" in *New Life*, London, 1958, 14, 1–60.

creases from 5 to 48 per cent in the case of boys, and from 5 to 36 per cent in the case of girls.[8]

TABLE 5

Religious participation of English Catholics (boys and girls) from 15 to 24 years of age, according to the religious instruction received. Answers are by percentage.

	Assistance at Church		
Degree of Religious Instruction	Weekly	Irregularly	None
Catholic school and catechism	86	9	5
Only Catholic school . . .	75	17	8
Only catechism . . .	74	18	8
Neither Catholic school nor catechism	25	33	42

Source: "Youth and Religion" (1958), 45.

On this point, we could also cite the results obtained by Nimkoff[9] who observed the behavior of Catholic students living at a predominantly Protestant college. The Catholics were afforded every opportunity to assist at Sunday Mass; but Nimkoff noted a considerable difference in the regular religious attendance of these Catholic students. Two very distinct groups appeared: those who had previously studied at a Catholic school and those who had come from a non-

[8] Although they look impressive, these figures should be carefully interpreted. As the authors of the survey point out (46), "religious instruction" should not be considered an independent variable, that is, without any reference to the religious fidelity of the parents themselves. It is clear that the most Christian families are generally those who are most faithful in sending their children to catechism and Catholic schools. The conclusions given in our preceding chapter concerning the privileged role of parents and primary groups in the spiritual formation of the young also prevent us from separating "religious instruction" from the "parents' attitude" or from "family influence." The relationships between these different types of influence will be more explicitly examined at the end of this section; see 150–154.

[9] M. F. Nimkoff, and A. L. Wood, "Effect of Majority Patterns on the Religious Behavior of a Minority Group" in *Sociology and Social Research*, 1946, 30, 282–289.

144

Catholic institution. In the first group 19 per cent missed Mass on five consecutive Sundays, while in the second group 40 per cent missed.

These figures seem to confirm the usual observations, and we in no way find fault with them. There are, however, other facts which deserve mention, and which oblige us to examine more closely the conditions for the success of religious instruction. A person's religious belonging should not be considered an extrinsic category. One must discover the de-

TABLE 6

Adhesion of French youth from 18 to 30 years of age to the teaching of the Catholic Church. Answers are by percentage.

Points of Doctrine	Affirmation
The Existence of God	73
The Divinity of Christ	62
The Other World	55
The Trinity	51
Original Sin	49
Influence of the Present Life on the Future Life	46
Heaven, Purgatory, Hell	38
Resurrection of the Body	32

Source: *Information Catholiques Internationales,* Dec. 15, 1958; 15 (Survey of I.F.O.P.).

gree to which religious affiliation assumes the sense of a real, psychological participation for the subjects whom one is studying. As we will see, there is a wide range between nominal and effective church belonging, and between declared affiliation and full commitment.

The inquiries reveal notable differences in the degree and mode of adhesion to the Christian community. Let us consult, for instance, the survey[10] conducted among French

[10] "La nouvelle vague croit-elle en Dieu?" (investigation of I.F.O.P.) in *Informations Catholiques Internationales,* 1958, 86, 11–20; see also the commentaries published by G. Hourdin, *La nouvelle vague croit-elle en Dieu?* (Paris: 1960).

youth by the Institut Français d'Opinion Publique in 1958. The population consists of young people of whom eight out of ten have received religious instruction (preparatory to First Holy Communion) and of whom three-fourths claimed at the time to have been Catholics. Yet it is clear that there are considerable differences in their adhesion to Church doctrine; this fact is clearly evident from table 6.

These answers pose a certain number of problems to the observer. In the first place, there appears a relation of cause and effect between religious instruction from which 82 per cent of these young people benefited and the fact that 76 per cent claimed they belonged to the Catholic Church. But when one examines the content of this attitude which is thus expressed one notes pronounced divergences: participation in the membership community does not convey the same significance for all. For some people Church belonging is equivalent to a total acceptance of the message and prescribed norms; for others, adhesion comprises a focal identification which permits a more or less broad margin of nonparticipation.

This fact is confirmed by the percentages of religious practice which the survey reveals. Among the 76 per cent who claim to "belong" to the Catholic Church, 43 per cent are estimated to be nonpracticing, while only 33 per cent practice in a regular or occasional manner. It is obvious, then, that the same "religious belonging" often refers, in fact, to specific attitudes and behavior which are very different.

We will not deny, however, the influence of religious instruction on the development of the sense of church belonging, but we are inclined to ask a further question, namely, how does religious instruction usually succeed in arousing a spiritual attitude which is integrated within the totality of behavior?

146

3 DIFFERENTIAL INTEGRATION OF RELIGIOUS ATTITUDES

Let us start with the observations gathered and published by Woodruff,[11] since his study will allow us to bring out new facets of the problem. The author conducted a three-year survey among twelve groups of youths belonging to different religious denominations. His purpose was to compare and evaluate the function of personal values in the youths' behavior and to link these values to the religious preferences of the subjects studied. By a multiple choice method, a comparative scale was set up indicating for each subject his appreciation of such values as religion, friendship, community service, family bonds, comfort, etc. An analysis of the results shows that the students can be divided into two groups: those who place religious values in the highest quarter of the scale and those who consign the same values to the lower three-quarters.

For the former, religious values dominate and control all other aspects of behavior. For the others, religion assumes a position apart; in the general pattern of personal values religion appears as a separated system in which rites and beliefs are not interrelated psychologically with the rest of behavior. On the one hand there is a relgious attitude which integrates the totality of values, and on the other hand a religious attitude which remains marginal.

Such differences in religious attitude have many causes, but if one looks for an explanation in the youths' early religious education, one will no doubt be confronted by two rather typical cases which Tuttle will help us understand.[12] For one category of young people, religious instruction con-

---

[11] A. D. Woodruff, "Personal Values and Religious Background" in *Journ. Soc. Psychol.*, 1945, 22, 141–147.
[12] H. S. Tuttle, "Aims of Courses in Religion" in *Journ. Soc. Psychol.*, 1950, 31, 305–309.

sisted in receiving concepts or a doctrine which was not integrated with their system of values or related in a lasting way to their general behavior. This results either from an overly academic form of instruction or from its premature interruption at the precise period of the development and individuation of a system of values. For others religious values were taught as a wisdom capable of motivating all behavior. Depending on the cases involved, then, one will be obliged to deal with religious attitudes or affiliations whose psychological significance and integrating function will vary considerably. From the viewpoint of the investigator analyzing collective conduct, a distinction will become evident from the cases observed: the "same" religious belonging does not imply for all the same models of behavior or a similar system of reference and motivation.

The basic explanation is, no doubt, to be found by considering the level of intimate integration of religious attitudes. The frequently cited work of French[13] on the structure of sentiments offer an interpretation which seems to take into account the facts uncovered by other researchers in this matter. Upon the completion of detailed psychological observations, French discovered that the religious sentiment of his subjects played an integrating role, which was more or less pronounced, on the totality of attitudes; and that religious beliefs even had a permanent effect on the personality itself. Religious sentiments were manifested in all, but in differently organized and integrated patterns. These different patterns are reflected in the integration of the inner self. In some instances religious sentiments are superiorly organized and therefore "constitute an integrating part of the self for the subjects who possess them." In others, religious sentiments exhibit less cohesion and organization. Their integration within the self is superficial: they remain at the

---

[13] V. V. French, "The Structure of Sentiments" in *Journal of Personality*, 1947, 15, 247–282; 16, 78–108; 209–244.

level of the outer self. "Solidly organized philosophico-religious feelings are the norms of the self which give to those who possess them a positive orientation while less well organized philosophico-religious sentiments afford a defense mechanism which serves as a protecting screen for the self." French's observations bear out the explanations which several researchers had already proposed concerning the psychological role of religious attitudes.

For Allport,[14] well developed religious sentiment tends to constitute the center which unifies all the values of the personality; it is the most comprehensive feeling of all. The integration of the religious attitude can only be progressive, and it is by the successive unification of interests that religious sentiment acquires maturity. Religious educators will wish to keep this fact in mind. Verbal transmission of the religious message is not sufficient for forging the bonds of church belonging. A slow process of integration will be necessary for religious beliefs to permeate the very structure of the personality and its unifying values.

What has been generally said concerning maturation of personal opinions and acquisition of a philosophy of life[15] should here be taken up again in considering the development of the fundamental religious attitude. It is important to emphasize the unifying role that religious sentiments play in the individual whose spiritual formation has been developed normally. It was in this way that Vernon and Allport[16] concluded their now classic test on personal values: "Religious interest seems to be the best defined and the best organized. If this interest plays any important role at all within a person, it will then color, in a consistent manner, his whole vision of life."

[14] See G. W. Allport, *Personality,* especially Chapter 8, 213–231.
[15] Consult on this subject J. Stoetzel, *Théorie des opinions,* 263–342.
[16] P. E. Vernon and G. W. Allport, "A Test For Personal Values" in *Journ. Abn. Soc. Psychol.,* 1931, 26, 231–248.

Recent studies in the sociology of education illustrate these conclusions. Hoult and Peckham[17] have verified in a survey of young students the hypothesis that religious homogeneity with the environment constitutes a decisive factor for cultural adaptation; the students' religion condition their cultural familiarity with their educational milieu, and their behavior—even their academic performance—benefits from this familiarity.

If one studies Woodruff's observation,[18] which we have already cited, he will understand better the distinction made by this author between the integrating and the marginal religious attitude. He will also grasp the profound differences that one or the other of these attitudes will imprint upon the behavior of the church member. In religious education, these explanations are not without interest. If social psychology cannot as yet give answers to all the questions that religious leaders would like to have from it, it has nonetheless studied the results of religious integration sufficiently to indicate the conditions which determine the inculcation of psychoreligious attitudes.

Several problems remain to be solved, and one of the most difficult is that which Harms has already pointed out: the individualization of religious sentiment during the adolescent and post-adolescent periods. How can religious sentiment become individualized while there remains a feeling of belonging to a church?[19] This leads us to the as yet

[17] T. F. Hoult and C. W. Peckham, "Religion as a Cultural Factor in One Aspect of the Personality of Selected College Students" in *Journal of Educational Sociology*, 1957, 31, 75–81.

[18] A. D. Woodruff, "Personal Values and Religious Background" in *Journ. Soc. Psychol.*, 1945, 22, 141–147.

[19] There is not necessarily any opposition between these two *feelings*, as we will later see. The sole reason for stressing this double dimension (psychological and social) is to lead the observer to examine the relationships which exist between the intimate dispositions of individuals and their socioreligious framework of references.

unresolved question of the development of attitudes and of their relationship to group affiliation.

The correlation which exists between personal attitudes and insertion groups has often been observed, but the general theorems derived therefore have hardly been verified at the level of youth education.[20] In the future, it will be necessary for social psychology to apply itself systematically to the problem of adolescent religious education and to summarize, in a modern synthesis the research initiated in the past by the work of Hall.[21]

Within the limits that we have outlined here we can draw some useful conclusions. First, one recognizes the real dependencies which relate the degree of religious instruction received during adolescence and the stability of spiritual affiliation. But church belonging will imply very diverse forms of religious participation. Studying the forms of this participation in youth, we have seen that one must go beyond declared or juridical religious membership in order to understand the manifestations of belonging which have a real psychosocial meaning. Several factors of differentiation have become apparent to us. The most important from the point of view of teaching is the level of integration which doctrine must produce within the very structure of the personality. Depending upon the case in question, religious belonging will vary from the main focus of interest to a marginal and insulated concern, or even to a simple identification which is purely nominal. The behavior of young

[20] We will dwell at further length on the problem of *reference groups* in education in our section on "The Abandonment of the Religious Practice by Youth;" see Chapter X, 241–243.

[21] C. S. Hall, *Adolescence:* "Its psychology and its relations to physiology, anthropology, sociology, sex, crime, religion and education," 2 vol., (New York: 1904); see L. Guittard, *L'évolution religieuse des adolescents* (Paris: 1952); see especially the bibliography compiled by Guittard at the end of his work.

church members has revealed to us all these nuances of behavior and, though the differences can be explained in part by the length of their previous religious education, it is also necessary to examine the way religious attitudes have been more or less integrated within the whole of their system of values.

These observations emphasize a fact which is frequently neglected by certain educators. Transmission of the religious message constitutes only one aspect of the spiritual education of youth. Religious knowledge will engender a comprehensive and stable attitude only by progressively unifying all levels of behavior. Religious belonging will only be psychologically significant and durable if it becomes harmoniously integrated with the value system which provides the personality with its major orientations. One becomes aware of all the difficulties that the educator faces when one considers the complexity of a religious doctrine. The educative task consists in encouraging the integration of all religious values within a personality which is in the process of growing and for which the affiliations themselves should be freely and gradually assumed and given value. It is generally accepted that the problem does not rest exclusively with the child, but also with his educators and parents. This again brings up the question of how religious instruction is valued among those who surround the adolescents. A survey of the I. F. O. P.[22] provides us with some information in this regard, to the extent, at least, that it makes us grasp the importance of the question. A group of young people (of whom 50 per cent were married) were asked: "Are you providing or will you provide your children with a religious education?" The answers were

[22] "La nouvelle vague croit-elle en Dieu?" in *Informations Cath. Intern.,* 1958, 86, 11–20.

as follows: 76 per cent Yes; 11 per cent No; 13 per cent Don't Know. When we examine the reasons advanced in favor of the reply "yes," we observe that the motivations are variable: family tradition: 30 per cent; moral reasons: 28 per cent; religious conviction: 12 per cent.

Only 12 per cent have recourse to strictly religious motives. It is true that these answers refer to the actual dispositions of the parents as well as to the attitudes of the unmarried about the future. One fact, in any case, is illustrated: if one wishes to understand the conditions for success or failure with regard to the religious formation of youth, one should keep in mind, as a basic fact, the cultural atmosphere in which their spiritual development takes place. To know the religious attitude of the parents themselves will usually be indispensable. But this leads us to a larger problem, for the resolution of which it will be necessary to examine not only youth's psychosocial universe but also the sociocultural conditions which affect the transmission of the religious message. This is the purpose of our next section in which the role of "preaching" in the formation of the sense of religious belonging will be analyzed. These observations will have reference to the religious life of the young as well as to that of the adults. If it were our intention to trace the spiritual evolution of adolescents stage by stage, we shall have to consider further how the views of youth with regard to the church are diversified. We shall treat these problems in Part III where we shall discuss explicitly the transformations of the religious attitude and particularly the abandonment of religious practice by youth. Let us pursue for the moment our study on the formation of the bond of religious belonging, let us see how the transmission of the religious message influences spiritual adhesion and affiliation.

153

III Preaching in Its Social Context

1 THE PREACHER AND HIS MILIEU

We shall not understand by preaching that only which is called sacred eloquence only; we wish rather to give the term a broad meaning to include all oral, written, symbolic or ritual forms used to transmit a religious doctrine. One can say that Wach's approach, discussed at the beginning of this chapter, offers a formal sociology of religious instruction. Viewed from this angle, the function of preaching is to reveal the sacred message and, consequently, to unite the listeners to the community of the faithful either by prompting their first adhesion through conversion or by strengthening the cult and life of the group.

From the social psychologist's viewpoint one may begin from this point to analyze the sociological concomitants of the forms of expression and communication of doctrine. If one admits that preaching is a way of forming the religious attitude, one will inquire into the conditions under which the diffusion of doctrine succeeds in transforming a milieu and gaining religious adhesions. One will also try to determine to what extent preaching itself is an integral part of a social and cultural reality.

Again there is no question of the sociologist judging the doctrinal content of preaching. But, in accepting this content as a point of departure, he can relate the message to the observable circumstances which condition the listener's receptivity or which color the social expression of the teaching itself.

First it will be useful to qualify certain oversimplified explanations—some of which are hardly more than ideology. To relate, for example, the success of religious instruction to the discontent of the masses and to the spiritual opportunism of preachers is only to reduce the problem of religious adhesion to the level of class protest. Max Weber, in a study on the social psychology of religions,[23] remarked that some preachers have been able at times, whether intentionally or not, to channel for their own purposes the resentment of the masses. But, he adds, a negative reaction such as social discontent could not account for the transcendent conceptions of the great religions; and one has rarely seen a great faith attached to the interests of a single class.

Another insufficient explanation grants an exclusive role either to the predisposition of public opinion or to the extraordinary power of a religious leader. Why, for example, did the Germans adhere to the Reformation of the sixteenth century? Some will say that it is due to Luther's revolt and teaching; others will claim that the true cause is rather found in the revolt which already pre-existed in the German mind and conscience. The analyses of Gravier,[24] utilized by Stoetzel, bring to this problem a solution which has more nuances than the preceding ones and which takes into account both the indispensable conditioning of public opinion and the decisive public role of Luther himself. Stoetzel notes how much Le Bon's affirmations on the omnipotence of opinion in this matter were exaggerated. Luther knew how to use public opinion, but one must remember that the Reformation was his own personal achievement. "Public opinion simply constitutes a favorable atmosphere for the action of individuals who know what they want, and who are determined to achieve their goals."[25]

[23] Max Weber, "The Social Psychology of the World Religions," in *From Max Weber: "Essays in Sociology,"* edited and translated by H. H. Gerth and C. W. Mills (London: 1947), 267–301.
[24] M. Gravier, *Luther et l'opinion publique* (Paris: 1942).
[25] J. Stoetzel, *Théorie des opinions,* 384.

Thus, we shall not explain the influence of preaching as if it were only a simple response to the demands of public opinion or even a form of socioreligious compensation. We shall admit, moreover, that religious instruction supposes an undeniable cultural interaction. Its success requires more than the triumph of a momentary indoctrination; preaching wishes to effect the emergence of a profound attitude by methods proper to education. Social psychology has succeeded in showing how difficult it is to change a person's attitudes if the social framework in which he is living is ignored.

To understand the solidarities which exist between personal attitudes and collective conditioning, one need not have recourse to any determinism of the milieu relative to the individual. Let us simply admit that, as Krech and Crutchfield have pointed out, the development of attitudes "bears the mark of the cultural milieu in which the individual is immersed." This leaves the properly doctrinal content of the religious message intact. Its formulation and pedagogical methods, however, must be in keeping with the cultural circumstances proper to each milieu. The experience of the great religions would be enlightening in this regard.

2 REORIENTATION OF
COLLECTIVE ATTITUDES

Beginning with the general theory of cultural change, one could ask how the Catholic Church, for example, came to modify the collective attitudes of a milieu in favor of Christianity. Jeffreys[26] handled this question in an interesting study of cultural anthropology in which he describes the

[26] M. D. W. Jeffreys, "Some Rules of Directed Culture Change Under Roman Catholicism" in *American Anthropologist*, 1956, 58, 721–731.

pedagogical rules followed by the Church in her traditional task of evangelization. Taking examples from religious history, he examines the methods employed by some spiritual leaders of the past.

A typical instance is the work of the Capuchin missionary Jerome Merolla da Sorrento who preached in The Congo in the seventeenth century. Jeffreys analyzes at length an ordinance of Merolla establishing directives for the religious teaching of the Congolese. The document is reproduced in two columns. In the first column the missionary starts with direct observation and describes the "Abuses," that is, a whole series of cultural traits or practices which are reprehensible from the Christian's point of view. A second column comprises "Prescriptive Ordinances," that is, reflections and practical decisions that each of the preceding practices inspired within the missionary. A last column is added by Jeffreys which contains the author's "Notations." Here he analyzes the missionary's pedagogy and remarks that the latter takes particular care to preserve those Congolese cultural traits which could be integrated with a Christian attitude. We shall later see the implications which Jeffreys, from the viewpoint of cultural anthropology, derives from this consideration.

Another document also attracted his attention and seemed to him meaningful for a pedagogy of cultural change. It is a letter of Pope Gregory I, delivered by a messenger to St. Augustine of Canterbury, in which the Pope indicates to missionaries how the pagan customs of the English were to be transformed into Christian practices. Let us cite some passages of this letter. One of the paragraphs concerns the reconversion of pagan temples: "Advise Augustine that, after much deliberation on those matters which pertain to the English, I have decided that it is not fitting to destroy the temples but only the idols. . . . For if these temples are

157

well built, they can be transferred from the cult of the demons to that of the true God. Thus, if the nation sees that its sanctuaries are left standing, it will abandon its errors, know and adore the Lord. It will more easily come to those places which it used formerly to frequent." In another part of his letter Gregory asks that the great annual festivals be transformed into Christian celebrations: "The English make great sacrifices of oxen to the devil. There again, one must change the custom into some Christian feast. . . . Around the temples, thus converted into churches, let them make for themselves some tents of foliage and let them celebrate the feast with religious banquets. Let them no longer immolate animals to the devil, but let them kill them for God's honor that they may thereby draw nourishment. . . . Thus, while they are provided with exterior joys, they are more disposed to receive interior joys. . . . Augustine who is on the scene will see what is proper to decide."

We can take several points from Jeffreys' analysis which have quite direct bearing on the process of the transformation of attitudes. First we note that, although these texts and facts are old, they do not necessarily stand alone and one can presume that they represent a long pedagogical tradition. The method which is revealed here is characterized by a positive desire to preserve and to integrate, within religious formation, the values and customs of the people who are being converted. Quite evident on the Church's part is a rejection of condemnation of practices irreconcilable with Christian morals. But aside from these elements impossible to assimilate, one should note the various cultural traits which the missionaries strive to convert, that is, to reorient. This procedure leads the author to think that the Church has known for a long time how to adapt her preaching to the laws governing the transformation of cultures.

158

How is this change brought about? Not by an abrupt break but by a slow process of substitution. Attitudes and behavior are not simply relearned; they are transformed from the interior whenever their content is assimilable. "This method," concludes Jeffreys, "succeeds in producing the change in the desired direction while creating the minimum disturbance at the core of the culture thus transformed." A cultural trait does not necessarily have to be uprooted; what is required is an alteration of its orientation.

The examples given by Jeffreys refer to relatively simple societies, but they elucidate, in outline form, the more general model to which we alluded when we stated that the formation of attitudes "bears the mark of the cultural milieu in which the individual is immersed." The process of conversion of attitudes supposes that, at the outset, preaching has responded to the present dispositions and commitments of the individuals involved and that, secondly, it applies itself either to the elimination of former cultural traits, or to their reorientation by a procedure of redefinition or substitution.

3 PREACHING AND
SOCIORELIGIOUS IDENTIFICATION

If we transfer this model to the modern situation, we realize that membership ties to a church are involved with complex ties to other aspects of the environing culture. A double identification will be perceived in these relationships: one which links the member to the church; the other which identifies the local church with a given socio-cultural milieu. Preaching will have to be done with this double process of identification kept in constant view.

On one hand, as has been observed, preaching will only succeed in permanently aggregating to the church those groups only whose culture will have been assumed or re-oriented toward the direction of Christian values. This is stated as a general observation and it does not exclude the possibility of abrupt conversions which are followed by a period of psychoreligious adaptation. From the psychosocial viewpoint it is not as an isolated individual that the faithful member usually belongs to the religious group, but as a person who is involved within a complex of groups which are favorable or unfavorable to the church. The role of preaching, then, will be to reach people in the context of their social and cultural ties. Studies in social psychology show that in this manner stable attitudes are generally formed.

A second aspect of identification remains to be explained. It consists in the identification of religious groups with a particular sub-culture within a minority. Here we are not speaking of the church considered in its universality, but of the forms that Christianity can assume in specific circumstances. Let us also add that here we are beyond summary identifications of the church with the privileged or outcast classes. Max Weber has opposed this type of explanation, and a study by Isambert[27] rejected analogous theses which pursued this line of thought. Going beyond the level of private interests, then, and applying ourselves to the level of cultural forms, we observe that local religious groups bear the imprint of a particular sub-culture. The religious organism is thus identified with the specific forms of intellectual formation and social perception and with a certain style of expression. The immediate transmittal of the religious message bears the mark of the sub-culture with which the local community of believers is specifically identified.

[27] F.-A. Isambert, "L'abstention religieuse de la classe ouvrière" in *Cahiers Intern. Sociol.*, 1958, 25, 116–134.

The double identification that we have just retraced permits a consideration which complements Jefferys' initial schema. A number of empirical studies allow, we believe, a high degree of confidence in the validity of these propositions. One of the best works on the question is Pin's[28] monograph, *Pratique religieuse et classes sociales*. Let us mention a few of the author's conclusions which will elucidate our present problem. Pin has shown how the outward form of urban Catholicism in France is identified with cultural traits which are practically foreign to the working class. Between the ordinary world of the workers and the Catholicism of the cities, contacts are occasional and superficial. Religion appears as a part of "all that which, in urban life, eludes the grasp of the proletariat." One is confronted with two types of cultural expressions which are mutually incomprehensible: "On the one side, a world in which the idea, critical reflection, acquired knowledge, defined social conventions mediate human relations, on the other, a world in which contact that is immediate, concrete, experienced, is the only approach to men and to things."[29] The Church's message will consequently assume, for the most part, a manner and style foreign to the worker milieu of French cities. The doctrine will certainly remain unchanged despite the audience to which it will be addressed, but in the face of different sub-cultures there will be emphasis on this or that particular aspect of the message. Here, there will be an insistence on personal salvation, maturity in the faith, eschatology. There, on class solidarity, the defense of justice, the Christian transformation of this world, etc. One will come to the conclusion that, if church belonging always preserves the same theological significance, it nevertheless gives rise to different psychological images according to the estima-

[28] E. Pin, S.J., *Pratique religieuse et classes sociales* (Paris: 1956).
[29] *Op. cit.*, 404.

tions of group opinion. Sometimes, it will be the image of a bourgeois or capitalistic or liberal church, at other times the image of a church devoted to action, to the people, to the workers, etc.

Whether or not these collective evaluations have any foundation, they still do not prevent the creation of a de facto situation characterized by the identifications of which we spoke earlier. Some psychosocial consequences will, of course, result. The member or the future member thinks of church belonging as religious adhesion (individual-church identification) and also as participation in a well defined sociocultural world (church-sub-culture identification). These identifications, again, do not necessarily effect a de facto assimilation between the church and a particular sub-culture. Still less is it a *de jure* identification. We are here on the level of appearances or images which are held by a segment of the public. Let us not forget however that public opinion itself is a social fact.

Analogous phenomena could be observed in various religious confessions. Léonard,[30] for example, has studied at length the process of social selection which has occurred among French Protestants, and he considers the expression "becoming bourgeois" an apt description of an entire phase of Protestant history in his country.

We have insisted enough on this matter to permit us to discern the main object of our concern. The pedagogy of religious formation requires that one keep in mind the identifications, conscious or not, which give a determined sociological significance to religious belonging. If a member becomes identified with his church, the church in its turn can be psychologically identified with the forms of expression which characterize a given culture. The transmission of the religious message, then, carries a particular imprint, the

[30] E. G. Léonard, *op. cit.;* see Chapter IV, 58–79.

psychosocial significance of which must be considered. It is only by advancing beyond the threshold of particular cultures that one will succeed in transmitting the message universally. Preaching which remained, in the judgment of public opinion, identified with a subculture would not be universally heeded.

PART THREE
DIFFERENTIATION OF THE
RELIGIOUS ATTITUDE

SECTION I

THE STRENGTH OF THE RELIGIOUS ATTITUDE

With our study of the formation of religious attitudes completed, we next examine their internal structure and the criteria which show us their strength, durability, how deeply they are rooted or, on the contrary, their lacke of integration, their psychosocial marginality, etc. This is the problem of the differentiation of the religious attitude in which the internal strength, as well as the *transformations* of the bond of religious belonging, will be investigated.

The present section will study the religious attitude in terms of the factors which contribute to its strength. Steadfastness of spiritual belonging is analyzed with relation to the cohesion of the religious group itself.

Sectarian groups (Chapter VII) and ecclesiastical communities (Chapter VIII) are considered in turn according to the specific cohesion that the two types of structures favor. A special chapter will treat the phenomena referred to as the psychosocial "representation" (Chapter IX); this will reveal how the image of the religious group contributes to reaffirm or to weaken the solidity of the member's bond of belonging.

CHAPTER VII

GROUP COHESION AND
THE BOND OF BELONGING

1 The problem. 2 Elements of a psychology of social cohesion. 3 Socioreligious cohesion according to types of communities. 4 The specific cohesion of sects.

1 THE PROBLEM

We have attempted in the preceding chapters to analyze the processes which give rise to the sentiment of religious belonging. We have emphasized the multpile personal or collective factors which produce differences in the stability and the psychological significance of religious attitudes as they are being formed. Undoubtedly the history and the development of our social ties constitute one of the major explanations for the diversification of our present attitudes. We acknowledge the fundamental role of education in the maturation of religious feelings; in this area, as in that of moral behavior in general, we admit the decisive influence of the years of formation and socialization.

However, once the process of early education is completed the sense of church belonging is established or stabilized within an individual or a group of individuals, are there any psychosocial phenomena which encourage or discourage religious fidelity? And if so is it possible to analyze the ways in which various factors influence, either positively or negatively, the strength of church adhesion? Such is the question we now ask. Obviously the answers cannot be of an absolute nature. If certain sociocultural regularities are observed in this area, they will still not constitute a uniform causal sequence. We intend to analyze, from the interior, collective differences in the stability of membership in religious groups. Why does such a class or such a group remain faithful to its religious affiliations, and why does another such group break away so easily? Does one not see that a particular form of spiritual action here arouses or strengthens religious participation while it proves to be inefficacious elsewhere? Is one not also impressed by the fact of religious minorities suddenly won over by a rapidly growing dissident movement? Is it possible for the sociologist to analyze these transformations or these variations of collective religious attitudes? How would he study the strenght of the tie of religious belonging?

Religious history claims a particular competence for explaining the collective evolution and the present quality of membership in religious groups. A complementary insight, however, is had from social psychology, and the methods that this discipline employs for evaluating the strength and the differentiation of attitudes would permit a better analysis of some still inadequately known aspects of collective religious behavior. Answers to all the psychosocial questions raised by an investigation of the differentiation of religious attitudes obviously remain impossible, and much patient monographic research is needed before general explanations can be reached. We believe, however, that it is possible to begin a provisory synthesis by gathering together the numerous elements which sociological observation has already accumulated.

We intend, then, to examine the processes of differentiation of religious attitude by using the work that religious psychosociology has up to the present made available to us. Once we have explained the notion of strength of attitudes, we shall attempt to establish a relationship between the quality of religious membership and three universal factors which for the moment we will characterize as the internal structure of the membership group, the external relations of the group, and the image of the religious group in the consciousness of the faithful.

2 ELEMENTS OF A PSYCHOLOGY OF SOCIAL COHESION

Two approaches will be particularly useful in the differential analysis of religious adhesion: the psychology of participation and especially that of social cohesion. Let us make clear that we do not mean participation in the sense in which Lévy-Bruhl used it, that is, as some kind of a primordial logic or a prelogical knowledge. Lévy-Bruhl himself later criticized this concept of participation.[1] Reiterating the critique, Bastide[2] has explained how religious ethnology leads to a consideration of participation not as a simple category of thought or even of affectivity, but rather as a category or action, a pragmatic category. Without neglecting the cognitive or affective connotations of the phenomena of social participation, we shall make use of the suggestion offered us by religious ethnology: to situate participation on the level of action and behavior.

But all action, all behavior does not necessarily mean an actual participation of the personality. Allport[3] has em-

[1] See M. Leenhardt, "Les carnets de Lucien Lévy-Bruhl" in *Cahiers Intern. Sociol.*, 1949, 6, 28–42.

[2] R. Bastide, "Contribution à l'étude de la participation" in *Cahiers Intern. Sociol.*, 1953, 14, 30–40.

[3] G. W. Allport, "The Psychology of Participation" in *Psychol. Rev.*, 1945, 52, 117–132.

phasized the fact that a person can devote himself to numerous activities without, however, becoming deeply involved in any. It often happens that ego involvement remains superficial, even in the pursuit of activities which are, moreover, of vital importance to the subject. But one will observe that, when the individual is not a true "participant," he tends toward indifference, protest, aggression. Often, even his psychological well-being is at stake. Allport suggests that a balanced personality requires an effective participation in the majority of the following value systems: political, domestic, cultural and recreational, economic, and religious. Compensations and specializations will evidently be possible. One will note with the author that the psychology of participation definitely brings us to the fundamental values which motivate the adhesion of individuals to human communities. Social affiliations, then, are to be conceived not only in terms of the receptivity of the groups, but also in terms of the motivations for involvement on the member's part.[4]

Regarding the motivational aspect of affiliation, one will find in the works of Deutsch and his colleagues a certain number of verified propositions which can be used in a differential analysis of religious attitudes. We could legitimately regroup these explanations under the title, "psychology of cohesion." Two interdependent phenomena are studied in their relationships: belonging of the member and cohesion of the group. Motive for belonging is the attribute of the member; cohesion is the attribute of the group. It is evident then that, by analyzing the cohesion of groups with this perspective in mind, one discovers the differentiations of the sense of belonging, and vice versa. A comprehensive view of the studies involved will afford a better

4 Also see G. W. Allport, "A Psychological Approach to the Study of Love and Hate" in P. A. Sorokin, (ed), *op. cit.*, 145–164.

understanding of the psychosociological implications of the theory of cohesion, and help situate methodically the analysis which follows.[5] We shall therefore briefly review the principal elements of this psychology of cohesion and attempt to apply them to socioreligious cohesion. Four important elements will be pointed out: the members' perception of their interdependence; the proper motivations of belonging; the prestige of the group; and the external status of the group.

In previous work, Deutsch[6] began by defining cohesion in relation to (a) the perception that the members of a group have of their interdependence and cooperation; (b) the "attraction" exercised by goals pursued in common. This definition, though emphasizing the basic element of interdependence, does not sufficiently extend beyond the perspective of efficiency to be completely suited to our purpose. One would like to have a study made on the precise bonds which link the members to the group. Inspired by other research, Deutsch introduced elements of a descriptive analysis.[7] Among the motives which keep the individual attached to the group, he distinguishes three possible factors: (a) the positive attraction exerted by the group on the members; (b) the influence of a negative valence, that is, the fear of losing his allegiance to the group; (c) the obstacles or the barriers which prevent an effective abandonment of the group.

When these last three motives are applied to religious belonging, we shall possess certain concepts which permit the analysis of the strength of the membership tie to a com-

[5] See the synthesis presented by M. Deutsch, "Field Theory in Social Psychology" in G. Lindzey (ed.), *op. cit.*, 181–222; also the conclusions of S. Schachter, *The Psychology of Affiliation:* "Experimental Studies of the Sources of Gregariousness (Stanford: 1959).

[6] M. Deutsch, "A Theory of Cooperation and Competition" in *Human Relations*, 1949, 2, 129–152.

[7] See his article in Lindzey, *op. cit*, 214–215.

munity of believers. If, for example, the community is perceived by the members as a sacramental group or simply as a fraternal group, there will occur an affiliation motivated by what Deutsch calls a positive attraction. Belonging, on the contrary, will present quite another aspect if its primary motive is a negative one: fear of being excluded from the community. This situation undoubtedly exists only rarely in its extreme form, but it is easy enough to imagine when the religious group is practically coextensive with the human or national group; exclusion from one then involves rejection on the part of the other.

Back's research[8] adds some useful refinements to the preceding explanations. The author has carefully studied the way in which the attraction of the group is exerted on the members. He discovered that this attraction is exerted in different ways on the two different members, and that group cohesion will persist in spite of diversely oriented motivations. Cohesion will sometimes be based on the mutual esteem of the members, at other times on esteem for the group as such, and occasionally on esteem for the group as the means of realizing its own ends.

Are these three motivational poles found at the level of religious affiliation? With regard to the first two motives, the answer seems evident: the faithful member will be linked to his group by a true feeling of fraternity, and he will have a high regard for the religious institution itself because of its intrinsic values. Nevertheless, we should point out that the motive of prestige which is included in the second motive, will have to be understood in a rather broad sense in order to include distinctions of the psychoreligious order, that is, the acquisition of statuses proper to the spiritual community. With regard to the third motive, interest, one is made aware by the ever possible case of more or less

8 K. Back, "The Exertion of Influence Through Social Communication" in *Journ. Abn. Soc. Psychol.*, 1951, 46, 9–23.

self-interested conversions that religious belonging at times runs the risk of resting upon foundations which are deceptive or at least questionable. In these instances, religious belonging will appear to serve other causes or interests, personal, political, etc. Let us only remember for the moment the analytical concepts here suggested. Later we shall have the opportunity of applying them to the facts themselves.

A last element borrowed from Thibaut[9] will help us appreciate the totally distinctive cohesion of such marginal religious groups as cults or sects. Thibaut noted that high status groups normally are strongly cohesive while the low status groups exert only a decreasing attraction on their members. In these latter groups, on the other hand, sentiments of hostility are developed with regard to the more prestigious groups from which one imagines oneself to be excluded, and this sentiment will as a consequence encourage a renewal of cohesion. By examining the characteristic behavior of members of certain sects who believe themselves rejected and persecuted, one will find that Thibaut's analysis is quite accurate. Religious belonging in that case involves a feeling in which social protest plays, more or less consciously, an important role. We will treat this point in more detail later.

These propositions concerning the interdependence perceived by the members, the motives for belonging, and the prestige of the group, have focused our attention on the internal process of group belonging. Following our initial resolution of fixing our attention on the communal aspect of the problem, i.e., on the aspect internal to the community, we should concentrate on the fact of belonging and not on its secular or civil referents.[10] But speaking for the moment of the variations in belonging, certain influences of secular

---

[9] J. Thibaut, "An Experimental Study of the Cohesiveness of Underprivileged Groups" in *Human Relations,* 1950, 3, 251–278.

[10] Compare the remarks made in Chapter I, 35 f.

structures should be mentioned inasmuch as they exert a direct action on the cohesion of spiritual communities.

From the group's point of view the surrounding social structures will make themselves felt, especially on two points: (a) the status of the religious community and (b) the psychological representation of the group in the consciousness of the faithful. It is understood that the status of religious groups, like that of other groups, may be sociologically evaluated in relation to environmental structures; and social prestige will vary to the degree that the community maintains a position of majority or minority, of a dominant culture or sub-culture. The image which a religious group creates for itself can, consequently, be modified. These factors will have a positive or negative effect on the cohesion of the groups and on the quality of religious affiliation.

To understand the differences in the intensity of religious belonging, one must treat both the internal and external factors which differentiate the active participation of the members and the cohesion of their religious group. The cohesion of the group will be examined in the light of internal and external situations and from the viewpoint of group representations within the consciousness of the members. We reserve the particular problem of "representations" for a later chapter and discuss here the internal and specific structures of religious groups.

3 SOCIORELIGIOUS COHESION ACCORDING TO TYPES OF COMMUNITIES

The typology of religious groups, which we studied in Chapter II, brought us into contact with communities of belief which serve as frameworks for specific behavior. It is likely that the internal structures of these different groups influence the coherence and significance of religious belonging. Thus it will be useful to examine methodically the different type of participation by which membership in a sect is distinguished from membership in a church. Let us begin with some criteria distinguishing the structures and the behavior seen in these two types of religious groups.

From the start a number of studies suggest that, psychologically speaking, one does not belong to a sect or to an ecclesiastical institution in the same manner. One will note, in fact, that religious groups have ideas of salvation which determine characteristic attitudes in their faithful. Johnson[11] emphasizes this aspect. The church, as he has observed, is the unique dispenser of the means of salvation; the member must necessarily adhere to it if he wishes to participate in spiritual justification. The sect, on the contrary, rejects all liturgical and sacerdotal mediations of grace; one belongs to the sect as one belongs to a voluntary association. One concludes from these remarks that religious affiliations are first differentiated according to the degree of institutionalization of the means of salvation.

A second criterion would be a differentiation of the sect or church by the very behavior which is usual in these two types of religious groups. Dynes,[12] for example, has compared the faithful who belong to sects with the members of Protestant denominations which approximate the ecclesiastical type. He observed that the religious affiliation of the former tends to integrate and include the totality of their interests. All their social participations are concentrated within the framework of their religious group. Their habitual friends, acquaintances and companions are one with their coreligionists. Religious belonging is clearly expressed by

---

[11] B. Johnson, "A Critical Appraisal of the Church-Sect Typology" in *Amer. Sociol. Rev.*, 1957, 22, 88–92.

[12] R. R. Dynes, "The Consequences of Sectarianism for Social Participation" in *Social Forces*, 1957, 35, 331–334.

"sectarian" behavior which is limited, as strictly as possible, to members of that sect only. In denominations, on the contrary, religious belonging permits a considerable amount of extra-ecclesiastical social participation; and these participations remain relatively independent of religious attitudes.

We thus have, according to Dynes' explanation, two socioreligious structures which furnish the elements for a new differentiation of spiritual attitudes. In principle we shall retain this suggested distinction between sectarian behavior and marginal behavior, but we shall refrain from any generalizations. It is not evident that sect belonging is always expresesed by behavior which is so "sectarian," or that church affiliation is always marginal with relation to the totality of social participations.

Let us examine more carefully the psychosocial significance of these religious affiliations. Some important data will complete the general observations which Dynes and Johnson have furnished us. Let us first treat the structures of the sects; in the following chapter we shall come to a more detailed study of ecclesiastical structures.

4 THE SPECIFIC COHESION OF SECTS

Recent sociological research on sects[13] supports the conclusion that the form of belonging which is referred to as sectarian is itself differentiated into several forms which depend on the fundamental orientations of the religious groups. Wilson[14] thus distinguishes the sects according to

[13] See B. R. Wilson, "Apparition et persistance des sectes dans un milieu social en évolution" in *Arch. Sociol. des Relig.*, 1958, 5, 140–150; and by the same author, "An Analysis of Sect Development" in *Amer. Sociol. Rev.*, 1959, 24, 3–15; cf. H. Desroche, "Autour de la sociologie dite des sectes" in *L'Année Sociologique*, 1955–1956, 3e série, 395–421; see P. L. Berger, "The Sociological Study of Sectarianism" in *Social Research*, 1954, 21, 467–485.

[14] See the second article cited in the preceding note.

four principal tendencies: the conversion sects, the adventist sects, the introverted sects, and the gnostic sects. Each of these sects, because of its socioreligious orientation, produces a particular type of belonging. In all of them there is evident the fundamental rejection of compromise with the world and on principle of all accommodation to the needs of the times. But once this is understood, one sees that renunciation of the world assumes different meanings and consequently determines diverse modes of recruitment, adhesion and belonging.

The conversion sects openly predict and prepare for the transformation of this world; they offer salvation to all. One becomes a member by conversion and by the confession that Jesus is the personal Savior. Such is the criterion of belonging among the sects such as the Pentecostals and the Salvation Army.

The adventist sects stand for the most radical social changes and are only awaiting the overthrow of the present order. Membership is limited to those whose beliefs and conduct make them eligible; it is not sufficient to affirm that one has been converted; one must be worthy of being chosen. This is the requirement for the Jehovah's Witnesses.

The introverted sects are often identical with the pietists. Here, it is interior illumination which is primary, while doctrine is less important; the spirit counts more than the letter. The members are considered the elect for they have been illuminated. All other social, that is, nonreligious affiliations have little importance for them. Certain Quaker groups approximate this type.

The gnostic sects are characterized by esoterism. The Bible and traditional Christian teaching are considered symbolic references giving confirmation to the secret gnosis of the sect. The adherent hopes, little by little, to pierce

177

the mystery of gnosis which takes the place of everything: science, cosmology, psychology. There are no conversions, properly so called. But the initiate, the neophyte, is progressively admitted to illumination. Sect belonging promises the member success, health, and harmony with oneself and with the cosmos. Christian Science would be an example of this type.

This typology of sects obviously cannot take into detailed consideration all of the forms of sectarianism. But since it has been elaborated a posteriori by a specialist on the sociology of sects, we accept at least its general lines. Analysis of these types of groups first reveals that sect adhesion produces very disparate socioreligious participations. Even within the generic category of sectarian behavior there is found a wide variety of specific forms. In some sects religious belonging will signify the rejection of the world and social revolt, in others an indifference or peaceful resignation and, finally, in still others a sublimation or an escape into esoterism. One could recognize under these types of attitudes the broad categories according to which Troeltsch and Wach had divided the sect themselves: those which are distinguished by radicalism and those which remain passive and resigned.[15]

One notes the ambivalent character of each of these attitudes. They can be described by calling them "socioreligious" attitudes for they comprise a double reference and they plumb two worlds, that of belief and that of social participation. Wilson's typology permits one to understand the psychological bond which links the beliefs of these faithful to their behavior as members of the group. Social psychology thus brings out one of the major problems of religious ethnology, the linking of collective attitudes to group be-

[15] See J. Wach, *op. cit.*, 174.

liefs. Speaking of the "social organization of worship," Pinard de la Boullaye once said that it was "the problem of problems." The preceding comparative analysis emphasizes this fact. Each belief is expressed by a particular behavior; each determines the proper social structures which, in their turn, condition types of adhesion and affiliation.

Pinard de la Boullaye has also emphasized the importance of studying the problem of cohesion in the light of the "dogmatic cleavage" manifested by the religious groups. He suggested, among other things, that one consider whether, in the religious referred to as dogmatic, the rigor of doctrinal authority can be mitigated. If dogma is alterable one usually witnesses a relatively low degree of socioreligious participation. "The more," he observes, "the number of beliefs agreed upon by the members of the same social group is reduced, the more is the uniformity of thought and feeling among them restricted. . . . Likewise, the more the number of common doctrines is reduced, the more does social union produce participation in the same liturgical action, or in the same temporal advantages. . . ."[16]

Following this line of analysis one can inquire whether the progressive secularization of sects, such as has been studied by Pfautz,[17] is not finally explained by an internal evolution of religious structures which, in their turn, would result from the instability of doctrines and beliefs. The sect seems destined either to an institutionalization of its teaching and its structures or to a progressive dissolution of its religious character. In the last stage of this dissolution the belief system will have lost all that content which was properly religious; as a result, religious principles will no longer be invoked on the basis of their own authority but as

[16] *Op. cit.,* II, 445.
[17] H. W. Pfautz, "The Sociology of Secularization: Religious Groups" in *Amer. Journ. Sociol.,* 1955, 61, 121–128.

means or as techniques of happiness and personal success. The gnostic sects described above offer the first indications of this tendency. One adheres to these groups, which often resemble simple social movements, by a sort of mystique or sublimation of personal interest.

The research of Schneider and Dornbusch,[18] which treats of the popular works of religious psychology which have appeared since 1880, reveals the results of this spiritual pragmatism which they call a spiritual technology. The communal and doctrinal aspect of religion has vanished; only the psychological function or utility of adhesion to a religious inspiration is retained. The membership group has disappeared; religion is nothing but a psychological instrument. The phenomenon, however, ends in its own self-destruction for, as the authors point out, this religious "funtionalism" separates the spiritual message from its specific content and reduces it to a secular technique. Here again one notices how belief plays the role of the specifying element in the area of religious attitudes and behavior.

Let us briefly conclude this analysis of sectarian behavior. Granted that the distinction of sects and churches justifies our differential approach to the question of religious belonging, it is necessary to push the inquiry still further, for membership in sects itself reveals many levels of socioreligious participation. Sect typology permits us to underline the fact that it is the element of belief which is most decisive in determining the psychosociological significance of belonging. Progressing further one will see the need of examining the actual lines of dogmatic cleavage in order to perceive

[18] See L. Schneider and S. M. Dornbusch, "Inspirational Religious Literature: From Latent to Manifest Functions of Religion" in *Amer. Journ. Sociol.*, 1957, 62, 476–481; and L. Schneider and S. M. Dornbusch, *Popular Religion:* "Inspirational Books in America" (Chicago: 1958).

stability, the tendency toward secularization, or a reduction to the secular. These are the elements which will contribute to the specification and the differentiation of religious membership and belonging.

CHAPTER VIII

THE COHESION
OF ECCLESIASTICAL COMMUNITIES

1 Degrees of communal participation. 2 Institutional bonds.
3 Role of the priest in the cohesion of the community. 4
Dimension of communities and their cohesion.

1 DEGREES
OF COMMUNAL PARTICIPATION

We shall now consider ecclesiastical structures and see
how collective feelings of religious belonging are sociologically related to them. We indicated earlier the sense in which
we are using the term "church." The principal object of our
study will be the Catholic Church, and relationships and
comparisons will be made with parallel ecclesiastical structures, as those of the Episcopalians, Congregationalists, etc.
But each time we shall specify the particular church with
which we are dealing. If one considers the influence that
socio-ecclesiastical structures are said to exercise on the
strength of religious affiliation, three groups of factors
merit, we believe, special attention: the communal and institutional aspects of religious participation, the specific status
and role of the priest in the community and, finally, the dimension of the community of worship. It will be useful

[1] Refer back to 75–78, and especially 95–97.

182

to note that we do not intend to understand ecclesiastical structures in the properly juridical or theological sense. Our viewpoint is that of social psychology which examines the empirical structures and their image in the consciousness of the church members.

For the last ten years or so the sociology of Catholic parishes has undergone considerable development;[2] and, several of its conclusions can be used to elucidate, from various angles, the differentiation of religious attitudes and religious participation. Among the most important of these works are those of Nuesse and Harte, Fichter and Pin. All the researchers, in comparing milieux, have been struck by both the variation in the stability of religious attitudes and the different levels of religious participation.

The problems of religious participation have been approached both on the level of conceptualization and on that of systematic observation. The cohesion of the religious group itself, as well as the communal participation of the faithful, has been studied from an empirical point of view. Among the attempts which have been made to conceptualize and analyze observed differences in participation, those of Pin[3] deserve particular attention. He proposed to compare the degrees of belonging with the degrees of intensity of sociability as indicated by Gurvitch,[4] that is, the three forms of fusion: the Mass, the community, the Communion. Let us keep this idea in mind, but at the same time note that

[2] The bibliography on the sociology of Catholic parishes is very abundant; let us be content with pointing out some names among the better known researchers (see bibliography at end of book): Boulard, Donovan, Falardeau, Fichter, Houtart, Isambert, Labbens, Le Bras, Leoni, Nuesse and Harte, Pin, Schuyler, Ward, Winninger.

[3] E. Pin, S.J., *Introduction à l'étude sociologique des paroisses catholiques:* "critères de classification et typologies" (Ronéotypé) (Vanves: 1956).

[4] See G. Gurvitch, *La vocation actuelle de la sociologie* (Paris: 1957), 143–178.

183

empirical studies and comparisons are not sufficiently advanced to validate as yet the proposed analytical framework. The concept of Communion will serve, nevertheless, as a reference for the maximum intensity of religious or moral participation. "All religions, "writes Gurvitch,[5] "all churches, all great moral, intellectual, juridical or artistic experiences are based on collective participations, intuitions and judgments brought about by the interpenetration and fusing of separate consciousnessess into a single We; Communion constitutes the most intense degree of this unity."

This formulation helps us to understand that the phenomenon with which we are dealing is not reducible to the problem of the regularity of practice; it involves differences in psychosocial participation. Religious practice and religious participation are not phenomena without reciprocal action, but neither are they strictly equivalent. Isambert[6] came to grips with this problem in his survey of a Parisian parish.

By studying the levels of religious practice, this author succeeded in identifying an entire gamut of participation ranging from minus to plus, that is, from minimum involvement to total commitment: first, a simple awareness with regard to the church considered as a social group; then, the acceptance of the ethico-political principles attributed to the church; at a higher level there is the sharing of beliefs, properly so called, etc. For each level of practice, one will distinguish a particular level of integration in the parish group. "Integration in the Church through parish life is not univocal. At each level of practice, various forms of integration appear." The child, for example, will be brought for baptism either as an act of introduction to the Christian community, or as a simple family rite. To assist at Mass

[5] *Op. cit.*, 168.

[6] F.-A. Isambert, "Classes sociales et pratique religieuse paroissiale" in *Cahiers Intern. Sociol.*, 1953, 14, 141–153.

involves more and supposes "the acceptance of participation in a collectivity, of taking part in a community." To become a lay leader within the church is to assume a responsible role in "an organized and organizing community. The integration here is total."

These categories of observation merge with and extend Le Bras' typology which classifies practicing members as seasonal, as Eastertide worshipers or as Sunday churchgoers. Exterior practice is one criterion which provides information concerning the quality of belonging. To be sure, frequenting of the church is not an index which perfectly reveals the sense of religious belonging; but one will admit, with Le Bras, that regular or sporadic, or weekly or annual church attendance coincides on the collective level with different images of the bond of membership in the church. It is precisely to examine more carefully these psychological significations that research such as that of Isambert and Pin has been undertaken.

The question also arises concerning the extent of differential practice according to milieux or classes. Some social and historical factors are surely involved,[7] but Pin's hypothesis is the one which is most generally accepted at present. If the existence of subcultures in the interior of urban Catholicism is postulated, does not the proportionate inequality of practice (according to milieux) show the existence of a religious mentality which would be proper for each class or social category? One will admit, with the author, that this proposition is hypothetical and not definitive, although it already has been partially verified.[8]

Another question, moreover, would clarify the preceding one. Is not the dominant culture of a parish community an element determinative of religious affiliation as well as of

[7] See F.-A. Isambert, "L'abstention religieuse de la classe ouvrière" in *Cahiers Intern. Sociol.*, 1958, 25, 116–134.

[8] See E. Pin, S.J., *Pratique religieuse et classes sociales.*

practice? Do not the customs, manner and form of such parishes give a particular psychological coloration to their members' sense of affiliation—though it be only at an unconscious level of identification, projection, or the desire for social approval? There is always, to be sure, the same theological tie to a specific religion, but is the psychosocial content always the same? Granted the present condition of research, one can only state the problem. Let us hope, nevertheless, that these questions and hypotheses will encourage empirical studies of the matter, and that some day we will be in a better position to penetrate the mentalities or the cultural characteristics of parish communities. It appears more than likely that the strength of religious affiliation involves close interrelations with phenomena of this order.[9]

2 INSTITUTIONAL BONDS

Along with the more psychological or cultural aspects of attachment to the parish community[10] there are also situational aspects which we would like to consider. If the parish is considered from the perspective of the sociology of groups, one can inquire how the meaning of membership is capable of varying according to the differentiation of statuses and roles in the interior of the local Christian community. The group with its structures and with the statuses and roles proper to it will be called the institution.[11] The

[9] The reader is referred to the stimulating, documented article of J. Maître, "Religion populaire et populations religieuses" in *Cahiers Intern. Sociol.*, 1959, 27, 95–120.

[10] Participation is here envisioned in the perspective of religious *parish* practice. While admitting that the parish constitutes the habitual reference group for the majority of Catholics, it should be recognized that an appreciable number of the faithful seek satisfaction of their religious needs outside the parish framework: in churches located out of the parish, chapels, religious institutions, monasteries, at services conducted for particular groups, etc. This is frequently the case in the large cities. The religious participation of the faithful cannot be minimized, even if it seems to be "on the periphery" of the ordinary parish activity. Because

186

relationships between the behavior of the faithful and the internal structure of the group will be designated institutional bonds. Here the institution does not imply a strictly theological or juridical significance.

The institutional and structural aspects of the parish organization have been emphasized both in theoretical studies[12] and in empirical research.[13] With regard to our problem it is of some importance to inquire, as is done in these studies, whether the Catholic parish always constitutes a truly sociological group or whether, in the great urban centers, it often becomes an anonymous collectivity in which community life is impossible for the majority of the faithful.

Opposing Nuesse and Harte,[14] who present the Catholic parish as a formal group, Fichter[15] maintains that very large parishes no longer possess the strict characteristics of a de facto social group, at least in the sense defined by sociologists such as Hiller.[16] As a social group it lacks that minimum of interaction and interpersonal participation required for a real community life on the psychosocial level. We shall encounter this problem again when we treat the dimension of parishes as a variable influencing community behavior. Without treating for the moment the question of size and without posing the theoretical question of the reality of social groups, let us nevertheless note the conse-

---

of these facts, the studies on *parish sociology,* in spite of their immense interest, do not exhaust the sociology of *religious participation.* With regard to this subject, see the remarks of E. Pin, S.J., *Introduction à l'étude sociologique des paroisses,* 40–42.

[11] See J. O. Hertzler, *Social Institutions* (Lincoln: 1946).

[12] See the studies of Falardeau, Donovan and Schuyler mentioned in the bibliography.

[13] See, among others, the works of Fichter, Pin, Ward.

[14] Consult C. J. Nuesse and T. J. Harte (ed.), *The Sociology of the Parish:* "A Survey of the Parish in Its Constants and Variables" (Milwaukee: 1951), 65 f.

[15] See J. H. Fichter, S.J., *op. cit.,* 18.

[16] See E. T. Hiller, *Social Relations and Structures* (New York: 1947), 286.

quences which result from the de facto situation observed by Fichter.

If the parish is sufficiently circumscribed and forms a living group, identification with the immediate community will be facilitated, participation will be encouraged by interpersonal relationships, and religious belonging will assume local, direct references. If, on the contrary, the parish is immense and anonymous, participation on a social basis becomes practically impossible for most. Psychologically the member will no longer tend to refer his belonging to an immediate context, and only universal bonds will remain. One belongs to the Church but one has less and less a feeling of belonging to this particular church, to this particular and immediate community.

Fichter's[17] ten-year research led him to elaborate a typology which facilitates observation of the levels of participation in parish life. This typology is not presented as definitive; it is only an analytical model. But it illustrates certain criteria of behavior which serve to differentiate psychosociological adhesion to the parish community. Other types of parishioners will be observed in other milieux. Fichter noted four categories of parishioners; a particular degree of socioreligious participation corresponds to each of these categories: (a) the parish leaders and those whose fidelity and observance are the most clearly marked (nuclear); (b) the ordinary practicing members who constitute the majority of Catholics (modal); (d) those whose practice is sporadic and arbitrary with relation to Church requirements (marginal); (e) those who have practically abandoned Catholicism, but have not joined any other religious denomination (dormant). These four types are ex-

---

[17] See *op. cit.;* several other studies by the same author are noted in the bibliography.

188

plained, in a sense, by the particular situation of the Catholic Church in the pluralistic society of the United States.

Among these categories determined by Fichter the last two (marginal and dormant) reveal the lower degrees of socioreligious participation. The attitudes corresponding to these types will be analyzed in our chapter on the "mobility" of religious attitudes. Here we shall discuss the first two types (nuclear and modal) in which Church adhesion remains steadfast and participation regular.

The central core of the parish (nuclear parishioners) is made up of faithful members whose motivations are thus described by Fichter:[18] (a) a perfect orthodoxy in the faith and a constant tendency to think with the Church in all areas; (b) an evaluation of cultural institutions in which the religious institution ranks first; (c) prime importance given to the roles prescribed by the Church—these institutionalized roles rank above all other norms of behavior prescribed by the social milieu; (d) a system of well integrated religious values which provide a philosophy of life; (e) relations with the clergy which are cordial and spontaneous.

Other criteria serve to distinguish this first type of parishioner: regularity of observance, other practices of devotion, membership in parish organizations, etc. These parishioners constitute a small minority within the totality; in the three parishes which Fichter studied they numbered only 5.7 per cent. From this description one will deduce that for these members religious belonging constitutes a fundamental attitude which tends to unify their roles, and which gives a religious meaning to all aspects of their behavior. Their involvement is resolute and, in some of them, it is expressed by their acceptance of a leader's role in the parish. One can push the description further and inquire whether there do

[18] *Op. cit.,* 29 f.

not exist some behavioral standards or anticipations which are gradually formed within a parish and which come to be imposed on the leaders or outstanding members of the laity. Fichter[19] mentions the results of some interviews which seem to indicate this. The qualities required for leadership will vary from one milieu to another, but it is interesting to note that habits, customs and norms—one would say a particular culture—develop in a parish, and these traits in some way impose a certain type of behavior and socioreligious participation on parish leaders. Since this type of parishioner is acquainted with a limited number of persons only, the interactions between them are frequent and the influences mentioned earlier are more pronounced. But this small group is not representative of the whole.

The type most often encountered is the modal parishioner. In this category, Fichter places about 70 per cent of parishioners. These are ordinary practicing members who are regular in their religious observance. Their psychology and their communal solidarity is of particular interest to us. What is the psychosociological significance of their membership in the church? How are their other roles, on the whole, integrated with their religious behavior? To answer these questions would be tantamount, as Le Bras has commented, to "measuring the vitality" of Catholicism in a given milieu. We will not look for any universal solution here; each community must be studied separately. For illustration, let us consider the results obtained by Fichter[20] in his study of social personality and religious values. Here is how he describes those of the ordinary Catholics whom he observed.

By using the concept of social character elaborated by Fromm and Riesman, he distinguishes in the modal Catholic three levels of value-norms. A first level comprises stable values (beliefs and norms stabilized by the force of habit);

[19] *Ibid.*, 31.
[20] J. H. Fichter, S.J., "Religious Values and the Social Personality" in *Amer. Cath. Sociol. Rev.*, 1956, 17, 109–116.

a second level consists of fluctuating values; and there is a third level in which values are confused (social and racial questions, etc.). This configuration of the value system does not allow for a religious role capable of unifying all other roles and of integrating the social personality or the social character.

In the totality of his social personality, this modal Catholic resembles the non-Catholic to a great extent. His behavior, however, is not entirely secularized, and his religious role distinguishes him from the non-Catholic. But the influence of this role is limited. In short, it can be said that in this type of Catholic, religious belonging remains a steadfast and fixed attitude with regard to ultimate values, but the religious attitude itself does not encompass the totality of values. Some areas appear which, in practice, are considered secular and, therefore, independent of religious norms.

If, as Spengler and Allport postulate, religious feeling is ideally represented as unifying all personal values, one will nevertheless admit that in the present case it does not extend to the totality of interests. A residue remains and is not integrated within the psychoreligious system. In behavior there are observed some dimensions which are not related psychologically to the religious attitude. Church belonging is formalized and has a tendency to become parallel, if not marginal, to other social affiliations.

Mention is even made of alienation with regard to this lack of integration in the value society.[21] It is clear, consequently, that the socioreligious participation of these members is ambivalent. A real fidelity to the fundamental values of the religious group is discovered in their behavior. On the

[21] R. E. Morris, "Problems Concerning the Institutionalization of Religion" in *Amer. Cath. Sociol. Rev.*, 1956, 17, 98–108; on the general problem of the *institutionalization* of religious behavior, see T. F. O'Dea, "Five Dilemmas in the Institutionalization of Religion" in *Social Compass*, 1960, 1, 61–67.

other hand, conduct is observed which is more or less at conscious variance with Church norms. Their behavior is inspired by value systems which coexist without becoming integrated and, one would say in sociological language, that there is an accommodation to cultural and moral pluralism.

Accommodation to the surrounding culture will be extended in certain cases to the religious and doctrinal domain. The patterns of cultural pluralism then come to mark the spiritual attitudes themselves. In a milieu where skepticism and secularism are accepted attitudes, accommodation will take the form of a general relativism. Absolute values will tend to be received with a sense of reserve or of conciliation which encompasses the opinions of every group or school of thought. The different religious denominations will be perceived through a pluralistic representation of religion in which differences are diminished for the benefit of a syncretistic and idealized image. One identifies himself with all believers rather than with a particular confession. Uniformity is overestimated and the distinctive traits of the denominations are passed over. We are here describing tendencies rather than attitudes which are always explicit and conscious, but research such as that of Thomas[22] or of Herberg[23] shows us that such a type of behavior exists, the consequences of which are clearly observable.

[22] Thomas has shown how the *patterns* of "mixed marriage" affect Catholics as well as Protestants and Jews in the United States. Some previous studies undertaken by Hollingshead and Kennedy suggested that Catholics underwent an "accommodation" which was considerably less noticeable in this regard; Thomas discussed these works and emphasized, to the contrary, the extent of "accommodation" among the Catholics; see J. L. Thomas, S.J., "The Factor of Religion in the Selection of Marriage Mates" in *Amer. Sociol. Rev.*, 1951, 16, 487–491.

[23] W. Herberg, *Protestant-Catholic-Jew* (New York: 1955). Herberg's competent and incisive description reveals how this tendency to embrace a common religion, a common faith, a religion of religions, etc., can exist in a specific situation. These phenomena recall other forms of socioreligious "accommodation" such as religious utilitarianism, the politicalization of religion, the secularization of religious groups, etc.—deviations which have threatened religious institutions of all countries in all countries and centuries.

Let us briefly conclude these first analyses of community behavior before coming to other aspects of ecclesiastical structure. Having started with the general notion of sociability, we endeavored to understand the forms according to which religious participation and community cohesion are differentiated. Beyond the levels of religious practice, we have seen degrees of participation which appear related to religious attitudes which are quite different for each cultural stratum of urban Catholicism. The institutional structures of the local community, depending on whether they permit an authentic group life or only an impersonal public, also play a differentiating role in the strength of religious attitudes. If one penetrates the psychology of the faithful, one observes that the levels of participation are themselves explained by models and norms of behavior whose psychoreligious integration is more or less perfect. In some, religious belonging motivates the totality of behavior; in others, church affiliation will certainly furnish specific motivations for religious conduct, but it will only superficially inspire that behavior which, in practice, is considered areligious, profane, or secular.

All the factors of behavior which we have just examined are closely related. As has been seen, the psychology of the participant is only comprehensible if it is related to sociocultural characteristics and to the institutional cohesion of the community of worship. There are no absolute principles. But it is advantageous to point out that explanations which rely on one factor are insufficient, whether that factor be moral, psychological or sociological. This fact becomes still more evident when one considers the inverse phenomenon to that of belonging, that is, detachment from the church. Dechristianization, indeed, is not reducible to simple moral deterioration or cultural nonadaptation, or depersonalization within an anonymous institution. On the individual level, of course, one or another of these processes may play

193

an important part in detaching the member from the group; but even so, the existence of social processes does not necessarily eliminate the free choice of the individual. On the collective level, moreover, attempts to explain the religious preferences of whole groups through some form of social conditioning appear even more inadequate. Ultimately, recourse must be had to a dynamism which is both interior to the subject and yet not unrelated to the external forces which are impinging on him. The member's choice is exercised on an absolute object but the subjective representation of this object will be conditioned by the particular culture.[24] Observation of religious collectivities reveals constants which prompt us never to trust as complete an evaluation of religious affiliations which does not consider the totality of factors which we have outlined above.

3 ROLE OF THE PRIEST IN THE COHESION OF THE COMMUNITY

Among the factors of institutional cohesion which we have mentioned, there is one which we must treat separately: the action of the priest in the midst of the community. The priestly role is both complex and many-sided, and we have no intention of probing into every ramification which would be of interest to social psychology. Our investigation will concern only the precise point treated in the present chapter; we shall inquire into the ways in which the different forms of sacerdotal action influence the cohesion of worship or of communities.

In conformity with the viewpoint adopted above, we shall limit our analysis to the Catholic priest; but in order to understand his specific role more fully, it will be useful to

[24] On this question see E. Pin, S.J., *Pratique religieuse et classes sociales,* 265–266. We will come back to this problem in Chapter IX.

compare briefly his over-all activity with that of ministers in other Christian confessions.

One is aware, for example, that certain sects do not recognize any specialization of sacred ministers. In general these are rudimentary religious groups corresponding to what von Wiese has termed cults. Pfautz,[25] who has studied the evolution of several of these cults, has shown how, at the very time that they are becoming interiorly differentiated, they produce leaders or officials within their midst. Frequently this may involve certain ambiguities and contradictions in the status and role of the minister. Wilson[26] has stressed this point with regard to the Pentecostal ministers.

If we examine the denominations, properly so called, two principal types of clerical action will become evident. Smith's systematic analysis of them[27] provides us with the following elements. In denominations of the Episcopalian type the clergy has functions which conform to a traditional and hierarchical order that follows ritual prescriptions. Here we speak of sacramental and hierarchical function. In denominations of the Congregational type, the minister depends directly on the local community which has chosen him and which has retained his services. Rites do not have any value in themselves, they are only exterior means, instruments of the minister. Personal style of preaching, individual contracts and community organizations play an important role in the activity of the minister. His function is instrumental and democratic, as Smith tells us. His role is in some way imposed upon him by the local congregation; higher authority—if the local community depends on it—

[25] H. W. Pfautz, "The Sociology of Secularization: Religious Groups" in *Amer. Journ. Sociol.*, 1955, 61, 121–128.

[26] B. R. Wilson, "The Pentecostalist Minister: Role Conflicts and Status Contradiction" in *Amer. Journ. Sociol.*, 1959, 64, 494–504.

[27] L. M. Smith, "The Clergy: Authority, Structure, Ideology, Migration" in *Amer. Sociol. Rev.*, 1953, 18, 242–248.

has only a minor influence on the exercise of the pastor's ministry.

In both cases communital cohesion is related to the action of the clergy, but the differences are immediately apparent. For the Congregationalists, a voluntary, local and autonomous association, the elected pastor has the role of interpreting doctrine and coordinating spiritual matters. Among the Episcopalians the pastoral function, for the most part, is regulated by the denomination's current customs and rituals. The minister exercises an intermediary role between the believer and the church. The members of the local community actually belong to the latter, but the action of the clergy constantly reminds them that the local church is only a part of a universal community.

Turning now to the Catholic priest, let us examine his action within a parish. The observer, from the first, is struck by the strongly institutionalized character of the sacerdotal function. This trait has often been brought out by sociologists. Max Weber[28] ranked "the Catholic priest or chaplain" among the professions which have undergone the highest degree of "juridical formalization." Hertzler,[29] a specialist on social institutions, while maintaining that no institution can of itself satisfy all the interests of a person, is ready, however, to make an exception in the case of the celibate priest. According to the observations of Krech and Crutchfield,[30] the priest (as well as certain other spiritual leaders) has no need to participate in groups outside his own. The church is the milieu in which he can express his total personality.

Along the same lines, Rogé comes to a similar conclusion

[28] Max Weber, "The Social Psychology of the World Religions," *op. cit.*, 299.

[29] See J. O. Hertzler, *op. cit.*, 181.

[30] Confer D. Krech and R. S. Crutchfield, *Theory and Problems of Social Psychology* (New York: 1948).

196

in his study on the psychology of the priest. For Rogé,[31] the priest would even be "the most institutionalized man of our time." The psychologist, as he explains, is surprised by the numerous regulations and norms (rules, diocesan statutes, canon law, traditions, customs, etc.) which frame the priest's behavior. He plays a role which is extremely confining in some respects. But to the observer another polarity of sacerdotal behavior is laid bare: the personal spontaneity which interiorizes institutional norms and inspires informal contacts in this pastoral ministry. If we consider the priest's role within the community of the faithful, we can see that his action bears the marks of a constant tension between the institutional and the personal. The two aspects of action, furthermore, seem necessary for the cohesion of the parish group. It is evident that community life effectually depends on the balance which is maintained between these two types of action described by Rogé.

On one hand the institutional functions of the priest contribute to the formalization of the relationships between the faithful and the group. The juridical framework, the ritual practices and the sacramental dispensation remind the parishioner of the supralocal dimension of his religious belonging and provide universal motives for his adhesion. But if because of circumstances—too large dimension of the group, overwork, habit, routine—the role of the priest is gradually reduced to the institutional works of his ministry, there will be the danger of religious functionalism which would, sooner or later, threaten the cohesion of the Christian community. Apropos of the impersonal character of the very large parishes, Falardeau[32] referred to priests who become "anonymous functionaries with whom one no longer

[31] J Rogé, "Psychologie du prêtre" in *Journal de Psychologie,* 1956, 53, 63–80.
[32] J.-C. Falardeau, "Parish Research in Canada" in C. J. Nuesse and T. J. Harte (ed.), *op. cit.,* 144, 323–332.

has anything but chance contact." A certain rationalization of the ministry is evidently indispensable, but it must leave room for more spontaneous forms of faithful-priest relations. Gustafson,[33] treating in general of the sacred ministry, points out in this regard that "a sociological realism admitting the necessity of an institutionalization of programs . . . tends to neglect the less structured means of communication."

After showing the integrating role of the institutional pastoral life, let us also show the necessity of a direct, interpersonal action without rigid forms. According to Rogé, this type of action is favored by the bishops who are seeking "to transform the practicing flock into a vital and missionary-minded community." The creation or intensification of community relationships supposes a priestly presence which is personalized, interested, accommodating. Community life in large measure arises from the direct and spontaneous interaction of the faithful among themselves (Catholic Action, lay initiative), but these relationships run the risk of deteriorating if sacerdotal action is purely formal.

Let us add, however, that the problem is not reduced to the form of sacerdotal action only. A more or less extensive institutionalization of the ministry, together with a more or less widespread and immediate adaptation of pastoral action, are problems which are of great interest to anyone studying the cohesion of Christian communities. But social psychology would like to advance further and probe the level of motivation itself. Here, we can use the distinctions proposed by Szabo[34] for analyzing the priestly role. Three elements are proposed by the author for examining the

[33] J. M. Gustafson, "An Analysis of the Problem of the Role of the Minister" in *The Journal of Religion*, 1954, 34, 187–191.

[34] D. Szabo, "Essai sur quelques aspects sociologiques de la crise du recrutement sacerdotal en France" in *Bull. de l'Inst. de Rech. Econ. et Sociales*, 1958, 24, 635–646.

status and role of the priest: vocation or "call of God mediated by the Church;" profession or "function and kind of life . . . a combination of traits which distinguish the man of God;" and activity or the "daily routine of the ministry."

From these three aspects of the sacerdotal status-role it should be possible to discover the balanced norms to which priestly action should conform in order to contribute to the parish dynamism and cohesion. The question is, first of all, normative. But even at the level of behavioral models one cannot refrain from observing the interactions between these three constituents of sacerdotal action.

That the vocation aspect plays a prominent part in the motivational system of the priest and the faithful is a fact which seems evident to those who have analyzed the sacred character inherent in sacerdotal functions. The study of Burtt and Falkenberg on the influence than the clergy of the sacred ministry in general is pertinent here. If the majority in a Christian group exerts a greater influence on the faithful member with reference to political and social attitudes, the clergyman, due to his sacred character, has an unrivaled power of persuasion with regard to matters which directly touch upon the religious sphere.[35]

The sacred character can, however, become blurred if the faithful see nothing but the exterior, professional facet of the priest. Jammes,[36] in his work on the role of the priest, points out the painful contradiction which is sometimes encountered between the professional detachment of the

[35] See H. E. Burtt and D. R. Falkenberg, "The Influence of Majority and Expert Opinion on Religious Attitudes" in *Journ. Soc. Psychol.*, 1941, 14, 269–278; consult also C. Y. Glock and B. B. Ringer, "Church Policy and the Attitudes of Ministers and Parishioners on Social Issues" in *Amer. Sociol. Rev.*, 1956, 21, 148–156.

[36] J.-M. Jammes, "The Social Role of the Priest" in *Amer. Cath. Sociol. Rev.*, 1955, 15, 94–103; and J.-M. Jammes, "Les catholiques américains et le sacerdoce" in *Chronique Sociale de France*, 1955, 63, 23–36.

priest and the distressed attitude of the faithful who have recourse to him in time of distress. The disillusionment will be all the greater if they meet only the day-by-day routine attitude of the functionary.

We conclude with the observation that, beyond the daily activity and profession of the minister, we must penetrate to the fundamental beliefs and faith in a vocation if we wish to explain the specific efficacy of the sacerdotal role. The ultimate motivation is found at this level both with regard to the priest, who unifies the believers by his spiritual action, as well as the faithful, who visualize the priest as the institutionalized intermediary between themselves and God. In this sociotheological perspective, which results from empirical analysis, we accept Rogé's observation[37] for it will furnish us with a conclusion for this section on the sacerdotal role. Rogé conceives the specific action of the priest as a "relationship between four terms:" a person (a particular priest); "someone of social distinction" (the "good priest"); a Person viewed in faith (Christ); specific individuals (faithful or unbelievers).

4 DIMENSIONS OF COMMUNITIES AND THEIR COHESION

We have already intimated a number of times the importance that must be granted to the dimensions of the religious group if we wish to understand its internal cohesion and the quality of participation that it inspires. The dimensions of parishes or religious groups have been studied from several viewpoints: institutional aspects,[38] the pastoral

[37] See J. Rogé, "Psychologie du prêtre" in *Journal de Psychologie,* 1956, 53, 63–80.

[38] F. S. Chapin, "The Optimum Size of Institutions: A Theory of the Large Groups" in *Amer. Journ. Sociol.,* 1957, 62, 449–460.

[39] F. Boulard (Canon), "Aspects sociologiques: le problème des trop petites paroisses" in *La Maison-Dieu,* 1959, 57, 9–24.

aspect[39] and the sociojuridical aspect.[40] Here we will examine the problem in the perspective of communal cohesion and inquire into those dimensions of the community of worship which most favor participation and the sense of religious belonging. In a comparison between religious groups of different dimensions, Dynes[41] hoped to find out if there were not here some sort of optimum "beyond which the community of believers begins to lose its cohesion." This is the problem which we would like to investigate with regard to the Catholic parish.

For us, the easiest way of treating the question is to start with extreme cases and to attempt, by successive steps, to clarify what we mean by an optimum. In some large modern cities there are parishes whose members exceed 60,000 or 80,000. There is no need to point out that, with the possible exception of some restricted groups, participation is non-existent for the collectivity. It is interesting to note that the Church's traditional practice and even its spirit of canonical legislation confirm the requirements which the sociologist would propose regarding the dimensions of community groups. Winninger, who has specialized in this type of analysis, mentions an ecclesiastical principle of parish organization to which a psychosociologist would readily subscribe. This principle, incorporated into present-day Canon law, originates from the directive expressed in the past by the Council of Trent urging "that the parish priest know his sheep" (*debet suas oves cognoscere*).[42] According to this principle a parish will be considered unwieldy when its faithful are too numerous to be known by the parish priest. Following his historico-juridical analysis, Winninger

[40] P. Winninger, *Construire des eglises:* les dimensions des paroisses et les contradictions de l'apostolat dans les villes (Paris: 1957).

[41] R. R. Dynes, "The Consequences of Sectarianism for Social Participation" in *Social Forces,* 1957, 35, 331–334.

[42] See *Jus Can.* 467, 1; see Winninger, *op. cit.,* 23.

proposed the figure of 5,000 parishioners as the ideal parish dimension. While taking into account local conditions (the state of religious practice, the urban or rural character of the place of worship, etc.), he reports that experience shows that "a priest, capably assisted by several active members of Catholic Action, can effectively minister to 250 to 300 families, or 1,000 to 1,500 persons—figures broad enough to include that fringe, that kind of periphery which his influence can reach without having direct contact with it."[43] The possibility of personal contact between priest and faithful here seems to be the indispensable condition of community life. Two or three curates, with a pastor, will succeed in maintaining sufficiently close relations with a parish group of perhaps 5,000 people. To establish larger parishes with more curates would not have the same effect; for there would be no guarantee that the individual parishioner would be known to any one priest, and the total collectivity would be more anonymous because larger. Winninger admits that a parish of 15,000 inhabitants can remain balanced if it comprises, in addition to a main church, two secondary chapels with a resident priest. The number 5,000 if offered, in any case, as the unit-type, not as the general norm for the place of worship: "The figure of 5,000 inhabitants is not necessarily the order of magnitude for the parish, but it is rather the unit-type of a human group upon which a place of worship ministered to by one or more priests can efficaciously radiate."[44] We shall consider this figure as the upper limit of the unit-type of a community of worship; beyond 5,000, community cohesion tends to decrease because of obstacles which prevent a personalized pastoral approach as well as the possibility of an effective interaction between the faithful themselves.

[43] *Op. cit.,* 32.
[44] *Ibid.,* 38.

Conversely, could one find a lower limit below which parish life would lose its character of a coherent community? To answer this question, which is both theoretical and practical, we have at our disposal a study done by several researchers, notably Boulard and Winninger,[45] on the problems created by the small size of some parishes. Boulard states two principles which shed light on our problem. The author invites us to examine the question from the viewpoint of both the internal structure of the parish and its institutional functioning.

A human community which is too small "to assure the normal collective services of elementary social life," as Boulard explains, cannot constitute a coherent Christian community. It is difficult to determine absolute figures. Reasoning analogously from the facts that urban or rural sociologists have found, Boulard admits, *mutatis mutandis,* the limits set by Fogarty: "Recent studies, both urban and rural, concur with this idea that, to ensure human relations, the village, as well as the urban neighborhood, should have a minimum of 500 inhabitants. . . ." Fogarty would likewise maintain, following the research pursued by his colleague Adam Curle, "that isolated communities under 600 inhabitants, if they become self-centered (and this qualification is of the utmost importance), gradually fall prey to quarrels and cliques, and are less capable of upholding a satisfactory position of social organization and local government."[46] Evidently there is no complete parallel between the civil community and the parish, but if one probes into the collective psychology of these small human islands one realizes that the problems are analogous in the two types of com-

---

[45] Confer F. Boulard, "Aspects sociologiques: le problème des trop petites paroisses" in *La Maison-Dieu,* 1959, 57, 9–24; and P. Winninger, "[Le problème des trop petites paroisses]: aspects canoniques, que dit le Code?" in *La Maison-Dieu,* 1959, 57, 31–54.

[46] A report cited by Boulard, *art. laud.,* 15.

munities when the latter become too circumscribed: isolation, lack of differentiation, impossibility of improvement, impoverishment by depopulation or exodus of the young.

If the second criterion is next considered, that of the institutional functioning of the parishes, it becomes evident that an overly reduced population hampers the cohesion and the stability of religious participation. This fact appears clearly when one recalls the proper function of the parish group. This group is not only one whose task is simple cooperation or efficiency—in this case smaller groups are often more effective. The parish is a ritual community and because of this it requires stable institutions, a pastoral organization, and permanent social structures which will assure the functioning of parish service. The permanence of the institution, or at least its orderly functioning, would be compromised by the extremely small size of the parish group. Worship, religious instruction, equal distribution of work, temporal administration, support for places of worship and for the clergy all suppose that the parish is co-extensive with a relatively well developed and structured human group. The extreme diversity of situations prevents the determination of any precise figures. The principle however will be retained: the parish, being a worshiping community, needs dimensions which render it viable as an institution.

It will be noticed that the higher and lower limits thus proposed—which define the ideal unit-type—bring us indirectly to the two complementary aspects of sacerdotal action described earlier. The priest, as we have stated, exercises a role which is both personalized and institutionalized. If certain parishes are considered overextended, is it not due in part to the fact that, with an anonymous mass, the personal action of the priest is therein made impossible? If, on the other hand, parishes appear too restricted, is it not because of the practical impossibility of implanting or of maintaining within them an institutionalized sacerdotal action?

The preceding analysis gives a static view of the problem; the Christian communities have been considered according to their more or less stable or fixed dimensions. It would be also of interest to be able to evaluate the cohesion of religious groups with relation to their rate of growth. How many neophytes, for example, would it be possible to accept in proportion to the dimensions of the particular parish? The problem confronts all expanding religious groups, especially in mission countries. Indeed, it is not rare that a missionary must curtail the number of baptisms due to the lack of assurance that the neophytes will be harmoniously integrated within the Christian community.

Few works can give us precise information concerning this question. The only study of which we are aware is that of Chapin,[47] who does not consider Catholic parishes but eighty Protestant churches. His research deals with three factors: the number of present-day members (M), the number of new adherents (A), and a criterion of institutional cohesion (C). This latter is a composite measure based on religious practice, fidelity to the Sunday school, the condition of community services, the stability of organizations, etc. Chapin finds that the proportion $\frac{M}{M+A}$ is directly related to institutional cohesion (C) of the churches, provided one takes into consideration the absolute dimensions of the communities as well as their ages. While recognizing the differences in collective psychology which exist between Protestant communities and Catholic parishes, we can at least cite Chapin's general observations as useful hypotheses of research.

[47] F. S. Chapin, "The Optimum Size of Institutions: A Theory of the Large Groups" in *Amer. Journ. Sociol.*, 1957, 62, 449–460.

(1) The oldest churches have the largest actual membership, but their growth is ordinarily slow and their cohesion is average. Institutional cohesion, however, is better in those churches which do experience an influx of new adherents.

(2) Among the churches which are average with regard to age (about seventy-five years of existence) the rate of growth is moderate and institutional cohesion is quite strong.

(3) The more recent churches (an existence of ten or so years) have a high rate of growth but their institutional cohesion is rather weak.

Here is Chapin's attempt at an explanation: "Extreme rates of growth are associated inversely with institutional strength, because when growth rates are very high, the institution is weak due to lack of integration; and, when growth rates are very low, the weak institutional strength is due to lack of new blood."[48] This proposition in the author's opinion is still open to question, but one sees in it a concordance with a normative principle which the traditional pastoral approach knows well and which can be thus summarized: an efficacious missionary effort presupposes the cohesion of Christian communities and, inversely, the cohesion of Christian groups requires a constant missionary effort. Without developing these pastoral principles here, the preceding statements will be accepted in order to bring out some complementary aspects of the cohesion of religious groups. These remarks will serve as conclusions.

For a community to be vital, the member should have the sentiment of truly personal affiliation, that is, membership group should not surpass certain dimensions beyond which the parish would become an anonymous collectivity. On the other hand, the parish community, because it fulfills complex functions (worship, religious instruction, charitable

[48] *Art. cit.,* 452.

services, missionary action, etc.), has need of institutional structures which are sufficiently developed and this consequently requires a parish which is not too small.

These two aspects of community cohesion clarify, in turn, certain characteristics proper to religious participation and belonging. The sense of belonging will vary in intensity and strength to the degree in which both personal integration with the group and group institutional stability vary. The cohesion of the religious attitude rests on a balance—which here seems to us specific—between personal elements and institutional structure. We believe it would be difficult to find another type of social affiliation which, on the one hand, involves so deeply the whole personality and which on the other hand, requires an institutional support which is so complex.

Let us emphasize in this perspective of personal-institution relations a final characteristic of the religious attitude. We wish to speak of the missionary efforts which usually accompanies religious feeling. If a minimum of missionary action is considered indispensable for the cohesion of religious groups, one also observes that the sense of religious belonging rarely remains individualized to the point that the subject is completely unconcerned (even interiorly) with those who do not share his belief. The appraisal of this proselytism will permit an evaluation of the steadfastness of belonging to the Christian community. While recognizing the value of tolerance and of respect for the beliefs of others, we can assert that the Christian will be more closely attached to his church the more seriously he seeks—at least by his prayers—to have others share his faith. His religious affiliation, on the contrary, would assume little value in his eyes if he were to remain perfectly indifferent toward those who do not know the Truth acknowledged by him as the source of salvation.

CHAPTER IX

THE SELF-IMAGE OF THE RELIGIOUS
GROUP AS A SOURCE OF COHESION

1 The self-image of the group. 2 Image of the group: from subjective to objective? 3 The self-evaluation of the group. 4 The symbolic representations of the group.

1 THE SELF-IMAGE OF THE GROUP

Today "collective representations" are hardly mentioned. After many vicissitudes this concept, as well as the notions of collective soul and group mind, has finally disappeared from scientific thought. But while the psychic monism inherent in these conceptions is rejected, the idea of "representation" for analyzing social cohesion remains in use. Instead of conceiving "representation" as a supra-individual psyche, we shall rather study the group image within the consciousness of the members of a collectivity. This is a method which will help our understanding of the quality of social affiliations.

Expressed in general terms the problem comes down to discovering the image which the member forms of his group. And, as a related question, we might ask: what group image does the group present to those on the outside? A number of socioreligious studies have used this analytical schema, and an examination of them will be of use to us. This will allow, from a complementary viewpoint, the study of both the cohesion of groups and the differentiation of religious affiliations.

By way of example, let us mention the work of Mayer and Marx[1] who studied a Polish minority among whom an unfavorable self-image has been created by the dominant culture, orients the group toward a rapid identification with the surrounding majority as well as acceptance of its norms of conduct. Others have analyzed the religious denominations represented as hierarchical or equalitarian communities. In other studies religious confessions appear under the image of ethnocentric groups or become identified with a particular class, a particular politico-economic attitude, a particular cultural level, or a particular social status.[2]

For the purpose of our analysis, what psychosocial signification shall we give to the term "representation"? If one wishes to utilize the group image for appraising community cohesion, we think it necessary to examine three connected phenomena: the perception of the group; the self-evaluation of the group in relation to a given cultural context; the religious symbolization of the group in the consciousness of its members.

First, one determines how the group is perceived by members or outsiders. Is the group represented to the members' consciousness as a unified, expanding, accepted community, or rather as a rejected, retrogressive, sociologically amorphous group? If the group is represented as having a high status, cohesion between the members becomes more closely knit. It begins to wane in a group which is accorded

[1] A. J. Mayer and S. Marx, "Social Change, Religion and Birth Rates" in *Amer. Journ. Sociol.*, 1957, 62, 383–390.
[2] Numerous studies have used this process of analysis in religious sociology; see in the bibliography the works of Smith (1953), Goodnow and Tagiuri, Pope, Allinsmith, Cantril, Burchinal.

inferior status[3] or in a group which disappoints the "expectations" of its members.[4] What is the member's image of his attachment to the group? Is his sense of belonging fused with a collective and spontaneous identification, or is it personalized and made objective?

The image which the group offers of itself can remain more or less distinct in the eyes of the members, but an observer or a person exterior to the group will perceive its nature and cohesive force. Hoult,[5] for example, has noticed the economic conservatism of certain religious denominations, and he has observed how their faithful become identified with a common social consciousness. Both the doctrine which is constantly expounded to them and the religious journals which they read reflect, more or less consciously, the conservatism of the milieu from which members are recruited. Holt[6] had noted that, at the time of the economic depression before 1939, the churches offered an unfavorable image of themselves to the people who roamed about in search of work or aid. "The established churches," he writes "became for the wanderers the symbol of their isolation and also the symbol of the alien and harsh society that they had to confront."

From these examples it is evident that the image projected by a group plays a decisive role in strengthening the sense either of belonging or its rejection. Here we shall consider the first viewpoint, that of belonging. We shall also see in this perspective what psychosocial value the member at-

[3] See J. Thibaut, "An Experimental Study of the Cohesiveness of Under-Privileged Groups" in *Human Relations,* 1950, 3, 251–278; see also the remarks made on 172–174 concerning this subject.

[4] See E. Stotland, "Determinants of Attraction to Groups" in *Journ. Soc. Psychol.,* 1959, 49, 71–80.

[5] T. F. Hoult, "Economic Class Consciousness in American Protestantism" in *Amer. Sociol. Rev.,* 1950, 15, 97–100; 1952, 17, 349–350.

[6] J. B. Holt, "Holiness Religion, Cultural Shock, and Social Reorganization" in *Amer. Sociol. Rev.,* 1940, 5, 740–747.

taches to his religious belonging when his group is pictured within a sociocultural context whose values are in conflict with it. Finally, we shall examine the religious symbols which are present to the consciousness of the faithful and which contribute to a strengthening of their bonds of affiliation with their spiritual community.

2 IMAGE OF THE GROUP: FROM SUBJECTIVE TO OBJECTIVE?

The manner in which a member views his group both reveals and conditions his bond of belonging. We here touch upon the objective and subjective elements of religious affiliation. In this regard "representation" is a synthetic notion. In Van der Leeuw's opinion, "this idea [of representation] throws a very definite ray of light on the relationship between objectivity and subjectivity in religion."[7] Several times thus far we have thought it necessary to disregard the facile dichotomies which oppose personal religion and sociological religion, which oppose experience and rite or, again, the perceived group and its objective structure. Van der Leeuw mentions that "it is not permissible to pit institutional religion against the intimate experience of religion."[8]

With this in mind we shall inquire whether there do not exist significant differences between the private opinion of a faithful member and what is generally called his institutional attitude (F. H. Allport). In other words, what is his attitude when he perceives himself as a church member or, contrarily, when he has no awareness of his quality as a member? Schanck,[9] in 1932, obtained very interesting results on this subject. He questioned Methodists and Bap-

[7] *Op. cit.*, 209.
[8] *Ibid.*, 450.
[9] R. L. Schanck, "A Study of a Community and Its Groups and Institutions Conceived as Behaviors of Individuals" in *Psychological Monographs*, 1932, 43, n. 195, 1–133.

tists in order to discover a possible breach between their personal opinion and their institutional attitude with regard to the form of baptism. The answers, in percentages, appear in table 7. We have italicized some figures which in the investigator's judgment are characteristic. The results show that, when questioned as members of their denomination, the faithful respond according to the institutional viewpoint

TABLE 7

Private attitude and institutional attitude of Methodists and Baptists concerning the form of baptism.

Preference	As a Church Member		Private Attitude	
	Methodist	Baptist	Methodist	Baptist
By aspersion only	*90*	0	16	0
One form or the other	8	22	*71*	*59*
By immersion only	0	*67*	6	17
No opinion	1	11	7	24
Total	99	100	100	100
Source: Schanck, 1932.				

of their group, but when questioned without reference to their denominations they show a great deal less resoluteness and tend to agree on a common position. The consciousness or the representation of the bond of belonging seems determinative in certain respects: it conditions either an institutional behavior or a personal behavior.

Let us say from the first that, in spite of its thought-provoking character, this evidence does not appear conclusive. Too many questions remain unanswered. What is the quality of belonging declared by these subjects? Is it nominal or psychologically significative? What does private opinion mean here? Is it a firm attitude, a protestation, a preference? To what degree is personal attitude anchored or not anchored within the group?

Kelley has done research on problems of this type.[10] For example, he has studied the attitude of two hundred and seven high school and two hundred and forty-seven university students belonging to different religious denominations in order to determine to what degree the "present consciousness of belonging to a religion" (salience of membership) influences the steadfastness of opinions. His 1955 study dealt primarily with the Catholic group. By reading texts suited to each spiritual group, he first evoked in his subjects the awareness of religious affiliation; for Catholics, passages on the Pope, or Catholic missions, were read. Next a questionnaire provided the means of obtaining the students' reactions and of comparing their opinions before and after the readings. It becomes evident that the consciousness of the bond of religious affiliation makes attitudes a great deal more firm, and the experimenter observes that under these conditions attitudes offer much more resistance to change. Once the subjects' sense of belonging has been stimulated they cannot be induced to change their institutional opinions. Kelley states: "The attitudes a person holds depend in part upon his social contacts and particularly upon the groups in which he holds membership"; more exactly, upon the group to which he is aware of belonging.

Kelley has called attention to a distinction. The process of institutional representation seems more efficacious in younger than older people. The author remarks that the older students do not undergo the same degree of influence when the experimenter attempts to evoke in them the feeling of church identification. Can it be said that, with the development of the personality, there is a transition from spontaneous identification to objectivation?

[10] H. H. Kelley, "Salience of Membership and Resistance to Change of Group-Anchored Attitudes" in *Human Relations*, 1955, 8, 275–289; see also H. H. Kelley and E. H. Volkart, "The Resistance to Change of Group-Anchored Attitudes" in *Amer. Sociol. Rev.*, 1952, 17, 453–465.

We earlier encountered (Chapter V) these two concepts, borrowed from Lagache.[11] Recalling them, we inquire whether the progress of religious belonging does not follow stages which lead from spontaneous identification to deliberate objectivation. In other words, is religious affiliation reached by the member in such a way that one will find at the first level a simple sociological, shared identification rather than one consciously perceived and, at a higher level, an objectivation and a personalization of the bond of church belonging?

The problem thus stated seems to us badly formulated. There is no question of denying that religious maturity makes church affiliation more interiorized, more personal, and that the perception of the spiritual group becomes more conscious to the believer. But objectivation would be falsely conceived if it were supposed that it suppresses a more spontaneous or affective identification. After insisting on the importance of the phenomena of objectivation, Lagache points out that the inverse process ought not be minimized: "We have the tendency to fail to recognize the role of identification, as the fundamental process by which one man becomes like another. Man is literally condemned to identification."

These remarks seem to clarify and confirm the propositions we formulated previously with reference to the psychology of participation. The objective representation of the bond of belonging reveals only one of the aspects of our affiliations. The religious attitude in particular, whose comprehension we have many times emphasized, cannot be dissociated from its motivations which are both conscious or unconscious, from its resiliency which is both volitional and emotive, or from its personal and institutional dimensions.

[11] D. Lagache, "Quelques aspects de l'identification" in *Bulletin Intern. des Sciences Sociales*, 1955, 7, 37–46.

In this regard, it is revealing to consult research dealing with the faith of intellectuals. For example, Devolder[12] conducted a survey of 785 Belgian Catholics belonging to different professions (497 men and 288 women). It is interesting to discover the large role which the subjects attribute to "feelings" when they justify their religious affiliation; this is emphasized by nearly 50 per cent of the subjects. If these were regrouped to include all those who appeal to such motivations as identification with the family, the milieu, tradition, the total would be raised to 65 per cent. Barely a third of the men appeal to rational evidence to justify their religious positions.

A more recent survey conducted by Javaux[13] points in the same direction. A poll of 393 Catholic university students reveals two types of religious affiliation. All, as a whole, are fervent but, as the author explains, two groups are distinguished: in one, "a small elite who know how to reflect and act according to higher and conscious motives," while in the other is found "a mass, certainly well disposed, but living on a store of good habits and pious impressions acquired from the family or at the junior college. . . ."

Appreciably different conclusions can be drawn from these observations: some would assert a lack of religious formation to explain the fact that spontaneous identification plays such a noticeable role in the spiritual adhesion of these intellectuals. We should not absolutely contradict these explanations for it is quite evident that fidelity to the church will definitely become more meaningful by reflective adhe-directly that subjects lack religious formation from the sion to the faith. But it would seem imprudent to conclude

[12] N. Devolder, "Enquête sur la religion des intellectuels" in *Bull. de l'Inst. de Rech. Econ. et Sociales,* 1946, 12, 649–671; and N. Devolder, "Inquiry into the Religious Life of Catholic Intellectuals" in *Journ. Soc. Psychol.,* 1948, 28, 39–56.
[13] J. Javaux, S.J., "Une enquête religieuse en milieu universitaire" in *Nouvelle Revue Théologique,* 1957, 79, 828–848.

sole fact that they profess affective, spontaneous and collective motivations for their faith. Religious solidarities draw their support from various sources, and to distinguish the border lines of the personal and the institutional at the level of motivation seems to us sociologically arbitrary. Hertzler,[14] a specialist on the institutions, wrote that "to conceive a noninstitutionalized religion is sociologically meaningless; the great task [of religion] is precisely institutional reconstruction."

We can say, at the end of this discussion, that the dichotomy which separates religion that is determined by social pressure from that which is psychologically internalized is a false one. That there may be in the church member a maturation of religious feeling accompanied by a progressive objectivation is a fact which we have recognized and which we shall soon treat more explicitly. But we do not overlook the more spontaneous processes of religious identification by which the faithful member "gets a grip" on his group by directly and collectively participating in it. To identify with an institution and to view it objectively are not necessarily incompatible, and if one wished to personalize church adhesion, this would not be brought about by underrating collective solidarities but rather by permitting the faithful member to assume personally the multiple psychosocial bonds which link him with his religious group.

3 THE SELF-EVALUATION OF THE GROUP

In this chapter of the image of the membership group, we shall also examine how the faithful view their spiritual community when they compare it with surrounding institu-

[14] J. O. Hertzler, "Religious Institutions" in *Annals of the Amer. Acad. of Political and Social Science*, 1948, 256, 1–13.

tions and social systems. In this regard, we shall use the term "self-evaluation" of the group; it refers to the value judgments which the group makes of itself. The process explains, in some way, the strength of religious affiliations.

At the outset of this consideration of group self-evaluation we should recall an important distinction. We are dealing here with the matter of values, and values involve two different types of analysis. If a value system is viewed from its very interior, the analysis will be according to an ethical or doctrinal mode. But from the viewpoint of an observer who wishes to understand collective behavior the values represented in a group appear as motivations capable of explaining the conduct which he is studying. In this sense, Stoetzel[15] adopts Hartmann's principle: "Values are, in reality, both the basic data and the explanatory instruments for all the social sciences."

Adopting this latter approach, let us ask how the member appraises or perceives this attachment to the church. From a strictly religious viewpoint, he will accord absolute value to his church membership; and if in practice his adhesion weakens, it is at the level of belief or religious consciousness that the explanation for his delinquency must be sought. We shall come back to this point in our next section. But outside the framework of a strictly theological evaluation of religious belonging, the member will be led to compare his spiritual group and his religious beliefs with other value systems and institutions. From a psychosocial viewpoint, one will then note either conflict of allegiance or divergences in social loyalties or an accord between spiritual and secular affiliations.

In the preceding chapters we have already touched upon

---

[15] J. Stoetzel, *Théorie des opinions,* 344; see G. W. Hartmann, "Value as the Unifying Concept of the Social Sciences" in *Journ. Soc. Psychol.,* 1939, 10, 563–575.

a certain number of problems relating to the self-evaluation of the membership group. By way of example, a few of them can be here taken up again. We would, for instance, be interested in discovering what effect is produced on collective behavior when a group represents itself as a majority or a minority in a milieu. Also, how does a religious group which sees itself as a minority and frustrated come to assimilate the values of the majority? How does a Catholic minority behave when it becomes aware of conflicts occasioned by its moral positions, notably in the conjugal and family sphere? We shall likewise inquire whether the group is conscious of sharing the dominant culture, or a subculture, whether it feels accepted, tolerated, rejected or persecuted.[16]

In stating these problems one realizes to what degree all these representations are ambivalent as guides for action. A group which is considered a minority can quite easily disappear by simple assimilation just as it can become more tightly knit and indefinitely resist majority pressure. Persecution will at times weaken affiliation to a religious group, but it can also confirm and reinforce the bonds between the persecuted faithful. Furthermore, the conflict between religious and secular values can be a cause of internal disintegration for a community of believers, but it can also provoke a redefinition and a deepening of religious loyalties. Systematic explanations seem to us impossible here if we remain on the objective level. The fact of being a minority, a subculture, of being accepted or rejected is certainly not negligible. The repercussions of these situations on group cohesion will need to be considered. But we believe that the objective fact is less important than the manner in which

[16] These questions are suggested to us by various recent monographs; see, in the bibliography, the works of Nimkoff and Wood, Mayer and Marx, Thomas, Kanin, Le Moal, Pin, Thibaut.

it is valued, assumed and defined by group members. The representation of the fact and its evaluation bring us precisely to those borderlines of objectivity and subjectivity of which Van der Leeuw spoke and which must be reached if the profound motivations of religious behavior are to be grasped. We have previously affirmed the two sources of our attitudes, namely, the social framework and our personal way of perceiving and living an experience (Chapter I). At this point we wish precisely to examine those forms of perception and judgment which in some way interiorly condition the sense of belonging. We are curious to find out how the member judges his religious group when it is compared with outsiders and with the values of the milieu—values such as art, science, class solidarity, progress, etc. Let us add that it is not so much a question of doctrinal appraisal as of psychosocial judgment about the religious group.

Some particular instances will show the importance of this element of personal estimation with regard to religion and religious groups. Allport[17] and his collaborators had asked, in their survey of a group of students, the following

TABLE 8

Answers received from a question on the relationships between science and religion. Answers are by percentage.

Possible Attitudes	Answers Obtained
Religion and science clearly support one another	21
The conflict is negligible, more apparent than real	32
The conflict is serious, but probably not insoluble	17
The conflict is very serious, and perhaps insoluble	14
The conflict is absolutely insoluble	16
Source: Allport, Gillespie, Young, 1948, 18.	

[17] G. W. Allport, J. M. Gillespie and J. Young, "The Religion of the Post-War College Student" in *Journ. of Psychol.*, 1948, 52, 3–33; see 121–122.

question: "What do you think of the much-discussed conflict between the discoveries of science and the principal affirmations of religion?" A choice of answers was offered and the results are indicated in table 8. A brief explanation was requested of the subjects to justify the answer chosen. In summarizing these remarks the investigators discuss five student attitudes: the perplexed attitude (either religion or science is in error); the exclusively pro-religious attitude (science is evil); the exclusively pro-scientific attitude (science will eventually be able to explain everything); the dualist attitude (science can provide a solution up to a certain point beyond which a religious explanation is sought); the conciliatory attitude (science and religion will satisfy those who wish to believe in them).

Although 70 per cent of the students questioned tend to believe that conciliation between science and religion is not impossible, notable differences in the value assigned to such conciliation appear in their explanations. These estimations constitute value judgments on religion and, ultimately, on the religious group to which the subjects belong. On this point, certain psychosociologists prefer to speak of opinion, others retain the term "judgment." Krech and Crutchfield have emphasized the influence of these judgments on our attitudes. In the example that we have just cited, judgments constitute, certainly, a subjective element; but is it not ultimately the individual member's judgment which will condition his psychological attachment to his religious group? A scientist will not belong unreservedly to a religion which does not seem easily reconcilable with his position as a man of science.

Another case touching on the same problem is that of the position on social questions of the religious groups. How will the members judge the attitude of their church relative to social progress? Max Weber noted many years ago the significance of these problems of the opinion or mentality of religious groups. Here we will not enter into those general questions which have generated discussions among sociologists.[18] On the level of immediate evaluation, formulated by the church member, it is observed that for the faithful member the "feeling of the social efficaciousness" of his religion often plays a decisive part in his spiritual loyalties. On this point Allport[19] and his collaborators have noted in their survey of students that the reproach "religion has failed" recurs a great deal more often than the objection "religion is scientifically false." Kitay[20] reports that the most frequent justification used by Jewish students who had lost their faith is the spectacle of division, hatred and persecution engendered by religious conflicts. The consciousness of these cultural and spiritual antagonisms, they disclosed, separated them from all religion, including their own. Reconciliation between religious values and the values of social peace had become psychologically impossible for them.

On this question, it is meaningful to examine the way in which French youth represent the effect of religion on social progress. In the 1958 survey of the Institut Français d'Opinion Publique the question was asked: "Is religion opposed to social progress?" The proportion of negative answers was thus distributed: practicing Catholics, 84 per cent; nonpracticing Catholics, 57 per cent; atheists, 19 per

[18] Since Ernst Troeltsch and Max Weber, sociologists have continued to compare Christian confessions with reference to their contribution within the scientific, social, economic, etc., domain. These analyses, however, run the risk of not being entirely conclusive if they are not restricted to the examination of some empirically controllable factors. For more recent works see those of Mack, Murphy and Yellin, Field, Fischoff, Thorner, Russo; see Halbwachs.

[19] G. W. Allport, J. M. Gillespie and J. Young, "The Religion of the Post-War College Student" in *Journ. of Psychol.,* 1948, 25, 3–33.

[20] P. M. Kitay, *Radicalism and Conservatism Toward Conventional Religion* (New York: 1947).

cent.[21] These answers approximate those which had suggested an analogous question dealing with the relationships between science and religion. Among practicing Catholics, only 3 per cent see an opposition between the two; among nonpracticing Catholics the proportion climbs to 14 per cent; and among atheists, it reaches 51 per cent. These answers show that it is of some importance to religious groups whether their members have a favorable or unfavorable image of the sociocultural interactions of the church with secular values. We do not intend to suggest here any specific relation of causality among factors or maintain that the image may be determinative of religious participation or vice versa; we are only noting the parallelism. Representation serves, in any case, as an index for understanding either the quality of membership ties or the distance which separates the member from his community.

By way of conclusion, we would like to insist on the role that the estimation of the membership group plays in strengthening or weakening religious solidarities. In our opinion, the objective and subjective elements of the collective religious life have too frequently been separated in surveys. Besides the objectively observable socioreligious situations there are judgments which members make about their community. These judgments affect their representation of the religious group and condition the resoluteness of their adhesion. In the last analysis, it is a question of reconciling values on the motivational level. The church member is in perpetual question of interior unification. Pushing to the furthermost limits of empirical analysis, one can guess that the ultimate motivations of the member are inspired by his beliefs and his faith. Social psychology can discern these limits but it cannot, by itself, pass beyond them. It is pos-

21 "La nouvelle vague croit-elle en Dieu?" (survey of the I.F.O.P.) in *Informations Catholiques Internationales,* 1958, 86, 11–20.

sible, however, for it to investigate religious symbols in order to find in them a complementary aspect of religious solidarities.

4 THE SYMBOLIC REPRESENTATIONS OF THE RELIGIOUS GROUP

The world of symbols is indefinite. "Relations with God," as Le Bras[22] writes, "postulate a vast structure of intellectual and symbolic structuring of reality." Agreeing with the sociologist's observations, phenomenology emphasizes that man structures the world to the image of his beliefs.[23] For the religious man, everything speaks of God and, in this perspective, the symbol is coextensive with the spiritual universe. As such, it is not subject to analysis. From the viewpoint of the group's self-image, however, it becomes possible to examine the psychological significance of religious symbolization. The psychology of the unconscious, as the works of Jung[24] and Baudouin[25] attest, has contributed to the discovery—or the rediscovery—of the fundamental role of symbolism throughout the spiritual history of humanity with regard both to groups and to the individual himself.

While recognizing the general interest of these studies, here we will be more precisely oriented, and we shall restrict ourselves to symbolic representations, not of the religious universe, but of the religious institution itself. We shall study the symbols which represent the membership group in the consciousness of the faithful. We believe that this type of social perception reveals the quality and steadfastness of the bonds of belonging of the religious group. It makes a dif-

[22] G. Le Bras, *Études de sociologie religieuse,* II, 790.
[23] See G. Van der Leeuw, *op. cit.,* 663 f.
[24] *Op. cit.*
[25] C. Baudouin, *Psychanalyse du symbole religieux.*

ference for the cohesion of spiritual communities whether the member represents his group as a voluntary association, as a spiritual family or as a holy city.

When speaking of symbolic representation an important point should be noted: one must assume the viewpoint of the member and his faith if one wishes to understand the role of the symbol on his attitude and behavior. In this perspective the symbol is not only an image which serves to convey a further reality; the symbol communicates reality itself. For the member, God *is* a father, the church *is* a mother. There is agreement with Baudouin "to see in the symbol, not so much a mode of 'representation' of the religious facts (a position which could lead one to believe that there is something arbitrary in the choice of the sign, which is supposedly independent of the thing signified) but rather the most direct and spontaneous manifestation of these facts."[26] It is with this reservation that we shall here employ the expression "symbolic representation."

Halbwachs,[27] in his chapter on religious morphology, analyzed the problem of symbolic representations of ecclesiastical groups. He observed that for the member, the church is represented as an immense body with its distinct parts, its members, its functions. "It is all these elements that constitute the collective representation of religious space, common to the group, more or less precise and definite within the individual consciousness of its members." These observations permit an understanding of the psychological way in which the member is linked to the church; he sees himself properly as a member attached to a living body, and in this body he is situated within the universe. "In summary," Halbwachs observed, "we should not take the

[26] *Op. cit.,* 279.
[27] M. Halbwachs, "La morphologie religieuse," Chapter I of *Morphologie sociale* (Paris: 1938), 19–30.

expression the body of the church in a purely symbolic sense. The collectivity of the faithful is presented as a material mass, and nothing which is produced in it remains without religious significance."[28] The cohesion of the religious institution appears, then, as the cohesion of a living being; and one can predict that, on the psychosocial level, the bonds of affiliation will become tighter or more relaxed to the very degree that the symbol will be perceived as real or as devoid of content.

The symbols by which the membership group is represented will have a marked influence on all religious behavior. From this fact, we would like to investigate the psychosocial dynamism of symbolic representation. How do the symbols of the religious group act upon the psychology of the faithful?

A general answer to these problems is suggested by Jung who has studied particularly the effects which the removal of rites and traditional symbols has produced within Protestantism. Man has been placed alone before God. The intermediary of the maternal church has been minimized: "They have also more or less discarded the church's intercession between God and man" and, "in abolishing the protecting safeguards, the Protestant has lost the sacred images which express important unconscious factors. . . ." A Protestant himself, Jung corroborates the psychological tension which results from the lack of rites and sacred images: "The Protestant is left to the mercy of God alone. He has neither confession nor absolution. . . . He alone must cope with his sins and he is not too sure of divine grace which has become inaccessible because of the deficiency of an adequate ritual." Psychologically, there will result for the Protestant an acute awareness of his interior tension and of his sin which he alone bears under the gaze of God. This

28 *Ibid.*, 24, 29.

consciousness, according to Jung, attains "a degree comprehended with difficulty by the Catholic mentality, for confession and absolution are always on hand to mitigate tension when it becomes too great."[29]

The intensive studies which Murray[30] and his collaborators conducted among fifty university students seem to confirm Jung's assertions. Murray, in examining the interior life of his subjects, has taken into account the important role played by religious symbolism in their conscious and unconscious psychology. The image of the maternal Church in particular exercised a very clear function of integration among Catholic subjects. Catholic students, he notes, were "remarkably more self-assured and confident" than the others. From where did their psychological security come? "Their unconscious fears, it could be said, were calmed by the tutelary presence of the maternal Church. And if they were, at times, incapable of observing the precepts of their religion, they knew that pardon was always within their reach. A secret, repentant confession, and once again they would be benevolently accepted as members of the flock." For them, belonging to the maternal Church soothed the unconscious anguish which is involved in the quest for ultimate motives. The presence of "a wise, humane and indulgent Church" meant that they did not know "what it is to feel alone and abandoned in a swirl of incommunicable feelings and ideas." Speaking of another group of students who had a different religious affiliation, Murray remarks that they were "deeply aware of troubling impulses and feelings" and, in other regards, they "were not held in check by their religion and they never made use of its symbolism to describe their difficulties." Catholics also experienced difficulties but their recourse to the Church was almost spon-

29 *Op. cit.*
30 H. A. Murray, *op. cit.*

taneous: "It was as if their faith in an ultimate authority spared them the necessity of independently resolving fundamental problems. . . . Within the rationalized fantasy system of an effective Church there is a place for everything. . . . The problem of good and evil is resolved and only the problem of moral will remains."[31]

These observations bring us to the very limits of a psychosociological explanation. They reveal, we believe, an aspect of religious identification and affiliation which specifies the "sense of belonging"—a point to which we shall return. Spiritual belonging goes beyond the visible structures of an institution. The faithful member is a part of a body, he is a member of a family; he participates in the life of God. His attitude toward the sacred is not directed toward a category but, as Rogé notes, toward a Person. In Christianity this Person is Christ. It is definitely the reference to this Person which is the final explanation of church belonging and which assures the cohesion of the Christian community. Freud, whose theories on religious behavior have been challenged many times, has not, however, failed to perceive this fundamental fact. Let us conclude by quoting his observation: "It is not without a profound reason that there is an insistence on the analogy between the Christian community and a family, and that the faithful consider themselves brothers, that is, brothers by the love which Christ feels for them. It is incontestable that the bond which unites each individual to Christ is the cause of the bond which unites each individual to all others."[32]

[31] *Ibid.*
[32] S. Freud, *Group Psychology and the Analysis of the Ego* (New York).

Changes in Religious Attitude

Even in change the religious attitude reveals its specific character. We shall use the expression "weakening of religious commitment" to signify the negative changes of loss of integration of the belief system, lessening of religious practice and weakening of the sense of belonging. Positive change, a "strengthening of commitment," reveals itself in greater integration of beliefs, increased participation in religious practice, and a deepening of the sense of belonging.

In the next two chapters negative modifications and positive changes in the religious attitudes of a milieu will be treated. We shall point out in what sense religious change is said to be observable in a group, and we will emphasize the principal psychosocial manifestation of religious indifference, disaffection and disbelief (Chapter X). Lastly, the traits which specify the stability of religious sentiments will be analyzed together with the signs which accompany maturity of the religious attitude (Chapter XI).

Weakening of Religious Commitment

1 Observation of attitude changes. 2 The descriptive concept of religious change. 3 The leveling of religious attitudes. 4 The abandonment of religious practice by the young. 5 Loss of integration in the belief system. 6 Disbelief and the loss of membership.

1 OBSERVATION OF ATTITUDE CHANGES

What we already know about religious attitude and its relationship with the world of beliefs helps us to keep in mind the fact that religious sentiment partly eludes psychosociological observation. The question may then be raised whether, in studying the religious attitude, we are not entering into a deeply personal area similar to the area of the individual's free choice and, like the latter, beyond the reach of scientific observation. That the individual case defies systematic analysis is quite clear; but the observation of collectivities reveals changes which, at the statistical level, are empirically verifiable. It is to the examination of these changes and others empirically observed that we shall devote this last section of our analysis.

Some researchers have already tried to explain collective changes of religious attitudes. But the extent of these attempts, even in the opinion of their authors, remains limited, either because only one aspect of change was considered, for example, the stages of disbelief—or because the study has been restricted to a local community or a particular group.[1] To expand their explanations and to look for a general theory of religious change seems to us to be useless, at least in the present state of our knowledge. Thus it is not in this direction that we shall orient our present research. In this section we shall examine some observable characteristics of religious change and discover, if possible, the descriptive elements which help toward an understanding of it.

First, let us consider some means which the sociologist has at his disposal for discerning the phenomena of religious change. There are, in the first place, simple techniques which facilitate perception of general changes. A comparison of religious and civil censuses, for example, reveals the increase or decline in religious practice, especially with regard to births and baptisms, civil and religious marriages and funerals.[2] Following the lines of a similar survey, Fichter has used the relationship between the number of baptized infants and the number of those baptized who, as adults, are found in the Christian community. Of the three parishes thus studied he estimated that only a third of the baptized infants had ultimately remained connected with the parish community; somewhere along the way, the other two-thirds had left the religious group.[3] These methods, if they uncover the results of religious changes, give little if any information concerning the processes or stages of these developments. For this purpose other and more precise means are utilized.

[1] By way of example, see the bibliography for the works of the following authors: Vetter and Green, Schmitt-Eglin, Nelson, Telford, Gilliland.
[2] It is the method used, for example, by Le Bras, Schnepp, Thomas.
[3] *Op. cit.*, 75.

There is, for example, the method of religious profiles used in certain studies. The religious profile of a community indicates, with regard to easily observable religious practices, the age at which variations in the faithfuls' behavior occur. Two examples will illustrate the method. Fichter,[4] in one of his studies, sketched the following portrait of the modal Catholic after surveying a parish of 8,363 members who were 10 or more years of age: the modal Catholic is very religious during adolescence and post-adolescence (from 10 to 19 years of age): at 20 he becomes negligent; between 30 and 39 his religious delinquency is most pronounced. Then during the following decades religious practice is progressively improved but without, however, reverting to the level reached during adolescence.

Desabie[5] used the same method to interpret the religious survey conducted in the Seine (Paris and environs) during 1954. Here are his observations on the variations of religious behavior: maximum religious participation occurs at about 12 years of age at the time of First Holy Communion. There then follows a sudden drop in Sunday observance with this downward trend progressively continuing until about the age 35. After 35 there is an increase, first among women and then among men. Tables 9 and 10 summarize his results with relation to several variables.

Profiles thus set forth evidently ought to be interpreted with caution, especially if there is no possibility of obtaining them at a later period so as to follow the same persons at different ages. We should also keep in mind that these all-inclusive profiles simplify reality and they can even mislead the unwary observer who is not cautious enough to distinguish the percentages of practice according to milieux

[4] J. H. Fichter, S. J., "The Profile of Catholic Religious" in *Amer. Journ. Sociol.*, 1952, 58, 145–149.

[5] J. Desabie, *Le recensement de pratique religieuse dans la Seine* (Paris: 1958).

TABLE 9

Proportion, according to sex and age, of Seine Catholics at Sunday worship. Ratio is based on 100 persons of the same group residing at Seine.

Ages	Men	Women
11	49.7	53.7
12	52.7	57.7
13	33.2	36.0
14	25.7	28.8
15	22.2	25.9
. . . .	. . . .	. . . .
20	9.4	15.2
35	5.2	8.1
50	5.2	9.9
75	9.6	16.9

Source: Desabie, 1958b, 820–821.

TABLE 10

Proportion, according to sex, age and family condition, of Seine Catholics at Sunday worship. Ratio is based on 100 persons of the same group residing at Seine.

Family Condition	Age and Sex							
	20		35		50		75	
	M	F	M	F	M	F	M	F
Celibate[1] . . .	9.9	18.0	6.6	16.7	5.1	20.8	20.1	27.6
Celibate[2] . . .	9.9	18.0	5.2	14.7	3.8	18.3	14.0	23.8
Married	1.8	2.6	5.3	7.0	5.6	9.3	9.3	14.7
Widowed . . .	—	—	3.4	7.8	3.6	7.9	9.3	15.5
Total	9.4	15.2	5.2	8.1	5.2	9.9	9.6	16.9

[1] This includes priests, religious men and women.
[2] This does not include priests, religious men and women.
Source: Desabie, 1958b, 821.

or socio-professional categories.[6] As they stand, however, these modal images permit us to perceive patterns in the collective variations of religious behavior. Some constants are noted which will encourage more extensive research. These observations will orient those concerned with religious practice, notably in relation to the critical ages of abstention and of return.

Changes of religious attitude are also seen in studies dealing with the stages of personal religious development. We are already acquainted with Harms' analyses of the three ages of religious formation during childhood: the period of infancy, the period of religious realism and the period of individualized religion.[7] We shall later see the analysis that Allport offered on the maturation of religious sentiment. There is no need to emphasize the interest which these studies have for the psychosociology of the religious development, for they help to reconcile more general analyses which show how new integrations of attitudes are produced at the pivotal ages of life: around 5, 21 and 50 years of age.[8] The information thus obtained can help us to understand better how the statuses and roles are differentiated at different ages, and to see a little more clearly the psychosocial significance of changes in religious attitudes.

It is, then, by observing either collectivities (descriptive-statistical methods, religious profiles) or religious personality (genesis, maturation of religious sentiment) that one can study change in religious behavior. One can also start with religious change itself and study the processes which bring it about. We would in that case consider works on

[6] An excellent example of "profiles" differentiated according to "social categories" can be found in J. Labbens, *Les 99 autres* (Lyon: 1954), 116–132.

[7] E. Harms, "The Development of Religious Experience in Children" in *Amer. Journ. Sociol.*, 1944, 50, 112–122.

[8] See J. Stoetzel, *Théorie des opinions*, 299.

conversion itself, such as those of Penido on dechristianization, those of Schmitt-Eglin—on atheism, those of Vetter and Green.[9]

Let us bring our description to a close at this point; this brief presentation of methods suffices for our needs. We see in what sense variations of religious attitude are said to be observable. Let us now attempt to find the precise sociological meaning of religious change.

2 THE DESCRIPTIVE CONCEPT OF RELIGIOUS CHANGE

If we look closely at our descriptions up to this point, we note that the concept of socioreligious change is not univocal. Diverse phenomena are associated with the same descriptive word. For our analysis, we shall distinguish three viewpoints: the poles of essential change, the various degrees in change, and finally the direction of change.

We shall first consider the poles of essential changes which occur in religious attitudes. The two essential changes are from belief to nonbelief and vice versa; with these would be frequently associated new adhesion to or separation from a religious community.

Aside from these two essential changes in attitude, various forms of accidental changes or changes in degree, can be found. The number of such possible transformations is indefinitely large; they correspond to every variation from total church identification to marginal and sporadic participation. There is always evidence of an effective belonging to the religious group, but it is a belonging which produces more or less limited participation. Le Bras' typology, the classification suggested by Isambert, the categories utilized

---

[9] These latter works on dechristianization and atheism will shortly be discussed.

by Fichter will all serve to evaluate the practical meaning of all intermediary attitudes which range from fervor to practical indifference.[10]

We shall consider finally the orientation of change, and we can say that, viewed from the perspective of religious groups, these modifications have a positive or a negative sense. Belonging becomes more closely knit or more relaxed; the faithful's sense of affiliation is weakened or intensified by a more or less close adhesion to the religious group.

The three descriptive elements, thus explained, facilitate a methodical classification of the forms of religious mobility; this will help us in the analysis which follows. Regarding the extreme forms of change—conversion or affiliation on one side, separation on the other—let us note that we have already treated the first aspect in our chapters on the formation of religious attitudes. We shall therefore turn our attention to the second aspect which we will discuss in our treatment of the problem of transition to disbelief and atheism.

When we analyzed the cohesive factors of the feeling of belonging, we concentrated our attention on the intermediary variations of the religious attitude; we will here emphasize some complementary aspects: the successive rifts in "comprehension" of religious attitude. From a different perspective we will see how the maturation of religious sentiment is brought about psychologically.

With regard to the third consideration—the positive or negative orientation of change—there is involved, above all else, a reference to the value systems of the religious groups themselves. The religious group will evaluate the transformation of collective religious attitudes in terms of fidelity or infidelity (to the church, the community of faith). From a

[10] We have seen several of these typologies in Chapter VIII, 182–194.

strictly sociological viewpoint the positive or negative changes will be estimated according to their impact on a more or less close cohesion between the members and their group. The sociologist, however, will want to inquire into the specific motivations of spiritual belonging and, for that, he will have to rely on the judgments that the church offers regarding the signs of religious fidelity or infidelity.

We shall study at the end of this chapter the degrees of negative transformation: the forms of indifference, of de-christianization and of rejection because of atheism. We shall examine in the following chapter a complementary aspect of "religious change," that is, the particular persistence and stability of spiritual attitudes, and conclude with an analysis of the maturation of the religious attitude.

3 THE LEVELING OF
RELIGIOUS ATTITUDES

Considering the genesis of a skeptical attitude, Baudouin notes: "The psychological method must, with the same impartiality, take into account the drives which impel a person toward religion and those which turn him away from it."[11] The sociologist can follow this advice for his own purposes. Without limiting himself to the deep-seated "drives" of individual religious behavior alone, he will attempt to understand the sociological circumstances which accompany the modification and breach of affiliation bonds with a religious group.

One phenomenon among others which will be of interest to the observer is the socioreligious leveling that takes place in certain collectivities or multi-cultural groups. Even homogeneous communities can be affected by it. Schmitt-Eglin, for example, has done an analysis of the "mechanisms of

[11] C. Baudouin, *Psychanalyse du symbole religieux,* 38.

236

dechristianization" in a suburban community. Dechristianization appears to him as sociologically linked to the continual exodus of the elite to the city; this type of "outgoing advancement" deprives the village of the more dynamic elements which would keep the human and Christian community from falling into mediocrity, if not demoralization. In this regard conformity plays a very influential part and is practically irresistible; it crushes all efforts at social or religious reform. "Whoever is creative, makes progress, surpasses the group average, pushes himself ahead, becomes isolated and merits sanction. A feeling of unconscious culpability produces a reaction of compensation and excuse in the nonconformist: he masks his accomplishments and assumes extreme modesty in admitting his success."[12] This leveling has often been observed; it is even characteristic of certain rural communities. Other forms of leveling will occur in the cities.

Fichter[13] has described a similar phenomenon in urban Catholics. In Chapter VIII we described the process according to which average Catholics partially conform to a dominant non-Catholic culture. These analyses give a clear idea of the meaning of a modal religious personality. The observed behavior reveals that the integrating role of the modal Catholic is not derived from his religious status. Except for their references to supreme values, these Catholics in large part become identified with non-Catholics. A psychoreligious leveling has taken place within them.

Some still more noticeable effects of this leveling process have been seen by Telford[14] in a study of nearly 1,000

[12] P. Schmitt-Eglin, *Le mécanisme de la déchristianisation* (Paris: 1952), 151.
[13] J. H. Fichter, S. J., "Religious Values and the Social Personality" in *Amer. Cath. Sociol. Rev.*, 1956, 17, 109–116.
[14] C. W. Telford, "A Study of Religious Attitudes" in *Journ. Soc. Psychol.*, 1950, 31, 217–230.

university students (who were mostly Protestant). The fact is especially observable in a subgroup composed of armed service veterans. Telford compared their religious attitudes before and after the experience of military life. Various aspects of the leveling process become evident: it is not simply a general decline of religious sentiment ending in indifference for all; there is above all a sort of "collective compromise" in which the loss of religious sentiment by some is compensated by its acquisition on the part of others. If the more fervent become tepid, the initially hostile subjects, on the contrary, show themselves more sympathetic toward churches. "It is possible," suggests Telford, "that the experience of war had had a leveling effect on attitudes toward the church, making the better disposed less favorable and transforming the antagonism of the others into a more favorable outlook." This process of abandonment and compensation also appears elsewhere in their attitudes. On the one hand the veterans have a general disaffection with regard to their church as an institution, but on the other hand the majority of them exhibit a deeper appreciation of the moral and ethnical dimensions of religion.

It would be imprudent to make Telford's conclusions universal; they concern only a well determined milieu and refer only to subjects whose initial attachment to their church was not very strong. However, we shall keep in mind, as particularly suggestive, the author's remarks which indicate that socioreligious leveling is not, as one would be led to think, a sort of pure and simple reduction to the level of collective skepticism. If there is a decline of fidelity in some, there is a real discovery of the religious dimension on the part of others.

Nelson[15] has reported results comparable to the above

[15] E. N. P. Nelson, "Patterns of Religious Attitude Shifts from College to Fourteen Years Later" in *Psychological Monographs,* 1956, 70, n. 17, 1–15.

upon the completion of surveys conducted, with a fourteen-year interval, among 1,200 subjects belonging to twelve Protestant denominations. In 1936 these subjects were university students. They had, with others (3,749 in all), answered a questionnaire on religious attitudes according to the method of Chave and Thurstone. There was then obtained an evaluation of their attitudes: (a) toward God (existence); (b) toward God (influence on conduct); (c) toward the church; (d) toward Sunday observance. In 1950, Nelson resumed his investigation in a follow-up study of the 1,200 students he had questioned in 1936. Here again the same phenomena of leveling and compensation is observed. In some respects there was a lessening of the initial differences (observed in 1936) between students of different denominations, between students coming from denominational and nondenominational colleges, between students who came from diverse sections of the country, between students of both sexes, etc. With regard to all these variables the leveling is evident. But in other respects it was discovered that the general average of the second test was higher than the one obtained fourteen years earlier, at least with reference to the first three portions of the attitude scale (a, b and c). For Sunday observance there was a decrease (d). The author comes to the conclusion that on the whole the changes which occur tend to be favorable to religion despite a leveling of extremes.

A provisory conclusion is suggested to us by these observations. If it is necessary, on the one hand, to recognize the leveling downward of religious attitudes in a given milieu, one should be on his guard not to interpret this process as similar to a simple collective loss of religious feeling or to a generalized triumph of skepticism or indifference. The most favorable religious attitudes are not the only ones to undergo modification; the adversaries of religion also change in their views and feelings toward the church. Some observers will speak of pluralism, relativism, progressive secularization. It is even possible that this leveling results in a sort of religious syncretism. Sociologists and spiritual leaders will be interested in determining the social and spiritual significance of these phenomena. These remarks, as we have said, have only a provisory value; they must be completed by the analyses of our next chapter on the persistence and reinforcement of religious attitudes. What we have already stated concerning particular certitudes which accompany religious feelings will allow us to understand that reciprocal concessions are far from being the only phenomena observed in a context of religious pluralism. Other changes, which often are of a positive order, remain to be specified. We will return to this later. For the moment let us continue the examination of the negative modifications of religious attitudes. These modifications can evidently be as different as the religious choices of individuals are varied. The study of case histories can throw light on the way in which the individual becomes separated from his religious group. This type of analysis would, however, go beyond our present purposes. The sociologist will be more immediately concerned with the regularities, the patterns which seem to be manifested in the changes of religious attitudes within a group, a community, a social class, a region. It is this aspect which we shall examine here; we shall consider these sociological dimensions of the phenomenon in question. We shall orient our observations toward certain typical situations which have been more frequently studied during the last few years. We shall discuss in particular the abandonment of religious practice by the young, then unity rifts in beliefs, loss of integration in the belief system, and finally, loss of membership in the religious group itself and finally splits in religious belonging itself.

240

4 THE ABANDONMENT OF
RELIGIOUS PRACTICE BY THE YOUNG

Let us note from the start that this phenomenon of youth's religious disaffection is far from being a uniform occurrence. From one country or from one culture to another the religious state of youth will be quite different. To become convinced of this one has only to glance over the religious profiles shown at the beginning of this chapter. These profiles come from studies conducted among American Catholics (urban parish) and French Catholics (Paris and its environs). In the first case, as we have seen, it is precisely during adolescence and post-adolescence (between 10 and 19) that the modal Catholic shows the most fervor toward the Church. The most notable defections occur later, that is, between the ages of 30 and 39. In the second case, the Parisian Catholics manifest their greatest steadfastness toward the church about the age of 12; immediately after their first Holy Communion, their (modal) religious practice shows a very marked drop, and the curve continues to decline slowly till about age 35 when there begins a slow return to the Church.

This statistical comparison emphasizes the over-all differences of one milieu from another, but it does not however imply that the problem of youth's religious disaffection is confined to certain favored countries or milieux. One finds that adolescents and youth everywhere experience a critical stage of coming to maturation with regard to religious commitments. The stage can be short or long, of more or less benefit with reference to religious fidelity. It would evidently be imprudent to make generalizations in this matter since situations vary so much according to milieux, traditions and specific circumstances. But the basic fact, that is, the existence of a critical period in youth's religious commitments,

241

is quite unmistakable and demands some observations on the psychosociologist's part.[16]

This problem, it must be confessed, has thus far stimulated few methodical analyses. Surveys on religious practice, it is true, have furnished abundant descriptive material in past years. The facts themselves have been revealed and considerable knowledge is had concerning the age and circumstances in which youth ventures to break with religious practice and the differences that exist in this matter with regard to educational levels, socio-professional categories, family origin, etc. But no satisfactory general theory of this socioreligious phenomenon has as yet been offered. It would be vain to propose a priori explanations which are not founded on sufficient evidence. But would it not be enlightening to regroup methodically the different reasons postulated by researchers who have dealt with the problem of youth's religious disaffection? We believe that useful suggestions could thus be made with a view toward a systematic analysis which others could perhaps continue. Let us attempt, then, to review the principal reasons proposed up to this point, and let us next examine how these motives of disaffection could be combined in a useful synthesis which would serve as an explanatory hypothesis for further research.

To touch on a methodological point before commencing with our analysis properly so called: in what sense can we speak of explanatory reasons with reference to the phenomenon of religious disaffection? The sociologist and the theologian will understand what the type of explanation here considered signifies.

Strictly speaking the theologian can reject the social explanation as inexact since it is not an integral and religious

[16] Several authors have emphasized "the transformation of religious sentiment" as a "characteristic fact of adolescence;" see L. Guittard, *L'évolution religieuse des adolescents,* 69.

242

explanation of the fact of separation from the church. This explanation does not penetrate to the innermost motivation of religious involvement, to the very *ultima ratio* of adhesion to the faith.

But the theologian, like the social observer, will not fail to be struck by certain uniformities, certain patterns which are manifested at the level of collective behavior when large numbers are involved: differential percentages of faithfulness according to sex, age, milieu, tradition, etc. While keeping distinct, as we have said, the properly theological explanation of personal fidelity, are we not justified in seeking in collective behavior regularities or identifiable types of conduct which would indicate observable parallels between the fidelity of a group and a particular psychosocial context?

The sociologist will realize that the mere designation of these patterns is not an explanation of the secret of spiritual behavior, for the total cause of the religious experience extends beyond the field of his observation.[17] But he will attempt, nevertheless, from his viewpoint, to discern consistent tendencies or to perceive statistical constants in a given milieu. If he speaks of explanation or causality he does not intend by that to say the final word on religious behavior. But by not emphasizing the absolute relations of cause and effect he will seek to identify parallels, patterns or associations between a particular collection behavior and a particular social context.

It is, then, within the bounds of these empirical limits that we will attempt to analyze the phenomenon of youth's collective disaffection in certain milieux. Let us immediately

[17] G. Le Bras thus concluded his study of socioreligious explanation: "We know that our desire of understanding will never be satisfied, that the cause of causes will always escape our grasp. For religious men, it is God. . . ;" see G. Le Bras, "L'explication en sociologie religieuse" in *Cahiers Intern. Sociol.*, 1956, 21, 59–76; several other articles devoted to sociological *explanation* can be found in the same issue of *Cahiers*.

proceed to an examination of the motives ordinarily proposed by researchers.

A rapid inventory of the reasons which are generally offered to explain youth's discontinuance of religious practice reveals the following categories of causes: those which pertain to the pedagogical and moral order, those which pertain to the psychological order, and those which pertain to the cultural and sociological order.

At the first explanatory level, the decline of youth's religious practice is attributed to the lack of religious and moral instruction.[18] The explanation is not without some value. We saw earlier at what point doctrine plays a specific integrating role in the case of religious affiliation (see 138ff.). Let us add however that this type of analysis remains too general to be really enlightening. The surveys that we cited in Chapter VI show that the bonds between "religious instruction" and subsequent religious participation are far from simple, and the observer must, above all, seek to find out how and under what conditions (psychological, social, cultural, etc.) youth can by means of religious instruction attain a spiritual attitude which is integrated with his total conduct. This comes down to saying that the fact of having received early religious instruction does not of itself constitute an independent variable which is capable of explaining later fidelity to the church. Thus, it is sufficient for us to refer the reader to Chapter VI where we carefully examined religious attitudes. In addition to pedagogical factors, this

---

[18] The moralist, who speaks of the "awakening of the passions" and of the moral difficulties encountered by the young during adolescence or post-adolescence, also gives a very valuable explanation in his order. The moral orientation which will accompany biological and psychological maturation will be a basic factor for explaining the spiritual evolution of the adolescent. To understand the repercussions of this on religious affiliations, however, one must see how these problems, which are present in all youth, are differently resolved within the context of the family, the church, the school, groups of friends and companions, that is, within the framework of reference proper to each one.

the conditions which effect the differential integration of examination revealed other factors of a psychological and social nature which must be kept in mind in order to evaluate the success or failure of religious formation.

What explanation do the psychologists offer apropos of this phenomenon? When they analyze the conduct of youth who discontinue religious practice the majority of authors stress one or the other of the following motives: the rejection of parental authority or the development of a personal synthesis independent of religious values.

On the other hand, youth's religious crisis is interpreted from the standpoint of the child's psychological dissociation from his parents.[19] Pearson has described this as the "conflict of generations" in which religious crises appear in some youth to be a transposition and a projection of interior family conflicts.[20] The need for emancipation, the criticism of parents, the search for independence—all induce a youth to reject everything that once identified him with his family: values, traditions, religious attitudes themselves. This is evidently a description of an extreme case, but it helps toward an understanding of the nature of conflict situations which can influence the adolescent's spiritual dispositions. The reaction against parents will not usually reach the point of total rejection, but a great number will face this conflict in its milder forms. Citing several previous studies, Allport affirms that this reaction against parental teaching occurs in about two-thirds of all children.[21]

[19] It is clear that here our perspective is one in which the parents give a minimum religious formation to their children. In the cases in which youth's discontinuance of practice is linked to the parents' religious indifference, one must no longer have recourse to a psychological explanation but rather to a more general solution such as one we will later suggest.

[20] G. H. Pearson, *Adolescence and the Conflict of Generations: "Introduction to Some of the Psychoanalytic Contributions to the Understanding of Adolescence"* (New York: 1958), 79–81.

[21] G. W. Allport, *The Individual and His Religion*, 32.

Is there any necessity of emphasizing with what care this crisis should be approached lest the religious attitude be involved in the psychological conflicts which arise between one generation and another? Otherwise the rejection of the parents' religion, as Pearson has shown, forms part of the defense system by which the youngster opposes his family.

The psychologists, as we have said, insist on a second point: the absence of religious and integrating values at the time when youth's psychological maturation is accomplished. The formation of a personal value system occurs especially between the ages of 17 and 25. But it is during the entire previous period that the values which prepare for the individuation of a philosophy of life will be gradually assimilated. What we have already said about "marginal" and integrating religious values[22] permitted us to stress the organizational functions of the well developed religious attitude. This has suggested to us the complete insufficiency of a religious initiation which would not be psychologically bound up with the totality of behavior. The positive process that we have previously described now helps us to understand how there can arise a contrary phenomenon, namely, that of disaffection toward a religious practice which was superficially related to the youth's system of values. Here we have a mechanism of dechristianization which should be studied with the greatest of care. Empirical studies might be able to clarify the value conflict by which the youth is interiorly torn and which hinders in him the maturation of a religious sentiment which is well integrated with his total personality. But this mention of values soon leads us to cultural and sociological considerations.

The sociocultural explanations of youth's religious detachment uncover vast horizons for us: the entire history of a milieu, the whole tradition of a country, its customs, its

[22] See 147–153.

spiritual past, its cultural originality, its educational system, its civil and religious relationships, etc.—these are just a few of the aspects we could mention here. Without overlooking the complex role of these universal factors, we shall, from our viewpoint, confine ourselves to the immediate impact that they exert *hic et nunc* and their direct influence on youth's religious attitudes. We shall therefore consider the factors which mediate these general influences and which, in some ways, condition the religious behavior of youth.

One sociological datum that soon becomes apparent when we examine youth within his social environment is the confused character of his social role. In the majority of milieux where he lives—except perhaps among his friends and peers—the adolescent is in a state of nonadaptation and dissociation, if not antagonism. In his family, school, religious milieu, the child has a clearly determined place; his status is well defined, his role is neatly outlined. The adult as such also has a role which is precisely fixed and determined by his age, maturity and responsibilities. But the adolescent has a poorly defined status, which is neither that of a child nor of an adult. Here we have a source of personal disorganization which has often been noted, but whose social consequences are rarely investigated.[23]

Does not the ambiguous social status of the adolescent produce disorganization on the level of religious behavior itself? Clark does not hesitate to affirm this in remarking that nothing so humiliates the churchgoing adolescent as the fact of being confused with the children. On the other hand the adolescent does not as yet have the satisfaction of

[23] "It all seems," Fau writes, "as if the working world, with the exception of the pedagogical milieu, is unaware of adolescence. Apprentices and young workers are employed in workshops and factories as if they were adults, that is, as socialized individuals who are freed from their family and who have themselves created a new family unit." R. Fau, *Les groupes d'enfants et d'adolescents* (Paris: 1952), 103.

being treated as an adult. These are elements of non-adaptation and of conflict which can be counterbalanced only when the youth joins a group in which the status and role of adolescents will be clearly defined in relation to church life.[24]

These observations on the adolescent's social status and roles encourage us to push further with our analysis and to inquire whether certain competing groups could not come between the young and the church and shake the steadfastness of their religious allegiance. Problems of this nature call for an understanding of the reference groups to which the youth's behavior is linked. It is recognized today that the psychosociological explanation of attitudes supposes the knowledge of specific groups to which the individual is referred and identified. The theory of reference groups has shown that our attitudes are influenced by the values and norms of the groups to which we belong either actually or by desire. This analytical framework seems to us indispensable for an understanding of the spiritual evolution of youth.[25]

The different groups with which the young are psychologically involved have a major influence on the orientation of their conduct. The family group, the school group,

[24] See W. H. Clark, *The Psychology of Religion*, 120–121.

[25] We have treated this question in more detail in our article, "Le rôle des groupes de référence dans l'intégration des attitudes religieuses," an address delivered at the Sixth International Conference of Religious Sociology, Bologna, Sept. 5–8, 1959; see *Social Compass*, 1960, 2, 139–160. In this article, we listed an abundant bibliography on Reference Groups. Let us briefly indicate here: T. M. Newcomb, "Attitude Development as a Function of Reference Groups: The Bennington Study" in E. E. Maccoby, T. M. Newcomb and E. L. Hartley, *Readings in Social Psychology* (New York: 1958), 265–275; see also H. B. Gerard, "The Anchorage of Opinions in Face-to-Face Groups" in *Human Relations*, 1954, 7, 313–325. For pertinent information with regard to the adolescent, see the chapter entitled: "Adolescent Strengthening of the Ego through Use of Group Ideals" in G. H. Pearson, *Adolescence and the Conflict of Generations* (New York: 1958), Chapter Five, 82–100.

the peer groups, the leisure groups, the religious groups—all, with more or less persuasiveness, make demands on the loyalty of the youth who belong to them; they constitute the affective and normative frames of reference of his habitual behavior. These groups offer him status and particular roles; they impose values and norms upon him and control his conduct by manifest or latent sanctions. It is only by placing the young within their social context and within the complex of their community references that their total behavior as well as the meaning of their multiple affiliations will be understood.

All this finds its application within the area of religious belonging. By using this analytical schema, the solidity, the resistance or the fragility of the socioreligious affiliations will be discovered. We shall see what kinds of competition and antagonisms create in the young loyalties toward groups which are parallel, indifferent or hostile to the church.

Descriptions of some actual cases will reveal to us in what sense the theory of reference groups can be of use here. The parish priest of a very dechristianized parish (4 per cent who practice) related the following fact which illustrates how psychological dissociation is brought about in the young adolescent. "The children," he explained, "who attend my parish catechism class are, without fail, punished and ridiculed the following day at school by their teacher who is a militant communist." How can the behavior of these children be understood if no effort is made at coming to grips with the deep conflicts which arise within them because of the desire to belong completely both to a religious group and to the group of their classmates? Two psychosocial systems lay claim to the child's allegiance and cause interior conflict. The religious educator cannot treat the young Christian as a sociologically isolated being. The profound psychology of the child is as it were divided between two reference groups, the one favorable, the other hostile to religion. The conflict is not only in the exterior reality, it penetrates into the child's very attitudes. It is then by a consideration of the specific solidarities that surround and sustain the behavior of the young that knowledge can be had of the stability or precariousness of their psychological attachment to the church.

Grave conflicts can also spring up in the psychology of the child after the time of First Holy Communion. In many regions one observes that religious practice declines rapidly after the twelfth or thirteenth year. The adolescent then becomes detached from the religious group and becomes absorbed with competing groups, whose norms practically exclude church fidelity: these include leisure groups, work groups, etc. Beyond the statistics on religious practice and the curve of religious profiles (which reveal youth's abandonment of practice at different ages), one must know how to discern the truly significant influences which provoke these departures from the community of practicing members. Are not these influences in some way embodied in the different groups to which the adolescent's habitual behavior is specifically linked? Is it not because of this that a sort of psychological and moral competition is created in a more or less informal way by groups which are areligious or even hostile to the church?

Religious sociology has not as yet adequately investigated this area in a methodical way. There is scant information on the moral and spiritual influence of primary groups which the adolescent spontaneously joins when he becomes emancipated from his family. In this respect, the peer groups have particular importance. The few studies that are available on this subject seem to be eloquent proof of this fact. In a clear and very candid analysis Seidler and Ravitz[26]

[26] M. B. Seidler and M. J. Ravitz, "A Jewish Peer Group" in *Amer. Journ. Sociol.*, 1955, 61, 11–15.

studied, as sociologists, the influences they had personally experienced during their youth within a group which comprised twelve or so comrades. The culture of this group of friends profoundly influenced each of the group members to the point that the group became a substitute for the family, that is, a veritable primary group capable of supplanting the parents' moral and spiritual influence.

Religious sociologists, while studying the adolescent, would find it to their advantage to pursue their research in this direction.[27] Here again one can take over some of Bossard's general conclusions by applying them to the religious behavior of the child.[28] This author has shown how the peer groups each have their particular culture and their norms of conduct. These restricted groups have an impact which is often decisive on the personality of their young members; and the social control that they exert on the behavior of the young can, at times, destroy the influence of educators or even religious pastors.

Even while remaining on the level of purely religious affiliations, the theory of reference groups helps us to understand the differentiations which develop in youth's fidelity with regard to the church. If the analysis were advanced further, one would see by what process the child's religious attitudes, which at the beginning are anchored within the parental group, undergo during adolescence a kind of "institutional" transfer of such a type that the adolescent becomes more and more consciously identified with ecclesiastical groups as such. The sociologist Harms has described this type of sociocentric evolution in the child's psychology and

[27] The observations made by Cooley in the past remain quite pertinent: "It is a general fact that children—boys especially, a little after their twelfth year—live in a camaraderie in which their sympathies, their ambitions and their honor are often more deeply involved than they are within their family." C. H. Cooley, *Social Organization* (New York: 1911), 23.

[28] J. H. S. Bossard, *The Sociology of Child Development*, especially Chapter 23, "The Role of the Peer Groups," 523–549.

confirmed, in a sense, the more general propositions of Piaget, Murray and Bossard.[29] Deeper studies, however, would have to be made into the meaning of this institutional transfer which in the child corresponds to the personal discovery of the ecclesiastical community. Perhaps at the psychosocial level it would be found that the religious feeling of the young who leave the church so soon after their First Holy Communion had never been firmly related to the ecclesiastical group itself. The hypothesis merits testing by empirical methods. Would there not be found, in this line of research, one of the more profound causes of youth's religious separation? And if we confronted these observations with those we have already made about the influence of secular reference groups, we would probably understand how spiritual adhesions are strengthened or dissolved on the psychosociological level. We would also learn how the young are often psychologically and morally divided between different groups based on family ties, school, friends, leisure, the neighborhood, apprenticeship, etc. Each of these groups in varying degrees imposes its values, norms, rewards and sanctions. We could legitimately suspect that in a great number of cases, if the competition among these groups operates to the detriment of religious fidelity, it is because institutional transfer toward the church and subsequent psychological reference lacked consistency and true personal meaning for the practicing youngster.

Whatever the value of the particular hypothesis here described, we believe that the reference group framework opens up new approaches for the investigation of religious sociology. The appeal of this theory lies in the fact that it offers us an explicative framework which is both operational and comprehensive, that is, apt to include all the reasons

[29] We examined earlier the theory of these authors with regard to our interests; see 131–137.

proposed up to this point to explain sociologically the rejection of religious practice by the young.[30] These last considerations will serve as a conclusion and a recapitulation.

Examining the causes which would explain youth's transformation of religious attitude, we have attempted to review the principal reasons furnished to date by the authors cited. After distinguishing the pedagogical, moral, psychological, cultural and social reasons for the religious indifference of the young, we arrived at an explanation which we believe to be an adequate synthesis, and which proceeds from the analysis of reference groups, that is, groups to which the diverse allegiances of the faithful youth are concretely attached. We believe that each of the causes postulated above can be subsumed under the rubric of primary groups which encourage or claim the adolescent's loyalties. We see here the support that is afforded to the young by the affective and moral frameworks within which their spiritual evolution takes place. This provides a comprehensive and operational explanation which, while respecting the liberty of individual religious choices, takes into consideration both the wide differences and the similarities of pattern which are observed in the abandonment of religious commitments by youth.

Let us note in closing that the theory of reference groups will find multiple applications in religious sociology. In one sense, it is easier to use this analytical framework with re-

[30] Let us recall, nevertheless, the limit and exact extent of this explanatory analysis, which only includes the *sociological* aspect of the phenomenon of religious disaffection. Our empirical perspective requires a complement which only the theology of religious choices can furnish. For the theologian, "the psychosociological discovery of the ecclesiastical community" cannot explain the ultimate reason for religious adhesion. Only the personal judgment of the faithful can, from a theological viewpoint, serve as an ultimate explanation. See the remarks made on methodology, 243.

gard to the adolescent's primary groups. But the method can also be employed for the observation of religious behavior in general and for the analysis of the conflicts which influence the adult because of his participation in and identification with multiple groups. We shall have the opportunity of returning to this theory when we examine, in the following paragraphs, the way in which ruptures in the belief system and loss of religious belonging itself are brought about among the faithful.

5 LOSS OF INTEGRATION IN THE BELIEF SYSTEM

If the observer is to judge the stability or instability of religious commitments from the church's point of view, he must pay attention to the degree of conformity between the attitudes of the faithful and the norms and teachings of their church. From this point of view the sociologist will be able to identify the deviation of actual beliefs from the norms of faith proposed by the churches. He will also observe the divergences which appear between the faithful's theoretical and practical attitudes. Here we have in mind collective behavior of the type that can be investigated by the sociologist. There is no question, then, of considering the member individually in his moral conduct or according to his interior attitude of belief.

The sociological aspect of these modifications of attitude has been emphasized by surveys conducted for some years in different countries. The striking aspect in these studies on collective religious behavior is precisely the divergences which are observed either with regard to doctrinal teachings or on the level of practical religious involvement. Let us examine doctrinal adhesion in particular and see how the steadfastness of religious affiliation is related to it.

The 1958 poll undertaken by the Institut Français d'

Opinion Publique revealed, with regard to youth from 18 to 30 years of age, that there was a considerable variation in collective doctrinal adhesion.[31] Although 62 per cent of the French youth questioned believe in "Christ as the Son of God," only 49 per cent believe in original sin, and only 32 per cent in the resurrection of the body. Yet, from the Catholic Church's viewpoint, these members should accept with the same resoluteness every article of faith since each bears the same doctrinal authority.

The theologians, from their point of view, will appreciate the truly religious significance of these ruptures in belief. The sociologist, for his part, observes that the degree of doctrinal conformity or nonconformity indicates the steadfastness or weakness of visible affiliation with the community of believers. In this regard, researchers have noticed that there is a parallelism between firmness of faith and religious practice.[32] This seems to be suggested, for example, by the answers given by practicing and nonpracticing Catholics to the survey of the I.F.O.P. cited earlier. Here are the affirmative responses to three questions on faith:

	Practicing	Nonpracticing
Jesus Christ is the Son of God	97%	59%
The Trinity	90%	43%
Immortality	90%	43%

In various surveys, however, it appears that among Catholics the steadfastness of faith is more intimately linked to religious practice than it is among Protestants. Brown and Lowe,[33] for example, compared some Protestants and Cath-

---

[31] "La nouvelle vague croit-elle en Dieu?" in *Informations Catholiques Internationales,* 1958, 86, 11–20.

[32] See A. W. Eister, "Some Aspects of Institutional Behavior With Reference to Churches" in *Amer. Sociol. Rev.,* 1952, 17, 64–69.

[33] D. C. Brown and W. L. Lowe, "Religious Beliefs and Personality Characteristics of College Students" in *Journ. Soc. Psychol.,* 1951, 33, 103—129.

olics who no longer practiced any religion. If belief in traditional Christian doctrines is considered, the difference in orthodoxy is twice as great between practicing and nonpracticing Catholics than it is between practicing and nonpracticing Protestants. The Catholics who have abandoned all contact with the Church seem sociologically more separated from their coreligionists than unattached Protestants are from faithful Protestants. This confirms one of the remarks which ends the 1952 religious survey conducted in France: "It is perhaps easier to recognize oneself as a believer in a social milieu where the faith is not associated with strictly defined practices or with a discipline such as that which the Catholic Church imposes."[34]

Thus the loss of conformity to the belief system of the Church will, for Catholics, be expressed by a separation from the Church which is a great deal more pronounced than that created by an analogous doctrinal divergence within a community where the teaching is considered reformable. What is said here of Catholics could, in a sense, be applied to all Christians who have preserved an integrated doctrinal synthesis. In general, collective divergences in faith will, for these members, signifiy (either as cause or effect) a modification of religious belonging.

It is with this distinction in mind that the more general surveys on religious beliefs will be interpreted. Divergences in doctrinal matters will affect a milieu differently, depending on whether it is Protestant or Catholic in tradition. In this regard, it is interesting to consult the results of an opinion survey which was simultaneously conducted in twelve different countries at the end of 1947.[35] Two ques-

[34] "Le catholicisme en France" in *Sondages*, 1952, n. 4, 14, 1–56; cf. 42.

[35] "Une enquête internationale: la religion dans le monde" in *Sondages*, February, 1948, 10, 31–33.

tions were asked: "Do you believe in God" and "Do you believe in the immortality of the soul?" We here reproduce the affirmative responses to these two questions in the different countries (in per cent):

Country	Belief in God	Belief in Immortality
Brazil	96	78
Australia	95	63
Canada	95	78
United States	94	68
Norway	84	71
Great Britain	84	49
Finland	83	69
Holland	80	68
Sweden	80	49
Denmark	80	55
Czechoslovakia	77	52
France	66	58

Figure 3 brings out the divergences in the acceptance of these two points of doctrine. For some countries such as Australia, Great Britain and Sweden, there is a considerable margin between belief in God and belief in the immortality of the soul. Keeping our preceding remark in mind, the observer cannot conclude from this that in these three countries the separation or abandonment of institutional religion is more pronounced than in other countries. On the other hand, there is only a minor difference recorded for France, a country which by tradition is clearly Catholic. Here beliefs will have the tendency to evolve reciprocally and mutually. In France, as in the other countries, faith in God is firmer than belief in immortality. But in France more than the others there is a tendency to accept or reject the two propositions together. The compiler of the French poll states that "among atheists, 88 per cent do not believe in the immortality of the soul' and that "among those who do not believe in the immortality of the soul, 78 per cent are atheists." In France, then, it can be said that as a general

Affirmative answers to two questions of religious doctrine (belief in God and in the immortality of the soul), from a public opinion poll conducted simultaneously in twelve countries.

FIGURE 3

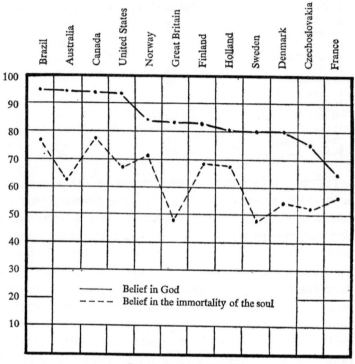

Source: *Sondages*, 1948, 33

rule "belief in the immortality of the soul involves faith in God."[36]

There are, then, two aspects to be considered regarding those phenomena that we have called a loss of integration of the belief system. On the one hand there is the fact that doctrinal acceptance is more or less firm (beliefs, properly

[36] *Ibid.,* 32.

258

so called), on the other, there is the impact of this acceptance or non-acceptance on the strength of religious belonging. The preceding analysis reveals how necessary it is for the sociologist when he is studying changes in religious attitudes to distinguish carefully the particular religious confession in question. It is in spheres such as this that formal sociology and the history of religion will be of great help to the researcher: they furnish him with information on the juridico-theological conditions of religious belonging. We shall retain here the insight divergences in the integrity of the faith have sociological consequences which are completely different for Catholics than they are for the faithful belonging to a religious confession in which doctrine would be less strictly defined. According to the cases observed, the religious attitude is differently anchored in the community of affiliation; variations between faith and belonging will occur in diverse ways. This latter aspect will also be brought out in our analysis of total loss of membership in the religious group.

6 DISBELIEF AND LOSS OF MEMBERSHIP

The extreme limit in "negative changes" of religious belonging is the break with the community of believers. Everyday forms of expression tend to confuse disbelief, atheism, agnosticism and irreligion, as though all refer to the same. Research which is now available shows that the social psychology of disbelief is more complex and that, even within this area, generalizations are difficult. Vetter and Green,[37] in a survey of six hundred atheists (three hundred and fifty valid answers), inquired into the personal factors

[37] G. B. Vetter and M. Green, "Personality and Group Factors in the Making of Atheists" in *Journ. Abn. Soc. Psychol.*, 1932, 27, 179–194.

and collective influences which contribute to atheism. Some of their observations merit examination and comparison with results obtained from other sources.

The formative years seem to exert a significant influence on the unbeliever's attitude. It has been pointed out that, among the more precocious unbelievers (those whose disbelief dates from about their twentieth year or earlier), half had already at this time lost their father and mother. As a group, 31.3 per cent stated that their childhood was unhappy. For the majority, the decision to give up all belief occurred early in life: at 19, some 42 per cent were atheists. Let us note that 90 per cent had attended Sunday School instructions until 15 years of age; and 61 per cent continued them after the age of 15. Yet, the survey revealed that parental lack of religion exerted little influence on the disbelief of the subjects studied: scarcely 5 per cent of the cases could be explained by a family background which was unfavorable to religion. Without denying a grain of truth in the statement that "atheism can just as well be the product of an excess of piety on the part of parents as it is of a free-thinking family atmosphere," we would hesitate, in general, to separate the unbeliever so completely from his family antecedents. In normal circumstances and from what we already know about the parents' role in the formation of spiritual attitudes (Chapter V), it is surprising to find here an atheism so independent of family religious climate.

The I.F.O.P. inquiry[38] into the faith of French youth shows, on the contrary, a similarity between the attitude of atheists and the religious opinions of their parents: *half* the atheists revealed that neither parent was a believer; and 67 per cent stated that neither parent was a practicing member. Without admitting an overly strict dependence of one generation on another here, one can at least rec-

[38] See footnote 31.

ognize that the parents' influence is far from being negligible; the supposition moreover would conform to the observations of Vetter and Green who show the importance of the young years in forming the attitude of disbelief.

If the subjective attitudes of disbelief are viewed in relation to church affiliation, it is observed that there is not a perfect parallel between atheism and the break with the church. This is shown in table 11. At the age of 19, some 54 per cent had left the church, but only 42 per cent were

TABLE 11

The age at which 350 atheists left their church and abandoned the faith. Answers are by percentage.

Ages	Left the Church[1]	Became Atheists[2]
Before 15	8.0	6.7
Between 15–19	46.0	35.2
" 20–24	21.7	24.0
" 25–29	6.7	10.2
" 30–34	3.8	4.2
" 35–39	2.2	3.8
" 40–44	1.9	2.6
After 45	3.2	4.2

[1] 6.4 per cent never attended church.
[2] 9.3 per cent admitted that they never had any belief.
Source: Vetter and Green, 1932, 188.

atheists at that time. Details of the answers provide more precise information about the two processes of separation from the church and the development of disbelief:[39]

— 46 per cent of the total stated that their attendance at church diminished progressively;

— 44 per cent made an abrupt break with their church;

— 6 per cent had already lost all religious sentiment before leaving the church;

[39] Vetter and Green, *art. cit.*, 189.

— 30 per cent admitted that they left the church and became atheists in the same year;

— 25 per cent became atheists a year or two after they
stopped attending church;

— 13 per cent: 6 to 10 years after;

— 4 per cent: 11 to 15 years after;

— 2 per cent: 21 to 25 years after.

These figures do not permit any conclusions concerning
the simultaneity of the two processes. It will be observed
however that the fact of leaving the church will not have
the same repercussion on the faithful of all denominations.
We have seen earlier that the relationship between faith and
institutional belonging is a great deal closer for the Catholic
than for the Protestant. Thus a Catholic who abandons his
Church will be more prone to reject belief in God itself. This
fact has often been verified and has led Jung to remark:
"The Catholic, who has turned his back on the Church, very
frequently develops a secret or avowed tendency for atheism, while the Protestant will, if possible, adhere to some
sect. The absolutism of the Catholic Church seems to demand a negation that is also quite absolute, when the
Protestant relativism allows variations."[40]

We believe that this fact elucidates the intimate bonds
which link personal religious attitude and institutional attitude, at least in the Catholic. It appears that the values and
norms of the religious institution play such an extensive
role in integrating personal attitudes that a rupture with the
religious group will bring about a dissolution of the very
synthesis of beliefs.

If the unbeliever's attitude is considered, what will be the
nature of his interior sentiments once he has psychologically
broken with the community of the faithful? What psychosocial content structures his new attitude? What does his

[40] *Op. cit.*

262

manifest behavior reveal in this regard? It is evidently impossible to make an analysis of all the attitudes which occur after a separation from a religious group. Among the facts discovered in surveys, we shall mention those which seem most significant for an understanding of changes in religious attitudes. We shall not offer any opinion on the possibility of a definitive cessation in psychoreligious evolution such that disbelief would be, psychologically, the final stage in a transformation of the spiritual attitude. For in this type of behavior there would no longer be any modification of religious sentiment to observe. We shall concentrate rather on the forms of atheism which present further spiritual variations in conduct and attitudes. Prescinding, then, from the possibility of an atheism which would involve an eventual psychological stabilization in disbelief, we shall examine two attitudes which have often been observed to parallel certain forms of modern atheism: a recourse to what may be called a substitute for a lost absolute; and instability.

The lack of resoluteness in convictions is one of the traits which has been indirectly pointed out in the behavior of atheists. This is probably the reason why the directors of the I.F.O.P.[41] thought it wise to introduce in their questionnaire a distinction between atheists who were "certain" of their position and those who were not "certain" of their disbelief. Now, upon closer examination of the young people who claim to be certain of their atheism, we find that 24 per cent admit that they often discuss religion—twice as many as the uncertain atheists. To the question "Is Christ the Son of God?" 54 per cent of the uncertain atheists and 20 per cent of the certain atheists do not know whether to answer yes or no. The question "Do you believe in the Trinity?" evokes, to a noticeable degree, the same type of uncertain answers (54 and 19 per cent indecisive answers,

41 See footnote 31.

respectively). To a question on the possibility of a life after death, 57 per cent of the uncertain atheists and 12 per cent of the certain atheists say they do not know.

Vetter and Green have observed a similar uncertainty which is characteristic of several cases studied in the survey. Among the atheists questioned, ninety-three had, in the course of their spiritual evolution, tried another religion different from that of their parents. Deism, Unitarianism and agnosticism were the principal intellectual positions embraced before abandoning all belief.[42]

Yinger, in his sociological study of the contemporary approaches to salvation,[43] reviews the many studies made on this subject by theologians or psychosociologists. It has been observed that humanitarian or spiritual projects undertaken outside the framework of institutional beliefs nearly always result in some initiation of the traditional forms of religion: creed, cult, authority, sacred history, new brotherly spirit, salvation, etc. Is there a question here of a genuine religious quest? Van der Leeuw would answer, as a phenomenologist, that these endeavors often assume the form of a "religion of flight" for modern man. Certainly, without further investigation it would be impossible to attribute this type of disguised religious motivation to all adherents of an abstract nonreligious cause; but the attitude of evasion seems characteristic of many social, humanitarian, etc., conversions which follow atheism. If these causes are espoused in the process of repudiating God, other gods are found and the flight continues. These people, as the phenomenologist notes, will never find the peace which the absolute offers: "Assuredly, there are always particular men who flee from God, but in this flight they cannot satisfy their need for religion. For, once they have barely escaped one power,

42 Vetter and Green, *art. cit.*, 190.
43 J. M. Yinger, *Religion, Society and the Individual*, 95 f.

they rush headlong into the jaws of another. . . . They can return from God to man or to humanity, but this flight simply brings them back to the original power."[44]

Transposed to psychosocial terms, these problems lead us back to the question of a substitute for religion in the integration of personal attitudes. Let us see how the question is treated in psychosociological analyses.

Recognizing that religious feeling is the all-comprehensive integrating factor, Allport states that other philosophies of life can also play the role of unifying synthesis at the level of personality.[45] Certain psychologists grant a para-religious significance to these values (esthetic, social, humanitarian, etc.).[46] Atheism itself can be understood in a religious perspective: "Atheism, rightly understood," wrote Spengler, "is the necessary expression of a spirituality that has exhausted its religious possibilities. . . . It is entirely compatible with an authentic desire for religion. . . ."[47] That absolute values are found, even in the very absence of religion, is a fact that the sociologist need not deny or affirm. Moreover, Spiegelberg's work on "the religion of no religion" reminds us that the absolute is, in fact, sought in other ways besides those which are traditionally considered spiritual.[48] But in the perspective of our methodological conception of the religious (cf. Chapter I), we shall not pursue our analysis beyond this point. We shall admit, however, that (from our viewpoint) nonreligious absolute causes may, in a sense, serve as personal integrating focal points and as substitutes for religion.

Nevertheless, the psychosociologists will try to determine

[48] F. Spiegelberg, *The Religion of No Religion* (Stanford: 1948).
[44] G. Van der Leeuw, *op. cit.*, 592.
[45] G. W. Allport, *Personality*, 226.
[46] Cf. P. C. Glick and K. Young, "Justifications for Religious Attitudes and Habits" in *Journ. Soc. Psychol.*, 1943, 17, 45–68.
[47] O. Spengler, *Decline of the West* (London: 1926), 408.

to what degree the substitution of religion by another absolute affords adequate compensation. A few, like Fromm and all the sociologists who have come under his influence, would not hesitate to raise to the dignity of religion every absolute about which a person's devotion revolves: religious values would always be present and "the question is not in knowing if there is religion or not, but rather which religion."[49]

Others, like Allport, Grensted, Sherman and Erikson, would raise a further question: even if these absolutes are considered as a religion of substitution, will the transfer of personal values be wholly realized? The answers provided by these researchers are generally negative.[50] In his analyses in social psychiatry, Erikson remains skeptical: "When organized religions have failed, there remains in man's life a fundamental void which is not filled by the simple negation of faith or by an irrational overestimation of the dogmas of substitution."[51] Allport for his part states that certain zealous endeavors can take the place of religion, "yet, even from the psychological point of view, we see that any secular interest, however vital, fails to cover the same ground. . . . A cause may be absorbing, but it seldom includes the whole of a mature individual's horizon. Residues are left over which only religion can absorb."[52]

Are we to conclude that the nonbeliever will not find any interior peace outside his former faith? The reserve which we have adopted from the beginning prevents any decisive judgment on this question here. Let us note that in the present case, we are considering a substitute for religious values which had been integrated within the personality,

[49] E. Fromm, *op. cit.*, 26.

[50] Cf. M. H. Sherman, "Values, Religion and the Psychoanalyst" in *Journ. Soc. Psychol.*, 1957, 45, 261–269.

[51] E. Erikson, "On the Sense of Inner Identity" in R. P. Knight and C. R. Friedman (ed.), *Psychoanalytic Psychiatry and Psychology* (New York: 1954).

[52] G. W. Allport, *The Individual and His Religion*, 77.

even if not actually practised. It is Allport who adds this remark. Jung's observation tends in the same direction when he described the religious psychology of his patients who were over 35 years of age: "Among my patients, who were beyond thirty-five years of age, there was not a single one whose fundamental problem was not that of religious attitude. In the final analysis, all had become ill from the fact that they had lost that which the living religions were, from all time, able to provide their faithful members. None were completely cured as long as they had not regained a religious attitude."[53]

There is no need to point out that these psychosocial observations have no import as a theological argument with regard to the reality of the religious object. We are still on the level of the subject's attitudes and his spiritual representations. However, we shall add by way of a corollary that denial of all objective reality beyond personal religious feeling is equivalent to dissolving within the subject's consciousness the specific object of his belief. The psychosociologist will note here how the faithful member sees the object of his belief as real; this is the very foundation of his faith and his religious attitude.

To conclude this final section briefly, we shall again insist on the importance of primary education in the formation and stabilization of religious attitudes. The history of disbelief as we have seen often begins in childhood. We also have pointed out the characteristic role played by the institutional framework in the faith of Catholics, at least. Their faith links them to their Church. For many, to leave the Church is tantamount to abandoning their faith.

If he pursues the study of the interior transformations

---

[53] C. G. Jung, *Die Beziehungen der Psychotherapie zur Seelsorge* (Zürich: 1932), 16; see R. Hostie, S.J., *Religion and the Psychology of Jung* (New York: 1957).

which take place in the unbeliever's attitude, the psycho-sociologist will be impressed by the two tendencies frequently encountered in the modern forms of atheism: a type of psychoreligious instability and the search for a new focus for his motivation. No general inference will be drawn from these observations. At most, we can state that certain forms of disbelief constitute an unstable attitude in which the quest for the absolute continues to the last.

CHAPTER XI

STABILITY AND MATURITY
OF THE RELIGIOUS ATTITUDE

1 Change and permanence of religious attitudes. 2 Persistence of religious attitudes. 3 Characteristic stability of religious attitudes. 4 The maturation of religious attitudes.

1 CHANGE AND PERMANENCE OF RELIGIOUS ATTITUDES

In his study on the individual's religious values, Woodruff[1] has observed that "to be truly meaningful, religious sentiment must include within its sphere of influence the total behavior of the individual, otherwise he runs the risk of having his religion seriously hindered by competing forces." This remark, in short, distinguishes two types of religious attitudes: one which we have described above as psychologically significant for the individual; the other, one which has not really succeeded in structuring the individual's values, is superficial and does not penetrate to the level of motivation. Religious change will be particularly noted in those whose attitudes incline toward this second category. This is most apparent in the case of adolescents whose re-

[1] A. D. Woodruff, "Personal Values and Religious Background" in *Journ. Soc. Psychol.*, 1945, 22, 141–147.

ligious instruction has not been continued long enough to support the formation of personal values. Departures from the religious group are particularly conspicuous in subjects of this age, as is evident in the religious profiles given in the preceding chapter.

The religious attitude of the psychologically mature, on the contrary, assumes a stability which, we believe, would be found with difficulty in other areas of psychosocial behavior. Certainly freedom of beliefs or spiritual attitudes persists at every level of personal development, but it is a fact—the significance of which we shall shortly examine—that the religious beliefs, once they are consciously embraced, are the most lasting and ineradicable psychologically. Our previous analyses provide us with a preliminary general explanation of this stability which seems unique. Thus: a) the religious attitude is linked with the individual's primary solidarities: his family, his relations, his own traditions and the culture to which he belongs; b) the religious attitude is among the most comprehensive of all attitudes since it unifies, centralizes and integrates all the individual's values within a personalized synthesis; c) the religious attitude is institutionalized, leading to identification of the member with a group which incarnates his beliefs and symbolizes the object of his devotion.

It is difficult to compare this last type of attitude with the religious feeling which is only superficial, as described above. Both attitudes present, however, a common characteristic: a certain resistance to change, resistance which will manifest itself differently in the two cases. Even in the case of superficial attitudes, changes in the religious sphere are paralleled by phenomena of persistence or even of durability which seems to us to be specific. With regard to attitudes of spiritual maturity, we shall see that they have a very particular stability; they play the role of central value in the behavior of the religious man and they are reinforced by a feeling of absolute certitude or conviction.

After treating of the changes produced in spiritual attitudes, it is well to insist on this complementary aspect of religious sentiments, that is, their relative resistance to change. Let us first examine the phenomena of persistence which accompany spiritual attitudes in general. Then we shall study the specific stability of religious feelings that are psychologically well integrated. We shall devote a final paragraph to an analysis of the problems which concern the maturity of religious feelings.

2 PERSISTENCE OF RELIGIOUS ATTITUDES

Ethnologists and psychosociologists are unanimous in acknowledging a characteristic persistence in religious values. A high degree of sociocultural stability is characteristic of the spiritual values of groups or individuals: and, it is noted that, even during changes of religious orientation, a certain stability is as evident in psychologies as in cultures.

At the level of personality, stability will be observed in the manifest behavior or in the unconscious dispositions of the subjects. Krech and Crutchfield[2] offer a general explanation of the stability of our attitudes and opinions. Their explanatory schema will facilitate our analysis of the stability or persistence of religious attitudes.

According to these authors, four factors explain the psychological resistance of collective attitudes. (1) First comes the nature of perception and memory. We understand why our attitudes are in some way stabilized by this factor of selection. We have seen, in fact (Chapter I), that attitude

2 D. Krech and R. S. Crutchfield, *op. cit.*

is essentially a structuring of our perceptive and motivational processes. Once an attitude is acquired, the subject sees things in a certain manner (favorably or otherwise). The attitudes assumed by a person influence the very structure of his cognitive processes. A positive or negative direction is given to his preferences. If the direction of his choices has been previously determined by religious values, an absolute preference has been registered in the structure of his behavioral system. These absolute preferences are the most enduring, and even if the attitude undergoes modification, certain structures in the personality will persist for many years. The adult, for example, thus remains marked by the structures imprinted upon him by the religious education which he had received during his childhood. On this point Allport observes: "In no other region of personality do we find so many 'residues' of childhood as in the religious attitudes of adults."[3]

(2) A second factor in the persistence of our attitudes, as Krech and Crutchfield tell us, is the "principle of cognitive constancy" which they describe as follows: "All other things being equal, a change introduced into the psychological sphere will be absorbed in such a way as to produce the least effect. . . ." The authors note that our most resolute cognitive structures are precisely those which rest on our beliefs (even in a broad sense). The subject will usually avoid any rude shock which might harm the acquired structures. He might apparently abandon his religion, but his cognitive and motivational synthesis will, nevertheless, continue to rest on values in which religious elements survive. Examples of this can be found in the numerous cases cited in the preceding chapter. Brown and Lowe[4] report behavior of this type among students whom they have questioned; 77 per cent, for example, doubt the necessity of being a Christian; 80 per cent, however, retain a certain

[3] G. W. Allport, *The Individual and His Religion*, 58.

272

faith in Jesus Christ as Lord and Savior. The phenomenon of persistence is evident here. It is, no doubt, not always as manifest as this. It will even happen that para-religious compensations may be sought in order to fill a spiritual need which was previously imprinted in the psychology, and which, afterwards, remained unsatisfied. The interest in certain sects or cults[5] and certain forms of superstition[6] play an evident compensatory role. Zucker's chapter,[7] in which he describes "modern man in a superstitious society," also leads us to think that superstition does indeed suppose cognitive patterns once inspired by religion.

(3) A third reason for the tenaciousness of attitudes comes from the spontaneous movement of retreat by which the subject usually protects his interior dispositions. Krech and Crutchfield cite the example of the anticlerical who will refrain from attending Catholic gatherings or from reading literature favorable to Catholicism in order to preserve his attitude. This form of behavior which is, in short, a process of negative selection of experiences, reinforces our attitudes; pushed to the extreme, it is a psychological escape. This attitude will be encountered in some people whose religious insecurity prevents them from accepting any new values. Some interesting studies on the Mormons have shown this attitude of retreat and self-protection in the faithful of the sect.[8]

[4] D. C. Brown and W. L. Lowe, "Religious Beliefs and Personality Characteristics of College Students" in *Journ. Soc. Psychol.*, 1951, 33, 103–129.

[5] See W. R. Catton, "What Kind of People Does a Religious Cult Attract?" in *Amer. Sociol. Rev.*, 1957, 22, 561–566.

[6] See E. E. Emme, "Modification and Origin of Certain Beliefs in Superstition Among 96 College Students" in *Journal of Psychology*, 1940, 10, 279–291; and E. E. Emme, "Supplementary Study of Superstitious Belief Among College Students" in *Journal of Psychology*, 1941, 12, 183–184.

[7] C. Zucker, *Psychologie de la superstition* (Paris: 1952), 188 f.

[8] See T. F. O'Dea, "Mormonism and the Avoidance of Sectarian Stagnation: A Study of Church, Sect, and Incipient Nationality" in *Amer. Journ. Sociol.*, 1954, 60, 285–293.

In a less conspicuous way, one finds other types of conduct which serve as a protecting framework for religious feeling. In addition to retreat or psychological escape, properly so called, there is an entire pattern of ordinary preferences, constants in personal tastes, which maintain religious attitudes in a well defined orientation. Each will in a different way choose his experiences according to social class, age, sex. Van Vleck and Wolf,[9] for example, have observed among the readers of a popular magazine that the choice of articles dealing with religion operates differently in men and in women. Men confine their choice to religious articles which are social in content and in which biographies of impressive and influential men are related, a more stalwart democracy is championed, the church is occasionally criticized, and the nontraditional aspects of ecclesiastical obligations are emphasized. Women readers will choose religious articles which are descriptive and esthetic in nature. They will, in particular, peruse biographical accounts relating humanitarian traits and hidden service. They like articles which stress moral renewal centered on the community. A conventional presentation of the church and spiritual things is more to their taste.

This manner of choosing and avoiding one's experiences reveals different types of religious attitudes. Religious dispositions can remain fundamentally the same, but particular accents will be impressed on each one's psychoreligious synthesis. These preferences and rejections exert a protective function on personal traits.

Even if the religious attitude is transformed, the habit of retreat will continue to operate. To this effect Telford has noted some curious traits of persistence in former members of a religious sect which was studied in one of his

<hr>

[9] J. Van Vleck and C. U. Wolf, "Reader-Appeal of Religious Articles" in *Amer. Sociol. Rev.*, 1942, 7, 828–832.

surveys.[10] The subjects had abandoned the sect but they continued, nonetheless, to follow certain restrictions which had been previously imposed by their religious group (avoiding alcohol, tobacco, coffee, etc.). Here we have an example of retreat, isolated even from the original attitude that it reinforced. These processes will, in a sense, explain many cases of religious stability. We can also understand that the individual's choices or selections are linked with patterns which are relatively constant in a collectivity. The negative movements of retreat are not the only ones which are operative; a positive selection is also at work, as we have seen. But the two factors exert their total action together and are to be understood in relation to each other.

(4) As a last factor, we shall mention social support from which a person's beliefs and attitudes usually benefit. Krech and Crutchfield state the general principle as follows: "The correlation between cultural types and types of beliefs or attitudes has the effect of giving social support to each one's beliefs and attitudes" (253). In addition to social support the subject, on the other hand, experiences at times a desire for approbation by the collectivity: "An individual's attitudes often operate in such a way as to give satisfaction to his social need for approbation or acceptance" (*ibid.*).

The specific bonds which link a spiritual attitude to a religious institution give this factor of social support an importance which is quite specific; we have often noted its effects on the cohesion and modification of religious behavior. Here we must add to the explanations of the authors cited earlier by stating that the church as an institution assumes a supreme value in the estimation of the member, and

10 C. W. Telford, "A Study of Religious Attitudes" in *Journ. Soc. Psychol.*, 1950, 31, 217–230.

the approbation that he seeks is not uniquely social, but moral and spiritual as well, for the church embodies his whole religion and not only the value he places on inter-personal relations.

When the religious attitude is less adequately integrated within the depths of the personality, it can happen that an individual remains "religious" for routine, habitual motives, or for social approbation—a state which tells us little about the person's properly theological orientation. In any case, we are discussing here only psychosocial motivations.

It is even possible to imagine gatherings for "worship" where the "religious" element has been practically elimi-nated. Krech and Crutchfield describe a situation of this type: the faithful continue to assemble, but their religious convictions have been gradually replaced by secular motiva-tions. "We could, in this regard, appeal to the gregarious tendency, the need for social approbation, the desire to flaunt one's wealth, the need for peace, etc. For all these people, the church assumes, today, quite another meaning than that which she had in the eyes of their ancestors. . . ." (*ibid.*, 42). Schneider and Dornbusch[11] relate several ex-amples of these gatherings for "worship" where promises of psychological consolation and secular fraternization have gradually supplanted the religious motivations, properly so called.

Supposing that a group has broken every visible bond with a religious institution, it remains true that social sup-port can still preserve certain religious values formerly dominant in the milieu. Properly religious values enjoy social support even in a context which is patently indifferent or even hostile to religion: "We must not allow ourselves

[11] L. Schneider and S. M. Dornbusch, "Inspirational Religious Lit-erature: From Latent to Manifest Functions of Religion" in *Amer. Journ. Sociol.*, 1957, 62, 476–481.

to be deceived," remarked Troeltsch, "by all the hostility to the churches and to Christianity . . . the present-day world does not live by logical consistency, any more than any other; spiritual forces can exercise a dominant influence even where they are avowedly opposed."[12]

This fact is confirmed by ethnologists who have studied, from a psychosocial perspective, the function of religious values in a culture. Wells thus describes the persistence of religion in a milieu undergoing a process of spiritual evolution: "There is a marked 'cultural lag' between secular technology as it affects material living standards and the individual's spiritual needs for belief; the latter change far more slowly. The result is, in the absence of doctrinal religious authority, the appearance of smaller religious groups. . . ." Among these will necessarily be forms liturgically and doctrinally cruder than the traditional because their function is to appeal scientifically to a simple level of religious need, without claim or aspiration to 'catholicity'."[13]

Wells terms this process a phenomenon of regression in adaptation. The religious fact persists but it has not been able to integrate new values.

Studies undertaken by Barnett[14] on the sociocultural meaning of the feasts of Christmas and Easter demonstrate how the external celebration of these two days has changed, especially during the past fifty years or so. But, with regard to Easter, he observed that "it is the religious aspect of the feast which manifests the greatest resistance to change." Religious values in some way form an integrating part of a culture. Beyond the changes of individuals'

[12] E. Troeltsch, *op. cit.,* 38.
[13] F. L. Wells, "Social Maladjustments: Adaptive Regression" in C. Murchison (ed.), *A Handbook of Social Psychology,* 845–915; see 863–864.
[14] J. H. Barnett, "Christmas in American Culture" in *Psychiatry,* 1946, 9, 51–65; and J. H. Barnett, "The Easter Festival: A Study in Cultural Change" in *Amer. Sociol. Rev.,* 1949, 14, 62–70.

opinions or convictions, these values continue to be supported by the collectivity and each one, unwittingly perhaps, has reference to them each time that he identifies himself with the culture of the milieu. "For this reason," affirms Allport, "the supplanting of one religion by another is not possible unless the culture itself is basically altered."[15]

The four factors of attitude persistency suggested by Krech and Crutchfield have permitted us to study the durability and persistency of religious sentiments in a general way. To these are added motives which explain the stability of religious attitudes in a still more immediate manner.

3 CHARACTERISTIC STABILITY OF RELIGIOUS ATTITUDES

One of the most captivating problems of religious psychosociology, as Howells acknowledges,[16] is the fact that different people can maintain with so much assurance attitudes which are diametrically opposed with regard to religion. Howells undertook, in this research perspective, a survey of five hundred and forty-two people, about a hundred of whom were split into two extreme groups: staunch radicals and conservatives. His analysis—the postulates of which seem contestable to us for reasons that we shall later indicate— emphasizes a specific trait of religious attitude: its absolute character.

Religious sentiment, consciously assumed by a person, will prevail over all the rest. The observer may speak of fanaticism, of absolute conviction or authoritarianism, ac-

[15] G. W. Allport, *The Individual and His Religion,* 27.
[16] T. H. Howells, "A Comparative Study of Those Who Accept as Against Those Who Reject Religious Authority." Iowa City, *University of Iowa Studies,* "Studies in Character," first series, no. 167, vol. II, 1928, 1–80; see 7.

cording to his own value judgments; but in the eyes of the believer his faith offers him motivations which he considers supreme. His attitude is rooted in the absolute, and it is for this reason that his religious feeling exhibits such stability. This is characteristic of attitudes inspired and motivated by the sacred, as Van der Leeuw informs us. "Whether it arouses sentiments of hate and fear, or of respect and love, the sacred always imposes an absolute obligation on man."[17]

Is it surprising then that the believer sacrifices everything, even his life, in order to remain faithful to his God, to his church? No cause inspires as many martyrs as those which are religious. In an opinion poll,[18] a forthright question was asked of the interviewed persons: whether they "would defend their faith even to the point of martyrdom." The answers were evidently difficult to interpret, but in their general tenor, they seem characteristic of the reactions of religious feeling: 15 per cent would undergo martyrdom; the others did not answer "no" categorically; 33 per cent still hesitated before a decision which implies an unmistakable absolute meaning.

The absolute which polarizes religious attitudes evidently answers to a need for understanding ultimate meaning; sociologists of religion have recognized this, but they have not, perhaps, always noted that the absolute also answers the needs of everyday life. This is a point on which Max Weber insisted and which Parsons[19] has reiterated. The sacred is not reserved to the World Beyond, it also inspires the believer's daily behavior. To see the action of the sacred only in the big events of existence would be a misconception of the permanent motivations of religious conduct. To abstract from this fact would be equivalent to examining

[17] *Op. cit.*, 36.
[18] "Le catholicisme en France" in *Sondages*, 1952, n. 4, *14*, 22.
[19] See T. Parsons, "The Theoretical Development of the Sociology of Religion" in *Journal of the History of Ideas*, 1944, *5*, 176–190.

279

the exterior frameworks of attitudes and perceiving only the reverse side of certitudes or convictions. The sacred here is a specific element. If it is neglected, religious sentiment runs the risk of being confused with certain forms of dogmatism (political, ideological, etc.) which are of another order. For the Christian, above all, the sacred is not a category, but, as Rogé stated, a Person. The devotion which it inspires is personal, absolute and gives meaning to everything. Brien[20] has shown that the fact of recognizing degrees of the sacred prevents the confusing of intermediary forms. This methodological remark seems to be of prime importance to us. To neglect it is to put the believer's absolute conviction and all forms of authoritarianism, which distort the personality, on the same level. Howells' study which was cited earlier does not avoid this confusion on the level of his research postulates. Rokeach's analyses of "dogmatism" also lack a frame of reference comprehensive enough to include the various forms of the "absolute."[21] In all analyses of this type one can, at times, perceive examples of religious fanaticism and intolerance. But the deep fervor engendered by a balanced devotion, zeal and a positive charity are hardly explained. Religious convictions also have their specific character and motivation. That deviations are possible is a fact that must be recognized. The researcher, however, should inquire into the motivational content to which the faithful attribute their attitude. The Christian is said to be committed because of a personal, absolute love; he is also motivated by an absolute belief. Let us examine this second trait which specifies the religious sentiment.

[20] A. Brien, "Valeur religieuse et équivoques du sens du sacré" in *Recherches et Débats*, 1957, 20, 111–130.

[21] M. Rokeach, "The Nature and Meaning of Dogmatism" in *Psychological Review*, 1954, 61, 194–204; and M. Rokeach, "Political and Religious Dogmatism: An Alternative to the Authoritarian Personality" in *Psychological Monographs*, 1956, 70, n. 18, 1–43.

We have already consulted Thouless' analysis[22] of religious certitude. Bearing on the religious fact, he concluded, attitudes are characterized by conviction (for or against); no other object inspires similar certitudes. One of the reasons suggested is the fact that religious positions lead to an immediate involvement on the level of practical behavior. The analyses of our preceding chapter oblige us to modify slightly Thouless' conclusions. Degrees and differentiations do exist within religious convictions. On the other hand, the involvement which religious beliefs arouse is not expressed in uniform types of affiliation and practices. As we have seen, it is especially noteworthy that opposition and rejection—what Thouless would call negative religious attitudes —often lack resoluteness. This fact became clear to us when we examined the forms of disbelief. And even in admitting that a firm "certitude" characterizes an attitude of disbelief, can one legitimately postulate that such a certitude is strictly comparable to that of the believer? We must here bypass the verbal aspect of attitudes and attempt to clarify their content.

In other words, the analyses of individual psychology, suggestive as they may be, ought to be replaced within a sociocultural context in which real behavior gives meaning to the declared attitudes of the persons questioned. These reservations once admitted, let us recognize in analyses such as those of Thouless the merit of having carefully examined certain psychoreligious processes. As a special treatment of the stability of religious attitudes and their resistance to change, Thouless advances an explanation which fits in well with the tendency toward certitude in the spiritual domain. "When," he says, "in a group of persons, there are influences acting both in the direction of acceptance and of rejection of

[22] R. H. Thouless, "The Tendency to Certainty in Religious Belief" in *British Journal of Psychology* (General Section), 1935, 26, 16–31.

a belief, the result is not to make the majority adopt a low degree of conviction but to make some hold the belief with a high degree of conviction while others reject it also with a high degree of conviction."[23]

Thouless' proposition appears enlightening, and it completes our earlier idea of the leveling of religious attitudes. While there exists a tendency toward religious indifference in a milieu where rival religious systems confront each other, one should not overlook the importance of a second type of psychoreligious reaction which can be called the reinforcement of religious attitudes. It is a well known fact that opposition, hostility and persecution often serve to reaffirm and anchor more deeply religious attitudes and affiliations. The confrontation, difficulties and obstacles encountered remind the member of the value of his spiritual commitment and give him the opportunity of relating his preferences explicitly to absolute motives.

Religious motives, however, are not always psychologically operative, but it is observed that where they do come into play they have a clearly dominant function with relation to secular motives. Clark[24] has emphasized this fact. In an investigation into the causes of personal creativity he observed that religion has an effective role only among a minority of the subjects observed; but where it is recognized as motivation, it holds the primary place. Woodruff arrived at analogous conclusions, previously discussed (Chapter VI).

The steadfastness that is thus observed in freely assumed religious convictions will explain the particular resistance of spiritual attitudes. It will appear still more clearly if the believer's absolute "convictions" are linked with a religious

[23] Art. cit., 24.
[24] W. H. Clark, "A Study of the Factors Leading to Achievement and Creativity, with Special Reference to Religious Skepticism and Belief" in Journ. Soc. Psychol., 1955, 41, 57–69.

institution which incarnates his faith, orients his behavior, and procures spiritual security for him. It is especially among Catholics that this last phenomenon has been noted. Making use of Gerard's expression, we will say that their religious attitudes are psychologically anchored within the Church and from this springs a characteristic resoluteness in their religious opinions and in their behavior.

Numerous attitude tests conducted among Catholics have brought out this fact. Nowlan[25] has made a summary of these studies, and he cites, among others, the conclusions of a survey run by Heath of two hundred and sixty-eight Harvard University students, of whom 10 per cent were Catholic. Heath and his colleagues thus describe the religious psychology of Catholic youth: "They manifest a substantial uniformity in questions of faith, with only some accidental divergences on certain dogmas, for example the nature of faith in God, the practice of prayer and of worship, faith in the future life. Their religious ideas and behavior clearly distinguish them from their friends who are mostly Protestant. Doubts and deviations with regard to the Catholic faith are rare and always associated with a conflict."[26]

Murray, as we have seen, reached a similar conclusion after his study in depth of fifty young men: "The Catholic subjects were conspicuously more solid and secure. . . . There was relatively little anxiety-linked material bubbling up in the minds of Catholics. . . . It was as if their faith in an ultimate authority relieved them of the necessity of independently resolving fundamental issues. Their unconscious fears, one might say, were quieted by the hovering presence of the maternal Church."[27]

[25] E. H. Nowlan, S.J., "Le 'portrait du catholique' à partir du test d'attitudes" in *Lumen Vitae,* 1957, 12, 284–296.

[26] See C. W. Heath, *What People Are: A Study of Normal Young Men* (Cambridge: 1945), 42.

[27] Cf. H. A. Murray, *Explorations in Personality.*

These observations involve multiple psychoreligious elements which Nowlan analyzes methodically. As far as we are concerned, we shall be content with emphasizing the one aspect of steadfastness which surrounds the fundamental attitude of Catholics; their conviction rests on a millenary institution. Properly doctrinal motives justify, in the eyes of the Catholic, his attachment to the Church. But even on the level of psychosocial observation, one notes the security that is afforded the faithful by the fact of belonging to such an ancient institution—the oldest in the west, as O'Dea observed—to which, according to Hughes,[28] "everything, sociologically speaking, has happened," and which has acquired such a vast amount of experience. The psychological repercussions of this fact ought to be emphasized. The image that the member has of the Church is deeply influenced by this and, in like manner, his behavior is oriented by it in varying degrees. Above all, his beliefs are firmly attached to the Church which formulates them, defines them, teaches them, and defends them. His religious belief does not lie on the level of personal opinion, his faith cannot be compared with a theoretical position; it is attached to dogma which his Church has taught for centuries. The stability of his belief is comparable, in a way, to the stability of the dogmas contained in a long tradition. Jung perceived the consequences of this fact: "Theory should abstract from the emotional values of experience. Dogma, on the contrary, is very expressive in this regard. A scientific theory is soon bypassed by another. Dogma lasts countless centuries."[29] The traditional element comes, moreover, to root the member's attitude within a history which is precisely that of his religion and his faith.

Let us briefly sum up these analyses. If we recognize in

[28] E. C. Hughes, "The Early and Contemporary Study of Religion" in *Amer. Journ. Sociol.*, 1955, 60, I–IV.

[29] C. G. Jung, *Psychology and Religion.*

religious sentiment a particular stability and a specific resistance to change, the fact is to be attributed, first of all, to the general factors enunciated by Krech and Crutchfield; but we must add to these factors a conservative tendency which is peculiar to religious attitudes. In addition to these explanations of a general nature, we believe we have discerned three causes which specify the stability of religious attitudes in a still more direct way: the absolute character which they possess by reason of their orientation toward the sacred, the supreme certitudes which accompany them, and the ecclesiastical and traditional references which guarantee them in the eyes of the faithful. The stability of which we are speaking evidently concerns the fundamental attitude of the believer, that is, the disposition by which he preserves his definitive attachment to the church. This basically stable attitude will be differentiated, however, in its intensity and its degree of integration with over-all behavior. This involves the maturation of the religious sentiment. Let us see now how social psychology succeeds in observing this movement, this particular dynamism of religious progress.

4 THE MATURATION OF RELIGIOUS ATTITUDES

Vast perspectives present themselves here for observation, but we must limit ourselves to those which most directly concern the matter at hand. We shall indicate, then, the very large area which we shall not treat in the present discussion. We are leaving out the properly psychological study of spiritual development. There is no question, for example, of dealing with the problems of asceticism or mysticism. To the extent that these subjects are dependent on psychosociology, they should be studied at the level of "supranatural" behavior, as we have stated in the first chapter.

Here we shall examine only the modes and manifestations of progress in the sense of religious belonging. We already have at our disposal many explanatory elements. Previous analyses on the causes of the strength of the spiritual attitude and on the variations of religious participation have permitted us to understand how the bonds with the church are solidified and made firm (Chapters VII–IX). We should like to pause here to consider the more immediate process and, if possible, to trace some ways by which the sense of church belonging psychologically acquires a more comprehensive meaning in the faithful's conduct.

In a chapter on "the religion of maturity" Allport[30] utilizes three criteria to judge the psychological maturity of a person: (a) the scope of his interests is enlarged; (b) the person knows himself and objectivizes himself more easily; (c) the person succeeds in unifying his psychological life into a dynamic synthesis. These three criteria—expansion, objectivation, integration—summarize, according to Allport, all the processes of psychological maturation; all the characteristics of personal development, as he says, can be reduced to them.[31] We would also have here the three characteristics of the sentiments characteristic of maturity. Let us see how these criteria will help us in analyzing the maturation of the member's sense of religious belonging.

[30] G. W. Allport, *The Individual and His Religion*, Chapter 3.
[31] These indications of personal maturity are not to be considered separately. A greater "breadth of vision," for example, of itself no more suffices to characterize adult psychology than does a more knowledgeable "objectivity." These traits can exist side by side with problems of affectivity or with difficulties of social adaptation. The adult reveals himself, above all, in the "possession" that he has of himself; fundamentally, the maturation of the person supposes, then, the acquisition of central values which integrate the totality of the psychological and moral life. This phenomenon of integration normally occurs between 17 and 25 years of age. Different causes can delay its realization: prolonged psychological dependence, lack of responsibility, early rejection of absolute values, etc. Let us add that maturation will not always be perfect; it often happens, even in the adult, that certain segments of the psychological life have not been harmoniously integrated within the structure of the unifying values.

If, in the first place, the psychology of maturity is characterized by the development of ever broader interests, one can suppose that the religious sentiment of the mature man will be recognizable by this, namely, that it, has incorporated interests which tend toward the universal. The adult believer, therefore, will learn to reconcile spiritually all the values (personal, collective, etc.) which lay legitimate claim to his concern. By means of successive reorganizations, his religious attitude will encompass an area which becomes richer and richer. Otherwise, atrophy or fragmentation will menace his religious psychology.

As an example, let us take the reconciliation of the values of social universality with the values inherent in socioreligious particularisms. A spontaneous, noncritical, religious sentiment will sometimes confuse religious membership with primary (national, racial, family, social class, etc.) solidarities. The faithful member who discovers the values of social unity ought to know how to include these new interests within his total religious concern. If he is not successful, often it is his psychosocial attachment to the Church which will suffer and which, in certain cases, will be rejected. As several authors have noted[32] this is a frequent cause for abandoning the faith. The I.F.O.P. survey of French youth[33] reports, for example, that 56 per cent of the youths who say that they are atheists state that "religion is opposed to social progress." One can surmise that these answers do not only express a form of *post-factum* rationalization, but that, in a good number of these youths, the maturation of religious sentiments has not kept pace with the rhythm of psychological development, and from this there result conflicts between values which appear contradictory. The same remarks could be made with reference to values in science, politics, esthetics, etc. For the religious adult,

[32] See P. M. Kitay, *op. cit.*
[33] See *Informations Catholiques Internationales,* 1958, 86, 11–20.

the only values appearing of themselves unassimilable will be those which will be judged irrelevant or antagonistic with relation to the absolute value which is his faith.[34] Choices which are more and more differentiated are imposed on him; his attitude comprises, in a conscious manner, spiritualized interests which are always in the process of broadening.

This supposes, and this is the second criterion, an acquired habit of personal objectivation, something, moreover, which in no way renders impossible the process of spontaneous identification, as we have seen (Chapter IX). Perception of the bond of church belonging becomes reflective, and religious attitudes make more and more of a conscious impression on all the aspects of behavior. In this regard, Allport recalls that religious sentiment has a functional autonomy which is so particularly noticeable that a mature religious attitude can transform the believer's entire life and change even his character.[35] Well developed religious sentiment, as he explains, possesses a directive character which influences constantly the whole personality, orients its morality, and motivates every action.

For the member who is aware of his spiritual affiliations, this signifies that his church membership increasingly assumes the form of a personal commitment. This sentiment can be developed rather early in the Christian. Harms[36] indicated very early traces of it in youngsters who range from 7 to 12 years of age, the very age at which the discovery of the religious institution normally takes place. The first discovery leads to others in which the church will appear to the member in all its socioreligious meaning.

[34] This is perfectly reconcilable with the practical renunciation that religious perfection might require. To renounce specifically a good (by asceticism, for a higher purpose, etc.) is not a denial of the value of this good; it is, on the contrary, seeing it in its hierarchical relationship with the ideal sought.

[35] G. W. Allport, *The Individual and His Religion*, 73.

Psychosociology is giving more and more of its attention to the frame of reference and the value system which surrounds the behavior of the individual. This approach will show itself particularly useful when the question of interpreting religious conduct arises. Manifest behavior is only half understood if it is not related to the deep motivations of the person. With regard to religious behavior, the characteristic motivation is the search for unity, the quest for ultimate meaning. Braden's study on religious motivation provides an interesting confirmation on this point. Braden[37] conducted his survey among 2,000 people, and he questioned them on the motives for their religious choices; sixty-five possible answers had been suggested in the survey questionnaire. The most frequent and typical answer was: "Religion gives a meaning to my life."

Religion gives the believer a meaning for everything; it relates him to the universe, history, God. Yet one sees that this psychoreligious unification is accompanied by a form of religious behavior which is not burdensome but progressively more simple. This is evident in the studies that have been conducted on the prayer of the faithful at different levels of religious development. Welford[38] indicates, for example, that the most advanced faithful prefer prayer formulas in which the discursive content yields to affective and symbolic expression. This will be the function, moreover, of rites which symbolically unite the religious universe of the person, while linking the latter with the spiritual community. Baudouin, who, like others, has recalled "the importance of an examination of the totality in religious

[36] E. Harms, "The Development of Religious Experience in Children" in *Amer. Journ. Sociol.,* 1944, 50, 112–122.

[37] C. S. Braden, "Why People Are Religious: A Study in Religious Motivation" in *Journal of Bible and Religion,* 1947, 15, 38–45.

[38] A. T. Welford, "An Attempt at an Experimental Approach to the Psychology of Religion" in *British Journal of Psychology* (General Section), 1946, 36, 55–73.

life," also stresses "the eminent function of the symbol in the manifestation of all spirituality."[39] Rite centralizes everything in God; Mauss and Hubert recognized this and made this penetrating observation: "Rite puts into motion the totality of sacred things to which it is applied."[40]

If rite plays a privileged function in unifying the community,[41] or in linking the faithful to it,[42] it is not the only form of spiritual unification. It is by his whole conduct that the member advances toward unity, thanks to the ultimate values which he pursues in communion with his Church. There he finds "meaning for everything"; the church is the "final word" about religious behavior, as Van der Leeuw remarks:[43] "The religious meaning of a thing is one beyond which there is no broader or deeper meaning. It is the meaning of everything. It is the final word. . . . *Homo religiosus* follows the road of omnipotence, of perfect knowledge, of ultimate meaning."

[39] C. Baudouin, *Psychanalyse du symbole religieux*, 278.

[40] H. Hubert and M. Mauss, "Essai sur la nature et la fonction du sacrifice" in *L'Année Sociologique*, 1897–1898, 2, 29–138; see 134.

[41] See G. George, S.J., "The Sociology of Ritual" in *Amer. Cath. Sociol. Rev.*, 1956, 17, 117–130.

[42] See W. S. Salisbury, "Faith, Ritualism, Charismatic Leadership and Religious Behavior" in *Social Forces*, 1956, 34, 241–245.

[43] *Op. cit.*, 663.

CONCLUSION
THE SPECIFICITY OF THE
RELIGIOUS ATTITUDE

CONCLUSION

As far back as we can trace the sciences of society, it is clear that particular attention has always been given to religious phenomena. Polybius in his history of Greece attempted an explanation of the mentality of Athens' enemies, the Romans, by their strange belief in the gods. Bacon, as did so many others, saw in religion the social bond par excellence: *Religio praecipuum humanae societatis vinculum.* In this line of research, modern sociology and social psychology have made remarkable progress for thirty years or so.

Despite so much interest, so many studies and surveys, the impression is had, however, that religious behavior remains an enigma for the scientific observer. For religion, especially the Christian religion, is above all a life; its main driving force is invisible: it is faith in the love of God. "What the science of religions calls the object of religion is for religion itself its subject. The religious man always holds as primary, fundamental, and determining that which concerns his religion." These words of Van der Leeuw[1] express rather well the feeling experienced by the sociologist when he examines the religious universe. What is the secret of religious behavior? Who knows the boundary between the sacred and the profane? What do sociologists and psychologists study when they observe religious conduct? Clark[2]

[1] *Op. cit.,* 9.
[2] W. H. Clark, "How Do Social Scientists Define Religion?" in *Journ. Soc. Psychol.,* 1958, 47, 143–147.

has reminded us of the hesitations that sociologists have when confronted with this question which is, however, fundamental for the sociology of religion.

This is precisely the paradox. Although it is easy enough to recognize, in a concrete situation, the typical behavior of the religious man, the scientific observer hesitates, nevertheless, to determine on the level of analysis the specific traits of the observed behavior. A religious act, a spontaneous prayer, a ritual manifestation can hardly be mistaken. But how does he explain his observations?

We have shown at the beginning of this book (Chapter I) the impossibility, in our opinion, of defining the nature of religion without the use of metaphysics. We have accepted this methodological limitation which is imposed on the observer. Yet we have recognized that one can define the religious either by using a nominal formula, a starting hypothesis, or by restricting the analysis to well determined forms of religious life. We studied in these pages only Judeo-Christian religions and, more precisely, Christian confessions.

Within this framework, can one discern traits which specify religious behavior? We thought that by situating religious conduct within the perspective of psychosocial attitudes (Part One) we could analyze these attitudes in their formation (Part Two) and in their internal differentiations (Part Three). Making allowance for the inaccessible and the mysterious, rejecting also the sociologist's illusion that science can discover the origins of religion—a false problem, as wrote Gernet,[3]—we have attempted to understand, from a psychosociological viewpoint, the observable traits which accompany sentiments of religious belonging.

Speaking on a matter such as religious belonging, of the

[3] See L. Gernet, "Histoire des religions et psychologie: confrontations d'aujourd'hui" in *Journal de Psychologie*, 1954, (numéro spécial) t. 47–51, 175–187.

specificity of attitudes, we run the risk of causing confusion. On several occasions, we have emphasized the comprehensiveness of religious attitudes (Chapters I and VI); the manner in which they comprise all interests (Chapter IX); the meaning of the totality which characterizes them (Chapter XI). It might appear that these traits clearly reveal a general attitude, but not a specific attitude.

Let us not enter here into those discussions on the generality or the specificity of psychosocial attitudes. We will simply answer with Newcomb[4] that a general or comprehensive attitude also possesses its specificity, and that it determines well characterized, specific behavior—for example, the liberal, progressive, or conservative attitude which provides a general orientation and yet inspires well defined and even predictable behavior. It is in this sense that we say religious attitudes are specific. The fundamental or general orientation that they imprint on behavior is clearly characterized. The acts of the religious man will be, by that very fact, identifiable, specified.

At every stage of spiritual development we have had the opportunity of pointing out the specific traits of religious behavior. If it is by a conversion that one is joined to the life of a religious group, do we not notice, from the start, the uniqueness of this form of affiliation? No other social adhesion will produce such an upheaval in a psychology. Conversion to a religion restores a new unity to the personality, reintegrates all its values, and obtains for it an identifying status within a religious group. In a word, it is with reference to these three functional elements that conversion is explained: a new self, situated in relation to a religious collectivity, and polarized by the consciousness of a divine call (Chapter II). These appear to us as distinctive traits.

[4] T. M. Newcomb, *Social Psychology*, 219 f.

We cannot compare, however, all conversions to the same model; and we have distinguished those to sects from those which introduce one into a church. Sectarian adhesion seems to us to be characterized by a manifest psychoreligious insecurity. We have refrained, however, from explaining sectarian conversions as if they were the result of traumatic socioeconomic situations or simple forms of social protest. On the contrary, we have discovered in sects the three specific elements of conversion: changes at the level of personality; acceptance of the status and role which a religious (and even rudimentary) group offers; and especially an element of belief which is determinative if one wishes to understand how one form of sectarian behavior is distinguished from another. Although it might be called by some an illusion, or religious immaturity, the faith of the convert to sects is the ultimate explanation of his conduct (Chapter III).

With church conversion, it is the institutional reference which has been especially emphasized (Chapter IV). The church affords a special institutional stability, and it is through the radiation of its influence that a person is converted to it; it offers complete salvation. The response of the convert takes the form of both an acquiescence and a ceremony. No psychosocial behavior contains as clear a unification of motivations as this: between the believer, his devotion, his faith, the rite of baptism, his church and his God, a spiritual continuity is built up which gives the religious personality its unity while intimately linking it with the community of believers.

On the level of religious symbols, a type of interpenetration is operative between sentiment and rite, rite and the church, the church and God. For the believer, to accept baptism is to become affiliated with the church and to become affiliated with the church is to become a son of God.

No behavior, other than religious conduct, embraces dimensions which are both as intimate and as universal.

The sense of religious belonging is cultivated also by means of education. We have here noted, as characteristic of religious sentiments, their amazingly early appearance (Chapter V). Among adult attitudes (political, social, etc), very few go so far back into early childhood. In general, the influence of the family and that of the primary milieu serve as essential frame of reference in developing the sentiments of religious belonging. Identification with the parents' religion is extended into a larger identification: it is the progressive discovery of the religious institution by the child. At about age 12, the adolescent seems to have grasped clearly the significance of his spiritual belonging; he possesses personal convictions—this is true when education has progressed normally. After becoming identified with the religious life of his parents, he now becomes identified with the life of his church, with that fervor of attachment which characterizes spiritual affiliations which are consciously assumed.

Religious instruction will perfect the psychosocial and spiritual integration of the member with the community of faith. Long experience has shown the church the manner in which minds and cultures are transformed. The religious instruction of the young is a basic task for the church; the very permanence of religious communities depends on it. An effective pedagogy, however, supposes that religious instruction has been prolonged for a sufficient period of time in the life of the adolescent, so that religious motivations will clarify and inspire the slow processes of individuation of values, and will bring about a profound integration of the personality (Chapter VI).

Regarding the more general diffusion of the religious message, we have seen the particular kind of interaction which is established between the preacher and his milieu. The religious educator transforms attitudes while keeping in mind the solidarities of his listeners which make them collectively favorable or unfavorable to the church. Granting that an extremely close identification links the member to his church, nevertheless the persistence of the primary solidarities, which reinforce and support spiritual attitudes even in the religious adult (Chapter IX), should not be forgotten. The ties which link so closely the religious attitude with surrounding cultural values and with the primary milieux seem to us to be a distinctive trait of the psychology of the faithful. No other attitude, we believe, involves a similar synthesis, even on the psychosocial level.

To understand the internal differentiations of the sense of religious affiliation, we have had recourse to the psychology of social cohesion (Chapter VII). The "participation" of the member and the cohesion of his group have been studied in their reciprocal aspects. In every religious group, including sects, the specifying element of social cohesion is the belief that one professes in it. It is this which definitively determines the orientation and even the psychosocial significance of religious affiliation. Only religious affiliations are thus absolutely rooted in faith and in a common hope.

Ecclesiastical communities have their own cohesion (Chapter VIII); they involve affiliations which are basically identical from the theological point of view (Chapter I), but which are expressed in acts and attitudes of participation which are more or less intense, with the result that the psychosocial status of the church member will govern more or less profound areas of his total behavior.

Among the factors influencing the cohesion of ecclesiastical communities, two have been emphasized: (a) the role of the clergy in its institutionalized and personalized aspects; (b) the numerical size of the parish, in relation to certain upper and lower limits for an effective community life. Here we have emphasized the relations which exist between community participation and a missionary spirit. The community affirms itself and is interiorly strengthened when it continues to admit new adherents.

From all this, the specific element of church belonging which we stress is the fact that it requires an eminently personal participation within a highly institutionalized framework. Few psychosocial affiliations thus involve the totality of the person, while requiring such complex institutional support.

The image that the member forms of his local religious group plays a major role in his appreciation of the community, and in the quality of his psychoreligious participation (Chapter IX). It is necessary here to go beyond the objective situations which seem to discredit the exterior status of the religious group (persecutions, rejection, etc.), and to see how these situations are understood, in faith, by the believer. The spiritual meaning of solidarities created by faith constitutes, certainly, a specific trait of religious affiliations. This is understood especially by an examination of the properly religious symbolizations of the Christian community: solidarities are conceived as vital relationships within the interior of a living body.

Even in its internal transformations, the religious attitude presents traits which differentiate it from profane attitudes (Chapter X). It is especially by loss of integration in the belief system that religious attitudes are dissolved, leveled and obliterated. We can thus trace certain patterns in the development of religious indifference, disaffection, dechristianization and disbelief. Are there secular absolutes which are capable of filling the void left by a lost faith? The negative answers that numerous psychosociologists give to this question bring out, we believe, the proper function of the sacred in the profound integration of the personality, especially if the sacred is both personalized and possessed in common.

It is because of the sacred, absolute motivations which accompany it that religious sentiment has a very particular stability (Chapter XI). Collective changes can occur in religious attitudes involving indifference or dechristianization, but even then persistence and tenacious durability will testify to the profound and almost ineradicable influences that religious habits have imprinted upon psychologies and cultures. Psychologists and ethnologists agree on this double, distinctive trait of religious feelings. No attitude offers as much resistance to change; none leaves such persistent traces on the mentality of people.

In a sense, it can be said that the characteristic par excellence of religious transformations is spiritual progress, the movement toward conformity with a supernatural ideal (Chapter XI). Within the perspective of church belonging, one sees that religious maturation is expressed by a tendency toward the universal, by the objectivation of personal convictions which transform one's entire behavior, and by the assimilation of a unifying wisdom. For the religious adult, to belong to the church is to situate himself in relation to the universe of men and God. Religious affiliation is, finally, faith's acceptance of the Word of God, a Word which itself inspires and vivifies in the eyes of the faithful the community of believers.

This basic attitude of the church member, we believe, gives us the answer to apparent antinomies which we have often encountered in these pages: the antinomy between liberty and socioreligious belonging, between institutional participation and interior sentiment, between internalized religion and religion imposed by social pressure. . . . The sense of belonging in the faithful member, transcends these overly simple distinctions. Social psychology, which does not intend to neglect either the individual or the collective, is useful as a privileged instrument for observing how, within an adult personality, the religious sentiment of the individual and his sense of belonging to a religious institution are intimately reconciled and mutually developed.

It is understood that the sociologist experiences a similar curiosity about religious behavior: here is found the best of personal and social values. In no other area will sociologists and psychologists have as much need for collaborating in order not to overlook anything in the study of a type of behavior which is so comprehensive. But we are here speaking of mature religious feelings. The human and spiritual balance is not always realized, and religious affiliations, as is often seen, do not necessarily coincide with the development of the individual and the peace of groups. Man's religious quest has continued for centuries; but not all have found wisdom and fraternity. The sociologist, as a man, can only desire the establishment of a human equilibrium in which liberties and solidarities can flower in harmony. As far as we are concerned, we shall make our own Pinard de la Boullaye's both realistic and optimistic reflections which he used at the close of his chapter on the sociological method in the religious sciences.[5]

"If the happiness of humanity is linked to the solution of religious questions, if the organization adopted in human groups has so profound an influence on the formation and evolution of attitudes, one sees, in the final analysis, what interest must center on the social organization of sects, churches, or religions. The most vital seed of life and of progress, be it discovered by the genius of a man or transplanted from heaven to earth by an intervention of Provi-

[5] H. Pinard de la Boullaye, *L'étude comparée des religions,* II, 487–488.

dence, can encounter, according to circumstances, institutions which favor its growth or which stifle it. In the multiplicity of combinations to which these institutions lend themselves, two essential forms can be distinguished: individualism and authoritarianism. That both incline toward extremes—anarchy and despotism—is a fact that history has only too often proven. That a reconciliation is impossible cannot be admitted unless one gives up faith in reason itself. On the contrary, we perceive that true liberty as well as legitimate authority can exist only within the limits of the True and the Right; and on such an hypothesis the individual would really be able to find the perfect exercise of his liberty under the direction of an authority: he would gain his share of independence by renouncing not to misuse it."

✓ for DISSERT H's.

ABBREVIATIONS

Amer. Cath. Sociol. Rev.	*American Catholic Sociological Review*
Amer. Journ. Sociol.	*American Journal of Sociology*
Amer. Sociol. Rev.	*American Sociological Review*
Arch. Sociol. des Relig.	*Archives de Sociologie des Religions*
Cahiers Intern. Sociol.	*Cahiers Internationaux de Sociologie*
Journ. Abn. Soc. Psychol.	*Journal of Abnormal and Social Psychology*
Journ. Soc. Psychol.	*Journal of Social Psychology*

BIBLIOGRAPHY

ALLIER, R., *La psychologie de la conversion chez les peuples non-civilisés,* 2 vol., (Paris: 1925).

ALLINSMITH, W. and ALLINSMITH, B., "Religious Affiliation and Politico-Economic Attitude: A Study of Eight Major U.S. Religious Groups" in *Publ. Opin. Quart.,* 1948, 12, 377–389.

ALLPORT, G. W., "Attitudes," in C. MURCHISON (ed.), *A Handbook of Social Psychology* (Worcester: 1935), 798–844.

————, *Personality:* "A Psychological Interpretation" (New York: 1937), 1949.

————, "The Psychology of Participation" in *Psychol. Rev.,* 1945, 52, 117–132.

————, GILLESPIE, J. M., and YOUNG, J. "The Religion of the Post-War College Student" in *Journ. of Psychol.,* 1948, 25, 3–33.

————, "A Psychological Approach to the Study of Love and Hate" in P. A. SOROKIN (ed.), *Explorations in Altruistic Love and Behavior* (Boston: 1950), 145–164.

————, *The Individual and His Religion:* "A Psychological Interpretation" (London: 1951).

ALPHANDÉRY, P., "Foules historiques: les foules religieuses" in *La Foule*, (Centre Intern. de Synthèse) (Paris: 1934), 53–78.

ARGYLE, M., *Religious Behaviour* (London: 1958).

BACK, K., "The Exertion of Influence through Social Communication" in *Journ. Abn. Soc. Psychol.*, 1951, 46, 9–23.

BARNETT, J. H. "Christmas in American Culture" in *Psychiatry*, 1946, 9, 51–65.

———, "The Easter Festival: A Study in Cultural Change" in *Amer. Sociol. Rev.*, 1949, 14, 62–70.

BASTIDE, R., *Eléments de sociologie religieuse* (Paris: 1935).

———, "Contribution à l'étude de la participation" in *Cahiers Intern. Sociol.*, 1953, 14, 30–40.

BAUDOUIN, C., *Psychanalyse du symbole religieux* (Paris: 1957).

BECKER, H., "Supreme Values and the Sociologist" in *Amer. Sociol. Rev.*, 1941, 6, 155–172.

BENEDICT, R., *Patterns of Culture,* second edition, (New York).

BERGER, P. L., "The Sociological Study of Sectarianism" in *Social Research*, 1954, 21, 467–485.

BOISEN, A. T., "Economic Distress and Religious Experience: A Study of the Holy Rollers" in *Psychiatry*, 1939, 2, 185–194.

———, *Religion in Crisis and Custom:* "A Sociological and Psychological Study" (New York: 1955).

BOSSARD, J. H. S. and BOLL, E. S., "Ritual in Family Living" in *Amer. Sociol. Rev.*, 1949, 14, 463–469.

———, *Ritual in Family Living* (Philadelphia: 1950).

———, *The Sociology of Child Development,* revised edition (New York: 1954).

BOULARD, F., (Canon) *Premiers itinéraires en sociologie religieuse* (Paris: 1954).

———, "Aspects sociologiques: le problème des trop petites paroisses" in *La Maison-Dieu*, 1959, 57, 9–24.

BOWMAN, C. C., "Must the Social Sciences Foster Moral Skepticism?" in *Amer. Sociol. Rev.*, 1945, 10, 709–715.

BRADEN, C. S., "Why People are Religious: A Study in Religious Motivation" in *The Journal of Bible and Religion*, 1947, 15, 38–45.

BRIEN, A., "Valeur religieuse et équivoques du sens du sacré" in *Recherches et Débats*, 1957, 20, 111–130.

BROEN, W. E., "A Factor-Analytic Study of Religious Attitudes" in *Journ. Abn. Soc. Psychol.*, 1957, 54, 176–179.

For 11 Stage 3

BROWN, D. C. and LOWE, W. L., "Religious Beliefs and Personality Characteristics of College Students" in *Journ. Soc. Psychol.*, 1951, 33, 103–129.

BURCHINAL, L. G., "Some Social Status Criteria and Church Membership and Church Attendance, *Journ. Soc. Psychol.*, 1959, 49, 53–64.

BURNS, J., *Revivals:* "Their Laws and Leaders" (London: 1909).

BURTT, H. E., and FALKENBERG, D. R., "The Influence of Majority and Expert Opinion on Religious Attitudes," *Journ. Soc. Psychol.*, 1941, 14, 269–278.

CAILLOIS, R., *Man and the Sacred* (Chicago: 1939).

CANTRIL, H. "Educational and Economic Composition of Religious Groups: An Analysis of Poll Data" in *Amer. Journ. Sociol.*, 1943, 48, 574–579.

CARRIER, H., S.J., "Le rôle des groupes de référence dans l'intégration des attitudes religieuses" in Communication at the Sixth International Conference of Religious Sociology, Bologna, Sept. 3–6, 1959; see *Social Compass*, 1960, 2, 139–160.

CATTON, W. R., "What Kind of People Does a Religious Cult Attract?" in *Amer. Sociol. Rev.*, 1957, 22, 561–566.

CAZENEUVE, J., *Les rites et la condition humaine* (Paris: 1958).

CHAPIN, F. S., "The Optimum Size of Institutions: A Theory of the Large Groups" in *Amer. Journ. Sociol.*, 1957, 62, 449–460.

CHAVE, E. J., and THURSTONE, L. L., *Scale for the Measurement of Attitude Toward God* (Chicago: 1931).

CLARK, E. T., *The Psychology of Religious Awakening* (New York: 1929).

———, "Non-Theological Factors in Religious Diversity" in *Ecumenical Review,* 1951, 3, 347–356.

CLARK, W. H., "A Study of the Factors Leading to Achievement and Creativity With Special Reference to Religious Skepticism and Belief" in *Journ. Soc. Psychol.*, 1955, 41, 57–69.

———, "How Do Social Scientists Define Religion?" in *Journ. Soc. Psychol.,* 1958, 47, 143–147.

———, *The Psychology of Religion* (New York: 1958).

COHN, W. C., "Jehovah's Witnesses as a Proletarian Movement" in *The American Scholar,* 1955, 24, 281–298.

COUGHENOUR, C. M., "An Application of Scale Analysis to the Study of Religious Groups" in *Rural Sociology,* 1955, 20, 197–211.

304

CUBER, J. F., "Marginal Church Participants" in *Sociology and Social Research*, 1940, 25, 57–62.

DESABIE, J., *Le recensement de pratique religieuse dans la Seine* (Paris: 1958).

——, "Sociologie religieuse dans la Seine: recensement du 14 mars 1954" in *Revue de l'Action Populaire*, 1958b, 120, 815–823.

DE SANCTIS, S., *La conversione religiosa:* "studio bio-psicologico" (Bologna: 1924).

DESROCHE, H., "Domaines et méthodes de la sociologie religieuse dans l'oeuvre de Gabriel Le Bras" in *Revue d'Histoire et de Philosophie Religieuses*, 1954, 34, 128–158.

——, "Sociologie et théologie dans la typologie religieuse de Joachim Wach" in *Arch. Sociol. des Relig.*, 1956, 1, 41–63.

——, "Autour de la sociologie dite 'des sectes'," in *L'Année Sociologique*, 1955–1956, 3ᵉ série, 395–421.

DEUTSCH, M., "A Theory of Cooperation and Competition" in *Human Relations*, 1949, 2, 129–152.

——, "Field Theory in Social Psychology" in G. LINDZEY (ed.), *Handbook of Social Psychology* (Cambridge: 1954), 1956, 181–222.

DEVOLDER, N., "Enquête sur la religion des intellectuels" in *Bull. de l'Inst. de Rech. Econ. et Sociales*, 1946, 12, 649–671.

——, "Inquiry into the Religious Life of Catholic Intellectuals" in *Journ. Soc. Psychol.*, 1948, 28, 39–56.

DEWEY, R. and HUMBER, W. J., *The Development of Human Behavior* (New York: 1951), 1954.

DONIGER, S., (ed.), *Religion and Human Behavior* (New York: 1954).

DONOVAN, J. D., "The Sociologist Looks at the Parish" in *Amer. Cath. Sociol. Rev.*, 1950, 11, 66–73.

DUFRENNE, M., *Phénoménologie de l'expérience esthétique*, 2 vol., (Paris: 1953).

DURKHEIM, E., "De la définition des phénomènes religieux" in *L'Année Sociologique*, 1897–1898, 2, 1–28.

——, *Les formes élémentaires de la vie religieuse:* "Le système totémique en Australie" (Paris: 1912).

DYNES, R. R., "Toward the Sociology of Religion" in *Sociology and Social Research*, 1954, 38, 227–232.

——, "Church-Sect Typology and Socio-Economic Status" in *Amer. Sociol. Rev.*, 1955, 20, 555–560.

————, "The Consequences of Sectarianism for Social Participation" in *Social Forces*, 1957, 35, 331–334.

EISTER, A. W., "Some Aspects of Institutional Behavior with Reference to Churches" in *Amer. Sociol. Rev.*, 1952, 17, 64–69.

————, "Religious Institutions in Complex Societies: Difficulties in the Theoretic Specification of Functions" in *Amer. Sociol. Rev.*, 1957, 22, 387–391.

ELLUL, J., "On the Cultural and Social Factors Influencing Church Division" in *Ecumenical Review*, 1952, 4, 269–275.

EMME, E. E., "Modification and Origin of Certain Beliefs in Superstition Among 96 College Students" in *Journal of Psychology*, 1940, 10, 279–291.

————, "Supplementary Study of Superstitious Belief Among College Students" in *Journal of Psychology*, 1941. 12, 183–184.

ENGLAND, R. W., "Some Aspects of Christian Science as Reflected in Letters of Testimony" in *Amer. Journ. Sociol.*, 1954, 59, 448–453.

ERIKSON, E., "On The Sense of Inner Identity" in R. P. KNIGHT and C. R. FRIEDMAN (ed.), *Psychoanalytic Psychiatry and Psychology* (New York: 1954).

FALARDEAU, J.-C., "The Parish as an Institutional Type" in *Canadian Journ. of Econ. and Polit. Sciences*, 1949, 15, 353–367.

————, "Parish Research in Canada" in C. J. NEUSSE and T. J. HARTE (ed.), *The Sociology of the Parish* (Milwaukee: 1951), 323–332.

FERGUSON, L. W., "The Measurement of Primary Social Attitudes" in *Journal of Psychology*, 1940, 10, 199–205.

————, "The Stability of the Primary Social Attitudes: I. Religionism and Humanitarianism" in *Journal of Psychology*, 1941, 12, 283–388.

————, "Socio-Psychological Correlates of the Primary Attitude Scales: I. Religionism, II. Humanitarianism" in *Journ. Soc. Psychol.*, 1944, 19, 81–98.

FICHTER, J. H., S.J., *Southern Parish:* "I. Dynamics of a City Church" (Chicago: 1951).

————, "The Profile of Catholic Religious Life" in *Amer. Journ. Sociol.*, 1952, 58, 145–149.

————, "The Marginal Catholic: An Institutional Approach" in *Social Forces*, 1953, 32, 167–173.

————, *Social Relations in the Urban Parish* (Chicago: 1954).

————, "Religious Values and the Social Personality" in *Amer. Cath. Sociol. Rev.,* 1956, 17, 109–116.

————, "Religion, Integrator of the Culture?" in *Thought,* 1958, 33, 361–362.

FIELD, A. J., "Comment on 'The Protestant Ethic, Level of Aspiration, and Social Mobility' " in *Amer. Sociol. Rev.,* 1956, 21, 620–621; [cf. article of Mack, Murphy and Yellin, *infra*].

FISCHOFF, E., "The Protestant Ethic and the Spirit of Capitalism" in *Social Research,* 1944, 11, 53–77.

FRENCH, V. V., "The Structure of Sentiments" in *Journal of Personality,* 1947, 15, 247–282; 16, 78–108; 16, 209–244.

FREUD, S., *Group Psychology and the Analysis of the Ego* (New York); cf. Chapter 5.

FROMM, E., *Psychoanalysis and Religion* (New Haven: 1950).

GEORGE, A., "Fautes contre Yahweh dans les livres de Samuel" in *Revue Biblique,* 1946, 53, 161–184.

GEORGE, G., S.J., "The Sociology of Ritual" in *Amer. Cath. Sociol. Rev.,* 1956, 17, 117–130.

GERARD, H. B., "The Anchorage of Opinions in Reference Groups" in *American Psychologist,* 1952, 7, 328 (abstract).

————, "The Anchorage of Opinions in Face-to-Face Groups" in *Human Relations,* 1954, 7, 313, 325.

GERNET, L., "Histoire des religions et psychologie: confrontations d'aujourd'hui" in *Journal de Psychologie,* 1954, (numéro spécial) t. 47–51, 175–187.

GESELL, A. and ILG, F. L., *The Child from 5 to 10* (New York: 1946).

GILLILAND, A. R., "Changes in Religious Beliefs of College Students" in *Journ. Soc. Psychol.,* 1953, 37, 113–116.

GIROD, R., *Attitudes collectives et relations humaines* (Paris: 1952).

GLICK, P. C. and YOUNG, K., "Justifications for Religious Attitudes and Habits" in *Journ. Soc. Psychol.,* 1943, 17, 45–68.

GLOCK, C. Y. and RINGER, B. B., "Church Policy and the Attitudes of Ministers and Parishioners on Social Issues" in *Amer. Sociol. Rev.,* 1956, 21, 148–156.

GOODNOW, R. E. and TAGIURI, R., "Religious Ethnocentrism and Its Recognition among Adolescent Boys" in *Journ. Abn. Soc. Psychol.,* 1952, 47, 316–320.

GRAFTON, T. H., "Religious Origins and Sociological Theory" in *Amer. Sociol. Rev.,* 1945, 10, 726–738.

307

GRAVIER, M., *Luther et l'opinion publique* (Paris: 1942).

GREGORY, W. E., "The Psychology of Religion: Some Suggested Areas of Research of Significance to Psychology" in *Journ. Abn. Soc. Psychol.*, 1952, 47, 256–258.

GRENSTED, L. W., *The Psychology of Religion* (London: 1952).

GRINKER, R. R., (ed.), *Toward a Unified Theory of Human Behavior* (New York: 1957).

GUITTARD, L., *L'évolution religieuse des adolescents* (Paris: 1952).

GURVITCH, G., *La vocation actuelle de la sociologie* (Paris: 1957).

GUSTAFSON, J. M., "An Analysis of the Problem of the Role of the Minister" in *The Journal of Religion*, 1954, 34, 187–191.

HALBWACHS, M., "Les origines puritaines du capitalisme moderne" in *Revue d'Histoire et de Philosophie Religieuses*, 1925, 5, 132–134.

———, "La morphologie religieuse," Chapter I in *Morphologie sociale* (Paris: 1938), 19–31.

HALL, G. S., *Adolescence:* "Its psychology and its relations to physiology, anthropology, sociology, sex, crime, religion and education" (New York: 1904).

HARMS, E., "The Development of Religious Experience in Children" in *Amer. Journ. Sociol.*, 1944, 50, 112–122.

HARTMANN, G. W., "Value as the Unifying Concept of the Social Sciences" in *Journ. Soc. Psychol.*, 1939, 10, 563–575.

HEATH, C. W., *What People Are:* "A Study of Normal Young Men" (Cambridge: 1945).

HERBERG, W., *Protestant-Catholic-Jew:* "An Essay in American Religious Sociology" (New York: 1955).

HERTZLER, J. O., *Social Institutions* (Lincoln: 1946).

———, "Religious Institutions" in *Annals of the Amer. Acad. of Political and Social Science*, 1948, 256, 1–13.

HILLER, E. T., *Social Relations and Structures* (New York: 1947).

HOLT, J. B., "Holiness Religion, Cultural Shock, and Social Re-Organization" in *Amer. Sociol. Rev.*, 1940, 5, 740–747.

HOSTIE, R., S.J., *Religion and the Psychology of Jung* (New York: 1957).

HOULT, T. F., "Economic Class Consciousness in American Protestantism" in *Amer. Sociol. Rev.*, 1950, 15, 97–100; 1952, 17, 349–350.

———, "A Functional Theory of Religion" in *Sociology and Social Research*, 1957, 41, 277–279.

————, and PECKHAM, C. W., "Religion as a Cultural Factor in One Aspect of the Personality of Selected College Students" in *Journal of Educational Sociology*, 1957, 31, 75–81.

————, *The Sociology of Religion* (New York: 1958).

HOURDIN, G., *La nouvelle vague croit-elle en Dieu?* (Paris: 1960).

HOUTART, F., *Les paroisses de Bruxelles, 1803–1951:* "législation, délimitation, démographie, équipement. (Louvain: 1954).

————, "Les variables qui affectent le rôle intégrateur de la religion" in *Social Compass*, 1960, 1, 21–38.

HOWELLS, T. H., "A Comparative Study of Those Who Accept as Against Those Who Reject Religious Authority" Iowa City, *University of Iowa Studies*, "Studies in Character," First series, no. 167, Vol. 2, 1928, 1–80.

HUBERT, H. and MAUSS, M., "Essai sur la nature et la fonction du sacrifice" in *L'Année Sociologique*, 1897–1898, 2, 29–138.

HUGHES, E. C., "The Early and Contemporary Study of Religion" in *Amer. Journ. Sociol.*, 1955, 60, I–IV.

I.F.O.P., (Institut Français d'Opinion Publique), 1948, 1949, 1952: see SURVEY (SONDAGES).

————, 1958: "La 'nouvelle vague' croit-elle en Dieu" (Survey of I.F.O.P.), *Informations Catholiques Internationales*, 1958, 11–20.

IISAGER, H., "Factors Influencing the Formation and Change of Political and Religious Attitudes" in *Journ. Soc. Psychol.*, 1949, 29, 253–265.

ISAMBERT, F.-A., "Classes sociales et pratique religieuse paroissiale" in *Cahiers Intern. Sociol.*, 1953, 14, 141–153.

————, "Développement et dépassement de l'étude de la pratique chez Gabriel Le Bras" in *Cahiers Intern. Sociol.*, 1956, 20, 149–169.

————, "L'abstention religieuse de la classe ouvrière" in *Cahiers Intern. Sociol.*, 1958, 25, 116–134.

JAMES, WILLIAM, *The Varieties of Religious Experience* (New York: 1902).

JAMMES, J.-M., "The Social Role of the Priest" in *Amer. Cath. Sociol. Rev.*, 1955, 15, 94–103.

————, "Les catholiques américains et le sacerdoce" in *Chronique Sociale de France*, 1955, 63, 23–36.

JAVAUX, J., S.J., "Une enquête religieuse en milieu universitaire" in *Nouvelle Revue Théologique*, 1957, 828–848.

JEFFREYS, M. D. W., "Some Rules of Directed Culture Change Under Roman Catholicism" in *American Anthropologist*, 1956, 58, 721–731.

JOHNSON, B., "A Critical Appraisal of the Church-Sect Typology" in *Amer. Sociol. Rev.*, 1957, 22, 88–92.

JOURNAL OF RELIGION, "The Definition of Religion: A Symposium" in *Journal of Religion*, 1927, 7, 112–135; 284–314.

JUNG, C. G., *Die Beziehungen der Psychotherapie zur Seelsorge* (Zurich: 1932).

————, *Psychology and Religion* (New Haven: 1960).

KANIN, E. J., "Value Conflicts in Catholic Device-Contraceptive Usage" in *Social Forces*, 1957, 35, 238–243.

KARDINER, A., LINTON, R., DUBOIS, C., WEST, J., *The Psychological Frontiers of Society* (New York: 1945).

KEEDY, T. C., "Anomie and Religious Orthodoxy" in *Sociology and Social Research*, 1958, 43, 34–37.

KELLEY, H. H. and VOLKART, E. H., "The Resistance to Change of Group-Anchored Attitudes" in *Amer. Sociol. Rev.*, 1952, 17, 453–465.

————, "Salience of Membership and Resistance to Change of Group-Anchored Attitudes" in *Human Relations*, 1955, 8, 275–289.

KERKHOFS, J., S.J., "Aspects sociologiques du sacerdoce" in *Nouvelle Revue Théologique*, 1960, 82, 289–299.

KITAY, P. M., *Radicalism and Conservatism Toward Conventional Religion* (New York: 1947).

KLUCKHOHN, C., "Culture and Behavior," in G. LINDZEY (ed.), *Handbook of Social Psychology* (Cambridge: 1954), 1956, 921–976.

KNOX, R., "Some Vagaries of Modern Revivalism" in *Enthusiasm: "A Chapter in the History of Religion"* (Oxford: 1950), 1957, 549–577.

KOLB, W. L., "Values, Positivism, and the Functional Theory of Religion: The Growth of a Moral Dilemma" in *Social Forces*, 1953, 31, 305–311.

KRECH, D. and CRUTCHFIELD, R. S., *Theory and Problems of Social Psychology* (New York: 1948).

LABBENS, J., "Paroisses, chapelles et concentration de la pratique dominicale" in *Chronique Sociale de France*, 1955, 63, 59–64.

————, *Les 99 autres . . . ou l'Eglise aussi recense* (Lyon: 1954).

————, *L'Eglise et les centres urbains* (Paris: 1959).

————, *La sociologie religieuse* (Paris: 1959).

LAGACHE, D., "Quelques aspects de l'identification" in *Bulletin Intern. des Sciences Sociales,* 1955, 7, 37–46.

LE BRAS, G., "Note sur la structure de la sociologie religieuse" in *L'Année Sociologique,* 1948–1949, 3e série, 284–287.

————, "Présentation—La sociologie du catholicisme en France" in *Lumen Vitae,* 1951, 6, 13–42.

————, *Etudes de sociologie religieuse,* 2 vol., (Paris: 1955–1956).

————, "L'explication en sociologie religieuse" in *Cahiers Intern. Sociol.,* 1956, 21, 59–76.

————, "Sociologie des religions: tendances actuelles de la recherche" in *Current Sociology,* 1956, 5, 5–17.

————, "Sociologie religieuse et science des religions" in *Arch. Sociol. des Relig.,* 1956, 1, 3–17.

————, "La sociologie religieuse parmi les sciences humaines" in *Recherches et Débats,* 1958, 25, 11–25.

LEENHARDT, M., "Les carnets de Lucien Lévy-Bruhl" in *Cahiers Intern. Sociol.,* 1949, 6, 28–42.

LE MOAL, P., "Continence conjugale et morale sexuelle: étude statistique du comportement sexuel de 292 couples catholiques en fonction de leur position en face de la limitation des naissances" in *Supplément de la Vie Spirituelle,* 1958, 11, 43–69.

LENSKI, G. E., "Social Correlates of Religious Interest" in *Amer. Sociol. Rev.,* 1953, 18, 533–544.

LÉONARD, E. G., *Le Protestant français* (Paris: 1955).

LEONI, A., *Sociologia e geografia religiosa di una diocesi* (Roma: 1952).

LEUBA, J. H., *La psychologie des phénomènes religieux* (Paris: 1914).

LÉVI-STRAUSS, C., "Social Structure" in A. L. KROEBER (ed.), *Anthropology Today* (Chicago: 1953), 524–553.

LEWIN, K., *Field Theory in Social Science,* D. CARTWRIGHT (ed.), (New York: 1951).

LIGIER, S., *L'adulte des milieux ouvriers,* "I. Essai de psychologie sociale" (Paris: 1951).

LINDZEY, G., (ed.) *Handbook of Social Psychology,* 2 vol., (Cambridge: 1954), 1956.

LOWE, W. L., "Group Beliefs and Socio-Cultural Factors in Religious Delusions" in *Journ. Soc. Psychol.*, 1954, 40, 267–274.

MACK, R. W., MURPHY, R. J., and YELLIN, S., "The Protestant Ethic, Level of Aspiration, and Social Mobility: An Empirical Test" in *Amer. Sociol. Rev.*, 1956, 21, 295–300.

MCDOWELL, J. B., *The Development of the Idea of God in the Catholic Child* (Washington: 1952).

MCLOUGHLIN, W. G., *Modern Revivalism:* "Charles Grandison Finney to Billy Graham" (New York: 1959).

MAILHIOT, B., O.P., "L'univers religieux de l'enfant d'âge préscolaire" in *Revue Dominicaine*, 1958, 64, 131–143.

MAÎTRE, J., "Les sociologies du catholicisme français" in *Cahiers Intern. Sociol.*, 1958, 24, 104–124.

———, "Religion populaire et populations religieuses" in *Cahiers Intern. Sociol.*, 1959, 27, 95–120.

MALINOWSKI, B., "Social and Individual Sources of Primitive Religion" in J. NEEDHAM (ed.), *Science, Religion, and Reality* (New York: 1925), 52–64.

MAUSS, M., *Sociologie et anthropologie* (Paris: 1950).

———, cf. HUBERT and MAUSS.

MAYER, A. J. and MARX, S., "Social Change, Religion and Birth Rates" in *Amer. Journ. Sociol.*, 1957, 62, 383–390.

MENSCHING, G., *Sociologie religieuse* (Paris: 1951).

MERTON, R. K., *Social Theory and Social Structure* (Chicago: 1957).

MORRIS, R. E., "Problems Concerning the Institutionalization of Religion" in *Amer. Cath. Sociol. Rev.*, 1956, 17, 98–108.

MURCHISON, C., (ed.), *A Handbook of Social Psychology* (Worcester: 1935).

MURPHY, G., "Social Motivation," in G. LINDZEY (ed.), *Handbook of Social Psychology* (Cambridge: 1954), 1956, 601–633.

MURRAY, H. A., *Explorations in Personality*, 2 vol., (Oxford).

MYSTICI CORPORIS, (encyclical of Pope Pius XII on the Mystical Body), *Acta Apostolicae Sedis*, 1943, 35, n. 7, 193–248.

NÉDONCELLE, M. and GIRAULT, R., *J'ai rencontré le Dieu vivant:* "témoignages avec deux études sur la conversion" (Paris: 1952).

NELSON, E. N. P., "Patterns of Religious Attitude Shifts from College to Fourteen Years Later" in *Psychological Monographs*, 1956, 70, n. 17, 1–15.

NEWCOMB, T. M., *Social Psychology* (New York: 1950), 1958.

———, "Attitude Development as a Function of Reference Groups: The Bennington Study" in E. E. MACCOBY, T. M. NEWCOMB and E. L. HARTLEY (ed.), *Readings in Social Psychology* (New York: 1958), 265–275.

NIMKOFF, M. F. and WOOD, A. L., "Effect of Majority Patterns on the Religious Behavior of a Minority Group" in *Sociology and Social Research.*, 1946, 30, 282–289.

NOWLAN, E. H., S.J., "Le 'portrait du catholique' à partir du test d'attitudes" in *Lumen Vitae,* 1957, 12, 284–296.

NUESSE, C. J. and HARTE, T. J., *The Sociology of the Parish:* "A Survey of the Parish in its Constants and Variables (Milwaukee: 1951).

O'DEA, T. F., "Mormonism and the Avoidance of Sectarian Stagnation: A Study of Church, Sect, and Incipient Nationality" in *Amer. Journ. Sociol.,* 1954, 60, 285–293.

———, "Five Dilemmas in the Institutionalization of Religion," Proceedings of the Sixth International Conference of Sociology of Religion, Bologna, Sept. 3–6, 1959; cf. *Social Compass,* 1960, 1, 61–67.

O'REILLY, C. T. and O'REILLY, E. J., "Religious Beliefs of Catholic College Students and Their Attitudes Toward Minorities" in *Journ. Abn. Soc. Psychol.,* 1954, 49, 378–380.

PARK, R. E., "Missions and the Modern World" in *Amer. Journ. Sociol.,* 1944, 50, 177–183.

PARSONS, T., "The Theoretical Development of the Sociology of Religion" in *Journal of the History of Ideas,* 1944, 5, 176–190.

PEARSON, G. H., *Adolescence and the Conflict of Generations:* "Introduction to Some of the Psychoanalytic Contributions to the Understanding of Adolescence" (New York: 1958).

PENIDO, M. T.-L., *La conscience religieuse:* "essai systématique suivi d'illustrations" (Paris: 1935).

PFAUTZ, H. W., "The Sociology of Secularization: Religious Groups" in *Amer. Journ. Sociol.,* 1955, 61, 121–128.

———, "Christian Science: A Case Study of the Social Psychological Aspect of Secularization" in *Social Forces,* 1956, 34, 246–251.

PIAGET, J., *The Moral Judgment of the Child* (Chicago).

———, "Pensée égocentrique et pensée sociocentrique" in *Cahiers Intern. Sociol.,* 1951, 6, 34–49.

PIÉRON, H., *Vocabulaire de la psychologie* (Paris: 1957).

313

PIN, E., S.J., *Pratique religieuse et classes sociales* (Paris: 1956).

——, *Introduction à l'étude sociologique des paroisses catholiques:* "critères de classification et typologies" (Vanves: 1956).

PINARD DE LA BOULLAYE, E., S.J., *L'étude comparée des religions,* 3ᵉ edition, 3 vol., (Paris: 1929).

POBLETE, R., S.J., *Puerto Rican Sectarianism and the Quest for Community.* Unpublished M.A. dissertation presented to Fordham University (New York: 1959).

POPE, L., "Religion and the Class Structure" in *Annals of the Amer. Academy of Political and Economic Science,* 1948, 256, 84–91.

RAHNER, KARL, "Belonging to the Church according to the Encyclical *Mystici corporis*" in *Theological Investigations,* vol. 2, Baltimore 1964.

RAPAPORT, I., *Introduction à la psychopathologie collective:* "la secte mystique des Skoptzy" (Paris: 1948?).

REUSS, C. E., "Research Findings on the Effects of Modern-Day Religion on the Family" in *Marriage and Family Living,* 1954, 16, 221–225.

ROGÉ, J., "Psychologie du prêtre" in *Journal de Psychologie,* 1956, 53, 63–80.

ROKEACH, M., "The Nature and Meaning of Dogmatism" in *Psychological Review,* 1954, 61, 194–204.

——, "Political and Religious Dogmatism: An Alternative to the Authoritarian Personality" in *Psychological Monographs,* 1956, 70, n. 18, 1–43.

RUSSO, F., "Rôle respectif du catholicisme et du protestantisme dans le développement des sciences aux XIVᵉ et XVIIᵉ siècles" in *Cahiers d'Histoire Mondiale,* 1957, 4, 854–880.

SALISBURY, W. S., "Faith, Ritualism, Charismatic Leadership and Religious Behavior" in *Social Forces,* 1956, 34, 241–245.

SARAH, A., "Religious Behavior of Church Families" in *Marriage and Family Living,* 1955, 17, 54–57.

SCHACHTER, S., *The Psychology of Affiliation:* "Experimental Studies of the Sources of Gregariousness" (Stanford: 1959).

SCHAFFER, A., "The Rural Church in a Metropolitan Area" in *Rural Sociology,* 1959, 24, 236–245.

SCHANK, R. L., "A Study of a Community and Its Groups and Institutions Conceived of as Behaviors of Individuals" in *Psychological Monographs,* 1932, 43, n. 195, 1–133.

SCHMITT-EGLIN, P., *Le mécanisme de la déchristianisation* (Paris: 1952).

SCHNEIDER, L. and DORNBUSCH, S. M., "Inspirational Religious Literature: From Latent to Manifest Functions of Religion" in *Amer. Journ. Sociol.*, 1957, 62, 476–481.

———, *Popular Religion:* "Inspirational Books in America" (Chicago: 1958).

SCHNEPP, G., *Leakage from a Catholic Parish* (Washington: 1938).

SCHUYLER, J. B., S.J., "The Parish Studied as a Social System" in *Amer. Cath. Sociol. Rev.*, 1956, 17, 320–337.

———, "Potential Elements of Organization and Disorganization in the Parish" in *Amer. Cath. Sociol. Rev.*, 1957, 18, 98–112.

———, "Religious Observance Differentials by Age and Sex in Northern Parish" in *Amer. Cath. Sociol. Rev.*, 1959, 20, 124–131.

SEIDLER, M. B. and RAVITS, M. J., "A Jewish Peer Group" in *Amer. Journ. Sociol.*, 1955, 61, 11–15.

SHERIF, M. and CANTRIL, H., *The Psychology of Ego-Involvements:* "Social Attitudes and Identifications" (New York: 1947).

SHERMAN, M. H., "Values, Religion and the Psychoanalyst" in *Journ. Soc. Psychol.*, 1957, 45, 261–269.

SIGHELE, S., *Psychologiedes sectes,* translated from the Italian by L. Brandin (Paris: 1898); Italian edition 1895.

SMITH, J. J., "Religious Development in Children" in B. F. SKINNER and P. L. HARRIMAN (ed.), *Child Psychology* (New York: 1941).

SMITH, L. M., "The Clergy: Authority, Structure, Ideology, Migration" in *Amer. Sociol. Rev.*, 1953, 18, 242–248.

SOROKIN, P. A., (ed.) *Explorations in Altruistic Love and Behavior: A Symposium* (Boston: 1950).

SOURIAU, M., "La conversion" in *Encyclopédie Française* (Paris: 1957), XIX, fasc. 34, 1–6.

SPENGLER, O., *Decline of the West* (London: 1926).

SPIEGELBERG, F., *The Religion of No Religion* (Stanford: 1948).

STARBUCK, E. D., *The Psychology of Religion* (New York: 1899), 1903.

STOETZEL, J., "La Psychologie sociale et la théorie des attitudes" in *Annales Sociologiques,* 1941, fasc. 4, 1–24.

———, *Théorie des opinions* (Paris: 1943).

———, "Sociology in France: An Empiricist View" in H. BECKER

and A. BOSKOFF (ed.), *Modern Sociological Theory* (New York: 1957), 623–657.

STOTLAND, E., "Determinants of Attraction to Groups" in *Journ. Soc. Psychol.*, 1959, 49, 71–80.

STROUP, H. H., *The Jehovah's Witnesses* (New York: 1954).

SURVEY (SONDAGES) 1948, "Une enquête internationale: la religion dans le monde" in *Sondages*, février 1948, 10, 31–33.

SURVEY (SONDAGES) 1949: "Les fêtes" (Numéro spécial) in *Sondages*, janvier 1949, 11, 1–12.

SURVEY (SONDAGES) 1952: "Le catholicisme en France" in *Sondages*, 1952, n. 4, 14, 1–56.

SZABO, D., "Essai sur quelques aspects sociologiques de la crise du recrutement sacerdotal in France" in *Bull. de l'Inst. de Rech. Econ. et Sociales*, 1958, 24, 635–646.

TELFORD, C. W., "A Study of Religious Attitudes" in *Journ. Soc. Psychol.*, 1950, 31, 217–230.

THIBAUT, J., "An Experimental Study of the Cohesiveness of Under-Privileged Groups" in *Human Relations*, 1950, 3, 251–278.

THOMAS, J. L., S.J., "The Factor of Religion in the Selection of Marriage Mates" in *Amer. Sociol. Rev.*, 1951, 16, 487–491.

———, "Religious Training in the Roman Catholic Family" in *Amer. Journ. Sociol.*, 1951, 57, 178–183.

THORNER, I., "Ascetic Protestantism and the Development of Science and Technology" in *Amer. Journ. Sociol.*, 1952, 58, 25–33.

THOULESS, R. H., *An Introduction to the Psychology of Religion* (Cambridge: 1928).

———, "The Tendency to Certainty in Religious Belief" in *British Journal of Psychology* (General Section), 1935, 26, 16–31.

THURSTONE, L. L., *The Measurement of Values* (Chicago: 1952), n. 77, 1–9.

TROELTSCH, E., *Protestantism and Progress* (New York: 1912).

———, *Die Soziallehren der christlichen Kirchen und Gruppen* (Tübingen: 1912).

———, *The Social Teaching of the Christian Churches*, translated by Olive Wyon, 2 vol., (New York: 1931).

TROUDE, R., "Le niveau moral de la Normandie selon quatre critères statistiques" in *Etudes Normandes*, 1958, 26, 1–11.

TUFARI, P., S.J., "Functional Analysis in the Sociology of Religion" in Proceedings of the Sixth International Conference of Sociology of Religion, Bologna, Sept. 3–6, 1959; cf. *Social Compass*, 1960, 1, 9–20; 2, 121–137.

TUTTLE, H. S., "Aims of Courses in Religion" in *Journ. Soc. Psychol.*, 1950, 31, 305–309.

VAKAR, N., "L'athéisme pieux" in *Cahiers de la Nouvelle Epoque*, 1945, 2, 109–118.

VAN DER LEEUW, G., *La religion dans son essence et ses manifestations:* "phénoménologie de la religion," translated into French by J. Marty (Paris: 1955).

VAN VLECK, J. and WOLF, C. U., "Reader-Appeal of Religious Articles" in *Amer. Sociol. Rev.*, 1942, 7, 828–832.

VERNON, P. E. and ALLPORT, G. W., "A Test for Personal Values" in *Journ. Abn. Soc. Psychol.*, 1931, 26, 231–248.

VETTER, G. B. and GREEN, M., "Personality and Group Factors in the Making of Atheists" in *Journ. Abn. Soc. Psychol.*, 1932, 27, 179–194.

WACH, J., "La sociologie de la religion" in G. GURVITCH and W. E. MOORE (ed.), *La sociologie au XXe siècle* (Paris: 1947), T. I, 417–447.

———, *Sociologie de la religion* (Paris: 1955).

———, *Types of Religious Experiences, Christian and Non-Christian* (Chicago: 1951), 1957.

WALLON, H., "L'étude psychologique et sociologique de l'enfant" in *Cahiers Intern. Sociol.*, 1947, 3, 3–23.

———, "Sociologie et éducation" in *Cahiers Intern. Sociol.*, 1951, 6, 19–33; 175–177.

———, "Les milieux, les groupes et la psychogenèse de l'enfant" in *Cahiers Intern. Sociol.*, 1954, 16, 2–13.

WARD, C. K., "Some Aspects of the Social Structure of a Roman Catholic Parish" in *The Sociological Review*, 1958, 6, 75–93.

WAX, M., "Ancient Judaism and the Protestant Ethic" in *Amer. Journ. Sociol.*, 1960, 65, 449–455.

WEBER, MAX, *Gesammelte Aufsätze zur Religionssoziologie* (Tübingen: 1920–1921).

———, *The Protestant Ethic and the Spirit of Capitalism* (New York: 1930).

———, "The Social Psychology of the World Religions" in *From Max Weber: Essays in Sociology*, edited and translated by H. H. Gerth and C. W. Mills, (London: 1947), 267–301.

317

WELFORD, A. T., "An Attempt at an Experimental Approach to the Psychology of Religion" in *British Journal of Psychology* (General Section), 1946, 36, 55–73.

WELLS, F. L., "Social Maladjustments; Adaptive Regression" in C. MURCHISON (ed.), *A Handbook of Social Psychology* (Worcester: 1935), 845–915.

WIESE, L. VON, and BECKER, H., *Systematic Sociology* (New York: 1932). Wiley and Sons, 1932.

WILSON, B. R., "Apparition et peristance des sectes dans un milieu social en évolution" in *Arch. Sociol. des Relig.*, 1958, 5, 140–150.

———, "An Analysis of Sect Development" in *Amer. Sociol. Rev.*, 1959, 24, 3–15.

———, "The Pentecostalist Minister: Role Conflicts and Status Contradiction" in *Amer. Journ. Sociol.*, 1959, 64, 494–504.

WINNINGER, P., *Construire des églises:* "les dimensions des paroisses et les contradictions de l'apostolat dans les villes" (Paris: 1957).

———, "[Le problème des trop petites paroisses]: aspects canoniques, que dit le Code?" in *La Maison-Dieu*, 1959, 57, 31–54.

WOODRUFF, A. D., "Personal Values and Religious Background" in *Journ. Sociol. Psychol.*, 1945, 22, 141–147.

WOOLSTON, H., "Religious Consistency" in *Amer. Sociol. Rev.*, 1937, 2, 380–388.

YINGER, J. M., *Religion, Society and the Individual:* "An Introduction to the Sociology of Religion" (New York: 1957).

———, "Areas for Research in the Sociology of Religion" in *Sociology and Social Research*, 1958, 42, 466–472.

YOUTH AND RELIGION 1958: "Youth and Religion: A Scientific Inquiry into the Religious Attitudes, Beliefs and Practices of Urban Youth" in *New Life* (London: 1958), 14, 1–60.

ZETTERBERG, H. L., "The Religious Conversion as a Change of Social Roles" in *Sociology and Social Research*, 1952, 36, 159–166.

ZUCKER, C., *Psychologie de la superstition* (Paris: 1952).

Author Index

319

Subject Index

Absolute
 religious attitudes, 271–78
 substitution of, 266–68
Accommodation
 to cultural pluralism, 192
 See Census
Adolescents
 and conversion, 68, 85–87
 religious formation of, 142–54
 imperfect role and status of, 248–49
 See Youth
Adults, religion of, 287–90
Adventists, 177
Affiliation
 personal and institutional, 203–06
 immediate process of, 121–25
 See Belonging, Participation
Age
 and consciousness of belonging, 214–15
 psychoreligious, 121, 231, 241–42, 246–47, 250, 287, 289
 See Adolescents, Adults, Infants
Alienation, socioreligious, 191–92

Ambivalence
 of religious adhesion, 192
 of religious crisis, 97–103
 of minority, 218
 of the sacred, 279–80
 of religious sentiment, 83
Anomy, 89
Anticipation
 of behavior, 67
 See Revivals
Apprenticeship, 127, 130
 See Socialization
Approbation, social, 275–76
Archetypes, 65
Atheism
 psychosociology of, 259–68
 and family climate, 123–25
 and loss of faith, 261–62
 and social progress, 221
 among students, 122–23
Attitude
 notion of, 54
 formation of, 63–66
 general or specific, 294
 egocentric or sociocentric, 131–33
 integrated or marginal, 147–54
 and belonging, 54–55
 and behavior, 53–55

324

327

328